TRANSFORMATECH INSTITUTE

Understanding Deep Learning:

Building Machine Learning Systems with PyTorch and TensorFlow

From Neural Networks to Natural Language Processing

Table of Contents:

Preface

Introduction to Deep Learning and Its Impact on AI

Deep learning has quickly become one of the most powerful technologies in artificial intelligence (AI). It's reshaping industries, enhancing our daily lives, and pushing the boundaries of what machines can achieve. From recognizing faces in photos to translating languages in real time, deep learning is the engine behind many of the AI-driven innovations we now take for granted.

But what exactly is deep learning, and why is it so transformative? At its core, deep learning is about training machines to learn from vast amounts of data using neural networks. These neural networks are designed to mimic the way the human brain processes information, allowing machines to make sense of complex patterns, recognize objects, and even generate new content, like art or music.

The reason deep learning has had such a huge impact is simple: it scales incredibly well. The more data and computational power you throw at it, the better it gets. This is different from traditional machine learning models, which often plateau once they reach a certain level of complexity. Deep learning's ability to improve with more data and computation makes it ideal for tasks that were once thought to be exclusive to human intelligence—like understanding language or driving a car.

Impact on Real-World Applications

In healthcare, deep learning is revolutionizing diagnostics. AI systems powered by deep learning can now analyze medical images with unprecedented accuracy, detecting diseases like cancer earlier and more reliably than ever before. In finance, deep learning models are being used to predict market trends, assess risk, and even detect fraudulent activity in real time. And in everyday life, deep learning powers personal assistants like Siri and Alexa, which understand and respond to our voices with increasing sophistication.

Self-driving cars are another example of deep learning's transformative potential. These vehicles rely on deep learning models to process vast streams of data from cameras, sensors, and radars, allowing them to make split-second decisions on the road. This technology, once seen as science fiction, is now becoming a reality thanks to deep learning.

Why It's a Game-Changer

What makes deep learning especially powerful is its ability to automate tasks that require human intuition. Traditional programming involves explicitly telling a computer how to solve a problem, step by step. With deep learning, however, we don't need to tell the machine what to do—we simply give it a large dataset and let it figure out the patterns on its own. This approach has opened up possibilities in areas where hand-crafted solutions would be impractical or impossible.

For example, natural language processing (NLP) tasks, like translation or summarization, used to require complex, rule-based systems. Now, with deep learning, models like GPT-3 can generate human-like text by training on vast amounts of data, without needing explicit rules. This same principle applies across other fields—whether it's predicting customer behavior, generating realistic images, or even composing music.

In short, deep learning is transforming AI from a tool that assists with decision-making into a system that can learn, reason, and generate ideas on its own. As you move through this book, you'll gain the knowledge and skills to harness deep learning for your own projects, from building neural networks to designing machine learning systems that solve real-world problems.

Purpose of the Book

The purpose of this book is simple: to help you understand deep learning and give you the tools to build real-world machine learning systems. Whether you're just getting started with neural networks or looking to deepen your knowledge, this book is designed to bridge the gap between theory and practical application.

Deep learning is an incredibly powerful tool, but it can feel overwhelming at first. This book breaks things down in a way that's accessible, without sacrificing the depth you need to fully grasp the concepts. By the time you're done, you'll not only understand how deep learning works but also how to use it effectively with frameworks like PyTorch and TensorFlow.

The content of the book is structured to guide you through the most important topics in deep learning—from foundational neural network concepts to more advanced architectures like transformers and GANs. It also focuses on practical skills, like how to set up your deep learning environment, how to fine-tune pre-trained models, and how to deploy models in production. In other words, this book aims to prepare you to confidently build systems that solve real-world problems using deep learning.

Another key purpose of this book is to provide a balanced view. While deep learning is a revolutionary technology, it comes with its own set of challenges—like overfitting, ethical concerns, and handling massive datasets. This book addresses these challenges head-on, equipping you with strategies to handle them, so you're not left guessing when things don't go as planned.

Ultimately, this book aims to empower you with the knowledge, tools, and confidence to apply deep learning to the projects that matter most to you. Whether you're working on computer vision, natural language processing, or something entirely different, you'll walk away with a strong foundation and the ability to build meaningful AI solutions.

Who Should Read This Book

This book is for anyone who wants to truly understand deep learning and apply it in a meaningful way. Whether you're just starting out or you're already familiar with machine learning concepts, this book has something to offer.

If you're a beginner, you'll find that the book explains the core ideas in a clear and accessible way. You don't need to be a math expert or a seasoned programmer to get started. We'll walk through the essential concepts step by step, making sure you feel confident before moving on to more advanced topics. The practical focus means you'll get hands-on experience with tools like PyTorch and TensorFlow, so you can start building your own deep learning models right away.

For those with more experience, this book digs deeper into some of the more advanced topics in deep learning—like transformers, generative models, and deploying models to production. You'll find sections that go beyond the basics, offering insights into real-world applications and best practices for designing and optimizing deep learning systems.

This book is also perfect for developers, data scientists, and engineers who want to add deep learning to their toolkit. Whether you're looking to expand your skills or apply deep learning to your current work, the book provides the knowledge and practical examples you need to build and scale deep learning models in your projects.

In short, if you're interested in how deep learning works, how to build systems with it, or how to apply it in your field—this book is for you. Regardless of your starting point, you'll leave with a solid understanding of deep learning and the confidence to use it in the real world.

How to Use This Book

This book is designed to be flexible, so you can approach it in a way that fits your goals and experience level. Whether you want to read it cover to cover or jump into specific sections, the structure makes it easy to find what you need.

If you're new to deep learning or machine learning, it's a good idea to start from the beginning. The early chapters cover foundational concepts like neural networks, gradient descent, and deep learning architectures. These are the building blocks for everything that follows, so taking the time to understand them will set you up for success in the more advanced topics.

For those with a bit more experience, you might prefer to jump straight into the sections that cover topics you're most interested in. Want to learn about transformers or generative adversarial networks (GANs)? Head to the chapters on advanced architectures and generative models. Need help with optimizing your model or deploying it into production? We've got sections dedicated to those topics as well.

Each chapter is designed to stand on its own, so feel free to move around and focus on what's most relevant to you at any given time. Along the way, you'll find plenty of hands-on examples, practical tips, and explanations of real-world applications. These will help reinforce the concepts and show you how to put deep learning to work in your own projects.

Finally, don't hesitate to come back to earlier chapters if you need a refresher. Concepts in deep learning build on each other, and it's completely normal to revisit foundational ideas as you tackle more complex topics. The key is to go at your own pace and apply what you learn in ways that matter to you.

Overview of Deep Learning History

Deep learning might seem like a recent buzzword, but its roots go back several decades. The concept of neural networks, which is at the heart of deep learning, originated in the 1940s. Researchers were fascinated by the idea of creating machines that could mimic the human brain's ability to learn and recognize patterns.

One of the first breakthroughs came in 1958 with the invention of the **Perceptron** by Frank Rosenblatt. The Perceptron was a simple neural network designed to recognize visual patterns, and it was a big step forward in artificial intelligence. However, it wasn't perfect. It had significant limitations, and interest in neural networks waned for several years.

In the 1980s, neural networks made a comeback with the development of **backpropagation**, an algorithm that made training multi-layer networks much more feasible. This was a crucial step forward because it allowed neural networks to adjust their internal weights more effectively, leading to better learning outcomes. This resurgence of interest led to early successes in tasks like handwriting recognition, but neural networks still faced challenges, particularly in handling large datasets and complex problems.

The real turning point for deep learning came in the 2000s when two key factors aligned: the availability of **massive datasets** and the rise of powerful **graphics processing units (GPUs)**. Neural networks, which had struggled with complex tasks in the past, could now be trained on vast amounts of data using GPUs to speed up computation. This combination unlocked the true potential of deep learning.

In 2012, deep learning gained widespread attention when a neural network called **AlexNet** won the ImageNet competition, a challenge focused on image recognition. AlexNet's performance was groundbreaking—it far outperformed traditional machine learning methods at the time. This success sparked a wave of interest in deep learning, leading to rapid advancements in the field.

Since then, deep learning has continued to evolve at a rapid pace. The development of new architectures like **Convolutional Neural Networks (CNNs)** for image recognition, **Recurrent Neural Networks (RNNs)** for sequential data, and **Transformers** for natural language processing has pushed the boundaries of what AI can do. Deep learning models now power everything from voice assistants and self-driving cars to medical diagnostics and even creative applications like generating music and art.

Today, deep learning is one of the most active and exciting areas of artificial intelligence research and application. With advances like **generative adversarial networks (GANs)** and **reinforcement learning**, it continues to open new possibilities in AI, enabling machines to tackle tasks that were once thought to be the exclusive domain of human intelligence.

1. Machine Learning and Deep Learning

1.1 Introduction to Machine Learning

1.1.1: Overview of Machine Learning Algorithms (Supervised, Unsupervised, and Reinforcement Learning)

Machine learning (ML) algorithms are typically categorized into three primary types: **supervised learning**, **unsupervised learning**, and **reinforcement learning**. Each type employs a unique approach to learning from data, addressing different challenges and tasks. **Supervised learning** relies on labeled data to train models to predict outputs based on input-output pairs. **Unsupervised learning**, on the other hand, works with unlabeled data to identify hidden patterns within the dataset. **Reinforcement learning** (RL) involves an agent learning through interactions with an environment, where it receives feedback in the form of rewards or penalties based on its actions. These three categories offer distinct solutions to various real-world problems.

Supervised Learning Supervised learning is one of the most commonly used ML techniques, where models are trained using labeled datasets. Each training example in the dataset is paired with a known outcome, allowing the model to learn to map inputs to outputs by minimizing the difference between its predictions and actual results.

Common Algorithms:

> **Linear Regression**: This algorithm is used for predicting continuous outcomes and models the relationship between independent variables and a continuous dependent variable.

> **Decision Trees**: These models use a tree-like structure to make decisions based on data features and can be applied to both classification and regression tasks.

> **Support Vector Machines (SVMs)**: Primarily used for classification tasks, SVMs find the optimal boundary that separates data points of different classes. Supervised learning is ideal for tasks with sufficient labeled data, such as spam detection, credit scoring, and medical diagnosis.

Unsupervised Learning In unsupervised learning, the algorithm operates with unlabeled data, aiming to uncover hidden patterns or groupings within the dataset. Without explicit labels, the model identifies inherent structures based on similarities among data points.

Common Techniques:

Clustering (e.g., K-Means, Hierarchical Clustering): Clustering algorithms group data points based on similarity, making them useful for tasks like customer segmentation and market basket analysis.

Principal Component Analysis (PCA): PCA is a dimensionality reduction technique that transforms data into fewer dimensions while preserving as much variance as possible. It is commonly used in data preprocessing and visualization.

Autoencoders: Although more prevalent in deep learning, autoencoders can also be considered an unsupervised learning technique, as they learn hidden patterns by compressing and reconstructing data. Unsupervised learning is commonly used in exploratory data analysis, anomaly detection, and pattern recognition, where the primary goal is to identify structures or associations within the data without prior knowledge of labels.

Reinforcement Learning (RL) Reinforcement learning differs from supervised and unsupervised learning by focusing on how agents take actions in an environment to maximize cumulative rewards. In RL, the agent interacts with the environment, receiving feedback (rewards or penalties) based on the outcomes of its actions. This feedback loop helps the agent optimize its behavior over time.

Key Concepts:

Exploration vs. Exploitation: The agent must balance exploration (trying new actions to discover their outcomes) with exploitation (choosing actions that yield the highest reward based on current knowledge).

Markov Decision Processes (MDPs): RL problems are often modeled using MDPs, which define the environment in terms of states, actions, rewards, and transitions.

Popular Algorithms:

Q-Learning: Q-learning is a model-free RL algorithm that seeks to find the optimal action-selection policy by maximizing the expected rewards over time. **Deep Q-Networks (DQNs)**: Extending Q-learning, DQNs use deep neural networks to estimate Q-values, enabling agents to learn complex policies in environments like video games.

Proximal Policy Optimization (PPO): PPO is an advanced RL algorithm that has achieved state-of-the-art performance in various environments, such as robotic control and autonomous driving. Reinforcement learning is widely used in fields such as robotics, game AI, and autonomous systems, where learning from interaction is essential.

Supervised Learning: In email spam detection, models are trained on labeled datasets, where each email is marked as spam or not spam. The algorithm learns to classify new emails based on features like text content, sender information, and metadata.

Unsupervised Learning: In customer segmentation, unsupervised clustering techniques are employed to group customers based on purchasing behavior, demographics, and other factors, allowing for more targeted marketing strategies.

Reinforcement Learning: Reinforcement learning has been applied in training robots to perform tasks like picking and placing objects. The robot learns optimal actions through rewards for successful operations and penalties for failures.

Recent advancements have improved each of these ML approaches. In **supervised learning**, transfer learning has made it possible to fine-tune pre-trained models for specific tasks, even with limited labeled data. In **unsupervised learning**, advanced clustering methods like DBSCAN and UMAP have enhanced accuracy and efficiency in pattern discovery within complex datasets. In **reinforcement learning**, breakthroughs with models like AlphaZero, which combines deep learning with RL, have achieved superhuman performance in games like chess and Go, showcasing RL's potential for complex decision-making tasks.

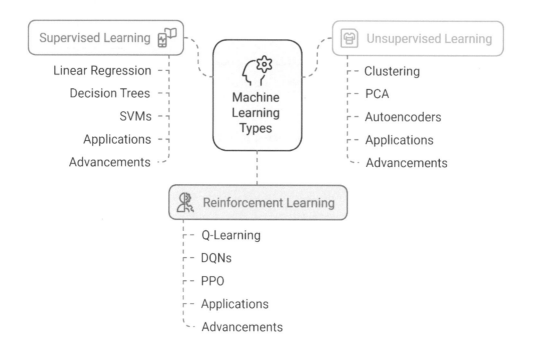

1.1.2: The Role of Data in Machine Learning Models

Data is the foundation of machine learning (ML), driving the effectiveness and accuracy of models across different applications. Whether we are predicting customer behavior, diagnosing diseases, or analyzing market trends, data plays a central role in determining the success of an ML model. High-quality, diverse, and sufficient data enables models to learn meaningful patterns, generalize to new situations, and make reliable predictions. Without good data, even the most sophisticated algorithms will struggle to deliver accurate results.

In machine learning, the type of data used can significantly impact model performance. Data typically falls into three categories: **structured**, **unstructured**, and **semi-structured**. Each category presents unique challenges and opportunities for model training.

Structured data is highly organized and often stored in tabular formats like databases and spreadsheets, with clear fields and columns. Examples include customer records, transaction logs, and inventory data. Machine learning algorithms such as linear regression, decision trees, and support vector machines (SVMs) are particularly suited for structured data, as they can efficiently handle numerical and categorical inputs. The predictability and consistency of structured data make it relatively easier for models to learn patterns.

In contrast, **unstructured data** lacks a defined format and is more complex to process. This includes text documents, images, audio files, and videos—data types that require deep learning models like convolutional neural networks (CNNs) and recurrent neural networks (RNNs) to extract features automatically. For example, processing a set of medical images for disease detection requires models that can identify patterns within the pixel data, which is far less straightforward than analyzing a well-organized table of patient information.

Semi-structured data falls between structured and unstructured data, containing some organizational elements like tags or metadata that provide partial structure. Emails, JSON files, and XML documents are common examples. Depending on the level of structure present, semi-structured data can be processed using a mix of traditional ML and deep learning approaches.

The success of machine learning models is also heavily influenced by three critical factors: data quality, data diversity, and data quantity. **High-quality data** is accurate, complete, and consistent. It is free from errors, missing values, and incorrect labels. If a model is trained on noisy or inconsistent data, it will struggle to generalize well and may produce biased or inaccurate results. For instance, if a spam detection model is trained on mislabeled emails, it could either flag legitimate emails as spam or fail to identify actual spam emails. Therefore, data preprocessing steps like cleaning, normalization, and validation are essential to maintain data integrity.

Diversity in training data is equally important. A diverse dataset exposes the model to a wide range of scenarios, reducing the likelihood of bias and improving generalization. Consider a facial recognition system trained on a dataset that represents various age groups, ethnicities, and lighting conditions. Such a diverse dataset helps the model perform consistently across different environments. On the other hand, training the model on a homogeneous dataset can lead to biases, as it may not perform well when faced with data that deviates from the training examples.

Quantity of data is crucial for effective model training, especially for deep learning algorithms, which require large datasets to identify complex patterns. When datasets are too small, models often suffer from overfitting—where the model performs well on training data but poorly on unseen data. Conversely, large datasets allow models to capture a broader range of patterns, reducing overfitting and improving overall performance. For example, language models like GPT require vast amounts of text data to learn the intricacies of human language, from grammar and vocabulary to context and semantics.

Bias in data is a significant issue that can affect model fairness and accuracy. When the training data is not representative of the broader population or contains systematic errors, models can make biased predictions. For example, a hiring model trained primarily on male candidates may inadvertently favor male applicants, leading to gender bias in the selection process. Mitigating data bias involves steps like rebalancing the dataset, augmenting underrepresented data, and implementing fairness-aware algorithms.

The impact of data on model performance is evident in various real-world applications. In healthcare, for instance, the accuracy of disease detection models largely depends on the quality and volume of medical imaging data. A deep learning model trained on high-resolution, well-labeled MRI scans can accurately identify tumors, while models trained on poor-quality or mislabeled images may lead to false positives or negatives, posing risks in clinical settings.

In the financial sector, data quality is equally critical for credit scoring models. These models analyze transaction histories, income levels, and debt-to-income ratios to assess creditworthiness. If the data contains gaps or errors, the model might misclassify low-risk individuals as high-risk or vice versa, leading to flawed lending decisions. By ensuring accurate and complete data, financial institutions can improve model reliability and make better-informed decisions.

Recent advancements in data collection, preprocessing, and augmentation techniques have further emphasized the importance of data in ML. **Automated data labeling tools**, such as Snorkel and Labelbox, have streamlined the labeling process, making it faster and more accurate, especially in scenarios where manual labeling is time-consuming. These tools use a combination of heuristics, weak supervision, and user input to generate labeled datasets efficiently.

Synthetic data generation has also emerged as a valuable technique, particularly when real-world data is scarce or sensitive. Synthetic data mimics the characteristics of actual data, allowing models to train on a broader set of examples without compromising privacy. For example, generating synthetic images of rare diseases can help medical models generalize better, even when actual medical records are limited.

Data augmentation techniques, such as rotating, scaling, and flipping images or replacing synonyms in text, are widely used to enhance training data diversity. These techniques increase model robustness by exposing it to a wider range of data variations during training.

1.1.3: Manual Feature Engineering in Traditional Machine Learning

Feature engineering is a fundamental process in traditional machine learning that involves selecting, transforming, and creating features (input variables) to improve model performance. In classic ML algorithms like linear regression, decision trees, and support vector machines (SVMs), the quality and relevance of input features play a critical role in determining the accuracy and interpretability of the model. While deep learning models excel in automatically extracting features from raw data, traditional ML models rely heavily on manual feature engineering to identify and emphasize the most relevant patterns within the dataset. This process requires domain expertise and a deep understanding of both the data and the problem being addressed.

Effective feature engineering can significantly enhance the predictive power and generalization capabilities of traditional ML models. It involves a variety of techniques, each designed to highlight different aspects of the data:

Feature Selection Feature selection aims to identify the most relevant variables for model training by removing irrelevant or redundant features. This process not only reduces computational complexity but also minimizes the risk of overfitting, where the model learns noise instead of meaningful patterns. For example, in a dataset containing dozens of variables related to customer demographics and behavior, only a subset of features—such as age, income, and past purchase history—might be relevant for predicting future purchases. Common methods for feature selection include **Recursive Feature Elimination (RFE)**, which iteratively removes the least important features based on model performance, and **feature importance scores** from tree-based models, which highlight variables that have the greatest impact on predictions.

Feature Scaling Feature scaling is the process of standardizing the range of independent variables, making them comparable. Algorithms like linear regression and SVMs are sensitive to the scale of input features, as differences in scale can disproportionately affect the optimization process. Two popular scaling techniques are:

Min-Max Scaling: This technique rescales features to a specified range, typically 0 to 1. It is useful for ensuring that all variables contribute equally to the model's learning process.

Z-Score Normalization: Also known as standardization, this method transforms variables so that they have a mean of 0 and a standard deviation of 1. It is particularly effective for algorithms that assume normally distributed data. By standardizing features, scaling ensures that models converge faster and perform better, especially in gradient-based optimization algorithms.

Encoding Categorical Variables Categorical variables represent data in discrete categories, such as gender, marital status, or product type. These variables must be converted into numerical representations before they can be used in ML models. The two most common encoding techniques are:

One-Hot Encoding: This method creates a binary column for each category, where the presence of a category is marked as 1 and its absence as 0. For example, a "color" variable with three categories—red, blue, and green—would be transformed into three separate binary columns.

Label Encoding: Label encoding assigns a unique integer to each category. While this method is more space-efficient, it can introduce unintended ordinal relationships between categories, making it less suitable for non-hierarchical data. Proper encoding of categorical variables ensures that models can correctly interpret and utilize categorical information during training.

Creating Interaction Features Interaction features are new variables that capture the combined effect of two or more original features. For example, in a financial risk analysis model, interaction features could include variables like "age multiplied by income" or "number of past defaults divided by total loan amount," which provide more nuanced insights into customer behavior patterns. Creating such features can improve model interpretability and enable algorithms to learn complex relationships that may not be evident when variables are considered independently.

Feature engineering is a vital step in many real-world ML applications. Consider a financial risk analysis model designed to predict loan defaults. In this scenario, historical transaction data can be used to create new features that capture user behavior patterns more effectively. For example, by combining variables like "average transaction amount" and "frequency of transactions," new features can be generated that provide a clearer indication of a user's spending habits and creditworthiness. Additionally, scaling numeric features such as "loan amount" and "annual income" ensures that the model interprets them correctly, leading to more accurate predictions.

Recent advancements in feature engineering have introduced automated tools and techniques that assist with feature selection, transformation, and creation. For instance, **automated feature selection tools** like RFE and **SHAP values** (from tree-based models) have made it easier to identify the most influential features in a dataset. SHAP (SHapley Additive exPlanations) values, in particular, provide insights into the contribution of each feature to the model's predictions, offering a clearer understanding of feature importance.

Moreover, modern ML workflows increasingly rely on **feature stores**, centralized repositories for storing, managing, and serving engineered features. Feature stores help standardize feature engineering processes, ensuring consistency and reusability across different models and projects. These advancements not only streamline feature engineering but also improve model accuracy and interpretability, as well as reduce the time and effort required to prepare data for ML.

1.2 Introduction to Deep Learning

1.2.1: How Deep Learning Differs from Traditional Machine Learning

Traditional machine learning (ML) relies heavily on manual feature engineering, where domain experts manually select and transform input features to train models like linear regression, decision trees, or support vector machines (SVMs). These models are designed to work well with structured data and often perform best when clear, well-defined features are provided. In contrast, **deep learning** (DL) is a subfield of ML that uses neural networks with multiple layers to automatically extract and learn features from raw data. Deep learning is particularly well-suited for handling large datasets and unstructured data, such as images, text, and audio. While traditional ML models typically require extensive preprocessing and manual feature engineering, DL models excel by learning features directly from the data.

The key differences between traditional ML and deep learning can be observed across several aspects, including feature extraction, scalability, and data requirements:

Automatic Feature Extraction One of the most fundamental differences is how features are derived. In traditional ML, feature engineering is a manual process that requires significant domain expertise and knowledge of the dataset. For example, in an image classification task, traditional ML models might require handcrafted features like edges, colors, or shapes to identify objects in images. In contrast, deep learning models, such as convolutional neural networks (CNNs), automatically extract hierarchical features from images through layers of convolutions and activations. This automated feature extraction is made possible by the network's ability to learn low-level features (e.g., edges) in the initial layers and more complex patterns (e.g., textures or shapes) in deeper layers.

Representation Learning Deep learning introduces the concept of **representation learning**, where the model learns data representations at different levels of abstraction. Traditional ML models, which rely on manually crafted features, typically struggle to capture complex relationships within the data. Deep learning models, however, use multi-layer architectures (e.g., CNNs, recurrent neural networks, and transformers) to learn representations that are better suited for tasks involving unstructured data, such as natural language processing (NLP) or speech recognition. For instance, while an SVM may require features extracted from text data (e.g., TF-IDF or bag-of-words), a transformer-based model like BERT can directly learn contextual representations of words and phrases, making it more accurate for tasks like sentiment analysis or text classification.

Scalability and Large Datasets Deep learning is highly scalable and performs well with large datasets, while traditional ML models tend to reach a performance plateau as the dataset size increases. Deep learning's scalability is largely due to its reliance on neural network architectures that can efficiently utilize parallel processing capabilities of GPUs and TPUs. This makes DL models suitable for tasks like image recognition, speech synthesis, and language translation, where training datasets often contain millions of examples. In contrast, traditional ML models are often limited by their computational complexity and may require sampling techniques or dimensionality reduction to handle large datasets.

Handling Unstructured Data Deep learning is designed to work with unstructured data, which includes text, images, audio, and video. Deep learning models are capable of processing raw input data directly, without extensive preprocessing. For example, a CNN can process raw image pixels, learning to identify patterns and structures automatically. Similarly, a recurrent neural network (RNN) or transformer can handle sequences of words or audio signals without manual feature extraction. On the other hand, traditional ML models generally require structured input data, which often involves converting raw data into tabular forms or extracting specific features for model training.

To illustrate the differences between traditional ML and deep learning, consider the task of **image classification**. In a traditional ML approach, features like color histograms, edge detectors, or texture descriptors might be manually crafted and used as input to an SVM or decision tree. While this approach can work reasonably well for simple tasks, it often fails to capture the full complexity of images, especially in diverse datasets. In contrast, a deep learning approach using a CNN automatically learns and extracts features from raw image data, progressively identifying more complex patterns through its layers. As a result, CNNs outperform traditional ML models in tasks like facial recognition, object detection, and medical imaging analysis.

Another example is **natural language processing (NLP)**. Traditional ML models, such as Naive Bayes or logistic regression, often rely on features like bag-of-words, TF-IDF, or n-grams for text classification. While these features capture word frequency and co-occurrence patterns, they often fail to grasp the contextual relationships between words. Deep learning models, like transformers (e.g., BERT, GPT), on the other hand, use attention mechanisms to understand context and relationships between words in a sentence, leading to superior performance in tasks such as language translation, sentiment analysis, and question answering.

Deep learning's rise in recent years has been fueled by advancements in neural network architectures, computational power, and availability of large-scale datasets. Models like **CNNs** have set benchmarks in computer vision tasks, achieving state-of-the-art performance in image classification, object detection, and segmentation. Similarly, **transformer-based models** have revolutionized NLP, with models like GPT and BERT demonstrating superior performance across a range of tasks by using self-attention mechanisms to understand the relationships between words and sentences.

Recent innovations like **Vision Transformers (ViTs)** have extended the use of transformers beyond text processing to image classification, showing that deep learning's architecture flexibility is a significant advantage over traditional ML. Furthermore, techniques like **transfer learning** allow deep learning models to leverage pre-trained representations from large datasets, making them more effective even when labeled data is limited. This adaptability and performance improvement across a wide range of applications highlight how deep learning has surpassed traditional ML models in many areas.

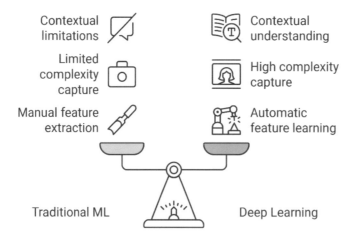

Traditional ML vs. Deep Learning in Image Classification and NLP

1.2.2: Understanding Neural Networks and the Rise of Deep Learning

Neural networks are the core building blocks of deep learning, revolutionizing the field of artificial intelligence (AI) by enabling machines to learn complex patterns from large amounts of data. These networks are inspired by the structure of the human brain, consisting of interconnected nodes (or neurons) that process information in layers. While early forms of neural networks were limited by computational constraints and small datasets, recent advancements have unlocked their potential, making them central to tasks like image recognition, natural language processing (NLP), and even autonomous vehicles. This section explores the fundamental structure of neural networks, their components, and the key developments that have contributed to the rise of deep learning.

At their core, neural networks are composed of layers of neurons that work together to transform input data into meaningful outputs. Here's a breakdown of the key components that enable neural networks to learn and perform complex tasks:

Neurons Neurons, or nodes, are the basic units of a neural network. Each neuron receives input signals, processes them, and produces an output signal. This output is typically passed to other neurons in subsequent layers. Neurons mimic biological neurons by activating (or firing) when certain patterns in the input data are detected. Each neuron has an associated weight, which determines the strength of the input signal it processes. These weights are adjusted during training, allowing the network to learn from errors and improve performance over time.

Activation Functions Activation functions play a crucial role in neural networks by introducing non-linearity, enabling the network to learn complex patterns. Without non-linearity, a neural network would be equivalent to a linear model, limiting its capacity to capture intricate relationships in the data. Common activation functions include:

Sigmoid: Outputs a value between 0 and 1, often used in binary classification problems.

ReLU (Rectified Linear Unit): Outputs the input if it is positive and 0 otherwise, making it effective for handling non-linear relationships.

Softmax: Used in the output layer for multi-class classification, transforming logits into probabilities that sum up to 1. The choice of activation function depends on the type of task and the specific requirements of the neural network model.

Layers (Input, Hidden, Output) Neural networks are organized into three main types of layers:

Input Layer: This layer receives raw input data, such as images, text, or numerical features, and passes it to the subsequent layers.

Hidden Layers: These layers are responsible for feature extraction and transformation. Neural networks can have one or multiple hidden layers, with deep neural networks containing many layers (hence the term "deep learning"). Each hidden layer extracts different levels of abstraction, allowing the network to learn complex patterns. For example, in image classification, the initial hidden layers might detect edges or colors, while deeper layers identify more abstract concepts like shapes or objects.

Output Layer: The final layer produces the network's output, which can be a class label (in classification tasks), a numerical value (in regression tasks), or another type of prediction based on the problem at hand. By adjusting the weights and biases in the neurons across these layers, neural networks can learn to minimize errors and improve their predictions, making them powerful tools for a wide range of AI applications.

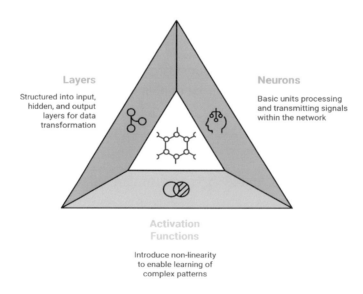

Neural networks have been at the forefront of many AI breakthroughs, enabling machines to perform tasks that were once thought to be exclusive to humans:

Speech Recognition: Deep neural networks are widely used in speech recognition systems, powering virtual assistants like Siri, Alexa, and Google Assistant. These networks learn to identify phonetic patterns in audio data, allowing them to convert spoken language into text accurately. Recurrent neural networks (RNNs) and transformers, which handle sequential data effectively, are commonly used for processing spoken words in real time.

Autonomous Vehicles: Companies like Tesla have integrated neural networks into self-driving software, enabling vehicles to recognize objects, interpret traffic signals, and make decisions based on their surroundings. Convolutional neural networks (CNNs), which are particularly effective for processing visual data, play a central role in analyzing images from vehicle cameras, helping the car navigate safely on the road.

Medical Imaging: In the healthcare sector, neural networks have transformed medical imaging by detecting abnormalities in X-rays, MRIs, and CT scans. Deep learning models trained on large datasets of medical images can identify diseases with high accuracy, assisting doctors in diagnosing conditions like cancer, pneumonia, and brain tumors.

The rise of deep learning has been driven by several historical milestones and technological advancements:

Backpropagation Algorithm The introduction of the backpropagation algorithm in the 1980s was a pivotal moment for neural networks. Backpropagation enabled networks to adjust weights efficiently by propagating errors backward through the network layers, allowing the model to learn from its mistakes. This advancement made training deeper networks feasible and laid the groundwork for the growth of deep learning.

Increased Computational Power (GPUs) The availability of Graphics Processing Units (GPUs) in the 2000s significantly accelerated the training of neural networks. GPUs, with their parallel processing capabilities, allowed deep learning models to handle large-scale data more efficiently. This improvement was crucial for training complex models like CNNs and RNNs, which require extensive computation.

Access to Large Datasets The rise of big data and the availability of large, labeled datasets have been key factors in the success of deep learning. For instance, the ImageNet dataset, containing over a million labeled images, enabled researchers to train models like AlexNet and ResNet, leading to major improvements in computer vision tasks.

Recent Advancements in Architectures Recent innovations in neural network architectures have further expanded the capabilities of deep learning:

Residual Networks (ResNet): Introduced in 2015, ResNet addressed the issue of vanishing gradients in deep networks by using skip connections that allow information to bypass one or more layers. This architecture enabled the training of much deeper networks, achieving state-of-the-art results in image classification.

Transformers: The introduction of transformer models revolutionized NLP by using self-attention mechanisms to capture relationships between words, regardless of their position in a sentence. Transformers, such as GPT and BERT, have become the backbone of NLP applications, enabling advanced language understanding and generation.

1.2.3: Why Deep Learning Excels with Large Datasets and Unstructured Data

Handling large datasets and unstructured data effectively has always been a challenge in machine learning (ML). Traditional ML models often struggle to process raw, unorganized data, like text, images, or audio, and typically require significant preprocessing and manual feature engineering. Additionally, as the size of the dataset increases, traditional models may encounter scalability issues, leading to diminishing returns in performance. Deep learning, on the other hand, thrives on large datasets and unstructured data due to its ability to automatically extract hierarchical features and utilize powerful hardware like GPUs and TPUs for parallel computation. In this section, we explore how deep learning overcomes the challenges posed by large and unstructured data, enabling superior performance across various tasks and industries.

Deep learning's capability to handle large datasets and unstructured data stems from its multi-layer architecture and self-learning feature extraction mechanisms:

Automatic Feature Extraction for Unstructured Data One of the key strengths of deep learning is its ability to automatically learn hierarchical representations of data, making it particularly well-suited for unstructured data types, such as text, images, and audio.

For example, convolutional neural networks (CNNs) are designed to process images by learning low-level features like edges and textures in the initial layers, and more complex patterns, like objects and scenes, in the deeper layers. Similarly, transformers in NLP applications can capture contextual relationships in text data, from individual words to sentence-level semantics, without requiring manual feature extraction.

This automated feature extraction allows deep learning models to handle a wide variety of unstructured data efficiently. While traditional ML models often require preprocessing steps to convert raw data into structured inputs, deep learning models can process raw inputs directly, making them more versatile and effective in diverse applications, from sentiment analysis to image classification.

Scalability with Large Datasets Deep learning models perform better as more data becomes available, unlike traditional ML models, which tend to plateau in performance as dataset size increases. This scalability is largely due to the neural network's capacity to adjust weights and learn more complex representations as data volume grows.

The use of GPUs and TPUs has significantly contributed to deep learning's success with large datasets. These hardware accelerators are optimized for parallel processing, allowing for faster computations during training. For instance, training a deep learning model on a dataset with millions of images can be achieved efficiently by leveraging multiple GPUs in a distributed setup, reducing training time from weeks to days.

Additionally, the batch processing capabilities of deep learning models enable efficient utilization of hardware resources. During training, models process data in batches, making use of parallel computation to handle large volumes of data simultaneously. This approach not only speeds up training but also improves model accuracy, as larger datasets provide a broader range of examples from which the model can learn.

The impact of deep learning's ability to handle large datasets and unstructured data is evident in numerous real-world applications:

Google Search Algorithm: Google uses neural networks to enhance its search algorithm, enabling it to deliver more accurate search results. Deep learning models process vast amounts of unstructured data, such as web pages, user behavior, and contextual relationships between queries. The models' ability to analyze millions of data points in real time helps improve the relevance and accuracy of search results, making Google's search engine more intuitive and effective for users.

Netflix Recommendation System: Netflix utilizes deep learning models to analyze user viewing patterns and preferences across massive datasets. The recommendation engine uses neural networks to process both structured data (e.g., user ratings, viewing history) and unstructured data (e.g., textual descriptions of shows, thumbnails, and video trailers). By leveraging large datasets, Netflix can generate personalized recommendations that enhance user engagement and satisfaction.

Autonomous Driving: Self-driving cars rely on deep learning models to process vast amounts of sensory data from cameras, LiDAR, and radar systems. These models use CNNs to interpret visual inputs, identifying pedestrians, road signs, and obstacles in real time. The scalability of deep learning models allows them to learn from extensive datasets collected over millions of driving miles, improving accuracy and decision-making in various driving conditions.

Recent advancements in handling large datasets and unstructured data have further propelled deep learning's capabilities:

Distributed Training Distributed training enables deep learning models to scale across multiple GPUs, TPUs, or even clusters of machines, significantly reducing training time for large models and datasets. Techniques like data parallelism (splitting data across multiple devices) and model parallelism (splitting the model itself across devices) have made it feasible to train models like GPT-3, which contain billions of parameters, on massive datasets.

Federated Learning Federated learning allows deep learning models to be trained across decentralized datasets, enhancing data privacy while maintaining performance. Instead of aggregating data into a central server, federated learning trains models locally on users' devices and aggregates the learned parameters, enabling deep learning to utilize diverse datasets without compromising user privacy.

Vision Transformers (ViTs) for Image Processing Vision transformers have emerged as an alternative to CNNs for image processing, demonstrating improved performance on large datasets. Unlike CNNs, which rely on convolutional layers, transformers use self-attention mechanisms to capture global dependencies in images. This approach has proven effective for large-scale image classification tasks, making transformers a promising architecture for processing unstructured visual data.

Large Language Models (LLMs) Recent advancements in large language models (LLMs), like GPT (Generative Pre-trained Transformer), have shown exceptional performance in handling large text datasets. These models are pre-trained on extensive corpora of text data, allowing them to generate coherent text, perform translations, and answer questions with human-like understanding. The ability of LLMs to process and understand vast amounts of unstructured text data showcases the scalability and flexibility of deep learning in NLP tasks.

1.3 Deep Learning vs. Machine Learning

1.3.1: Key Differences Between ML and DL in Practice

Machine learning (ML) and deep learning (DL) are both powerful tools for creating predictive models, but they differ significantly in their underlying approaches and practical applications. While both fields share the same fundamental goal—using data to make predictions—their methods diverge based on how they handle data, the complexity of the models, and the computational requirements involved. ML models are typically simpler, relying on manual feature engineering and smaller datasets, making them more suitable for straightforward tasks. In contrast, DL models use neural networks to automatically learn from raw data, allowing them to excel in handling large and unstructured datasets.

A closer look at ML and DL reveals key differences that impact their effectiveness in different situations:

One of the most significant distinctions between ML and DL lies in **feature engineering**. In traditional ML, feature engineering is often a manual process. Domain experts identify and create specific features from raw data, tailoring the input to improve model performance. For example, in predicting house prices, traditional ML models like linear regression or decision trees rely on engineered features such as "number of bedrooms," "square footage," or "years since renovation." These models perform well when the features are carefully selected, but the process is time-consuming and requires domain-specific knowledge. Deep learning, however, takes a different approach by eliminating the need for manual feature engineering. Instead, DL models use neural networks with multiple layers to automatically learn features directly from raw data. For instance, convolutional neural networks (CNNs) can identify edges, textures, and complex shapes within images without any manual intervention, making them particularly effective for tasks like image classification and facial recognition.

Another major difference is in **model complexity and computational requirements**. ML models are generally simpler, making them easier to interpret and quicker to train. Algorithms like linear regression, logistic regression, and support vector machines (SVMs) use straightforward mathematical relationships to make predictions, requiring less computational power. These models are suitable for scenarios where transparency is important, such as in credit scoring or medical diagnoses, where decisions need to be interpretable. On the other hand, deep learning models involve deeper architectures with many layers of neurons, enabling them to capture complex patterns in the data. However, this added complexity comes at a cost. DL models require significant computational resources, often relying on specialized hardware like GPUs and TPUs for efficient training. For example, training a large natural language processing (NLP) model, such as GPT, involves handling billions of parameters and vast amounts of text data, making it a computationally intensive process.

The **data requirements** for ML and DL also differ. Traditional ML models perform well with smaller datasets, provided that the features are well-engineered. For example, in a medical diagnostic system, a logistic regression model might accurately predict disease outcomes based on a limited number of patient features, such as age, blood pressure, and cholesterol levels. In such cases, having a smaller, well-curated dataset is often sufficient for accurate predictions. Deep learning, however, thrives on large datasets. The ability of DL models to learn from diverse and extensive datasets is what sets them apart. For instance, a deep learning model trained on millions of customer reviews can better understand nuances in sentiment analysis, capturing subtleties like sarcasm or slang. Additionally, DL's capacity to handle unstructured data—like images, audio, and raw text—makes it the preferred choice for complex tasks like speech recognition and self-driving cars, where massive and varied data sources are the norm.

In practical applications, the differences between ML and DL become even more evident. For example, consider predicting house prices. In a traditional ML approach, a linear regression model might use structured data, relying on features such as square footage, number of bedrooms, and proximity to schools. This approach is efficient and interpretable, making it suitable for real estate analysts who need clear explanations of how the model arrived at its predictions. In contrast, a deep learning approach might involve analyzing satellite images of neighborhoods alongside structured data, using a CNN to automatically detect patterns in the images. This allows for a richer understanding of the factors influencing house prices, but at the cost of increased complexity and data requirements.

Another clear example is found in **image recognition**. Traditional ML models, such as SVMs, can classify images if specific features like edges or color histograms are extracted manually. However, these models often struggle with more complex images that have overlapping objects or varying lighting conditions. Deep learning models, such as CNNs, excel in these tasks by processing raw pixel data and automatically learning the relevant features through layers of convolution. This makes DL models more effective for tasks like facial recognition, medical imaging, and object detection in autonomous vehicles.

In the realm of **text classification**, the differences are similarly stark. Traditional ML models often use techniques like TF-IDF or bag-of-words to convert text into numerical representations. While these techniques capture word frequency, they fail to capture context or relationships between words. Deep learning models, such as transformers (e.g., BERT), use self-attention mechanisms to understand the context, making them more accurate for sentiment analysis, translation, and language understanding.

Recent advancements have further emphasized these differences in practical applications. **AutoML**, for instance, has made traditional ML more accessible by automating tasks like feature selection, hyperparameter tuning, and model evaluation. This has allowed ML to remain relevant in smaller projects where labeled data is limited and computational resources are constrained. Meanwhile, deep learning has benefited from breakthroughs like **self-supervised learning**, which allows models to learn from large amounts of unlabeled data. This approach has been crucial for training large language models (LLMs) like GPT, enabling them to achieve remarkable performance without relying solely on labeled data. Additionally, advancements in **hardware acceleration** and **distributed training** have enabled DL models to handle unprecedented volumes of data, further underscoring their scalability and effectiveness with complex datasets.

1.3.2: Real-World Applications of Machine Learning vs. Deep Learning

Machine learning (ML) and deep learning (DL) are applied across a wide range of industries, each demonstrating strengths in specific types of tasks. The choice between ML and DL often depends on the complexity of the problem, the nature of the data, and the computational resources available. While ML models are typically more effective in handling structured data with simpler algorithms, DL models excel in processing large datasets and unstructured data, making them well-suited for complex tasks like image recognition, language processing, and autonomous systems. This section explores how ML and DL are used across different industries and compares their effectiveness in various applications.

The applications of ML and DL vary significantly based on the requirements of different tasks. Here's an in-depth comparison:

Machine Learning Applications ML models have found extensive use in areas that involve structured data and where interpretability, speed, and resource efficiency are critical.

Fraud Detection in Finance: In the financial sector, traditional ML models are widely used for detecting fraudulent transactions. Algorithms like logistic regression, decision trees, and random forests can effectively identify patterns in transaction data, such as unusual spending behavior, rapid transactions, or geographic inconsistencies. Because these models are relatively simple and require less computational power, they can quickly analyze structured financial data and make real-time predictions, making them ideal for fraud detection systems.

Customer Segmentation in Marketing: In marketing, ML models are used to segment customers based on demographic data, purchasing behavior, or online interactions. Clustering algorithms, such as K-Means or hierarchical clustering, help marketers identify customer groups for targeted campaigns. This segmentation allows for personalized marketing strategies that improve customer engagement and conversion rates.

Predictive Maintenance in Manufacturing: In manufacturing, ML models play a crucial role in predictive maintenance, where they analyze sensor data to predict when equipment is likely to fail. By identifying patterns in structured data—like temperature, vibration, or operational speed—ML models can alert maintenance teams to potential issues before they occur, reducing downtime and repair costs.

Deep Learning Applications DL models, due to their ability to handle unstructured data and large datasets, are deployed in more complex, data-intensive applications.

Image Recognition in Healthcare: In the healthcare sector, deep learning models are used for image recognition tasks, such as analyzing X-rays, MRIs, or CT scans. Convolutional neural networks (CNNs) can process raw image data, identifying anomalies like tumors or fractures with a high degree of accuracy. Unlike traditional ML models, which require manually extracted features, CNNs automatically learn the relevant patterns directly from the images, making them more effective for complex medical diagnostics.

NLP in Virtual Assistants: Deep learning has transformed natural language processing (NLP), particularly in the development of virtual assistants like Siri, Alexa, and Google Assistant. Recurrent neural networks (RNNs), long short-term memory networks (LSTMs), and transformers enable these systems to understand spoken language, generate natural responses, and even recognize user intent. These DL models can process massive amounts of text data, learning context and semantics at a deeper level than traditional ML-based chatbots, which often rely on decision trees or simpler models.

Self-Driving Cars: Autonomous vehicles heavily rely on deep learning to process sensor data from cameras, LiDAR, and radar systems. DL models, particularly CNNs and transformers, analyze images and sequences in real-time, identifying pedestrians, traffic signals, and road conditions. This capability allows the vehicle to make split-second decisions, a level of complexity that traditional ML models would struggle to handle due to their limitations with unstructured data and large-scale processing.

To better understand the differences in ML and DL applications, let's consider a few side-by-side examples:

Chatbots vs. Virtual Assistants: Traditional ML-based chatbots often use decision trees or Naive Bayes algorithms to generate predefined responses based on keyword matching. For example, a customer support chatbot might identify the phrase "order status" and direct users to a relevant information page. In contrast, DL-based virtual assistants, like Google Assistant, use transformers to understand the context of a query, enabling more natural conversations. These virtual assistants can interpret nuanced language, handle follow-up questions, and adapt to varied speech patterns, making them more effective for complex interactions.

Image Classification vs. Object Detection: Traditional ML models can classify images using algorithms like SVMs, provided that features such as edges or colors are manually extracted. For example, an SVM might be able to determine whether an image contains a dog or a cat, based on pre-extracted pixel features. In contrast, DL models like CNNs not only classify images but also perform object detection, identifying multiple objects within a single image. This capability is crucial in applications like facial recognition, where a model must locate and identify multiple faces in a crowd.

Sentiment Analysis in Text: ML models like logistic regression can perform sentiment analysis by using bag-of-words or TF-IDF features, which count word frequency to determine sentiment. While effective for basic sentiment detection, these models often miss context, such as sarcasm or nuanced language. Deep learning models, such as BERT or GPT, handle sentiment analysis more effectively by capturing word relationships and context. For instance, BERT can understand that "I love waiting in line all day" is likely sarcastic, while traditional ML models might misinterpret it as positive sentiment.

Recent advancements in both ML and DL applications continue to enhance their effectiveness in real-world use:

Federated Learning for ML: Federated learning has emerged as a significant development in privacy-preserving machine learning, allowing models to be trained across decentralized devices without centralizing the data. This approach is particularly useful in healthcare and finance, where data privacy is a major concern. For example, ML models can be trained on patient data across multiple hospitals without sharing sensitive information, preserving privacy while improving model accuracy.

Vision Transformers for DL: In DL, vision transformers have revolutionized image processing by replacing convolutional layers with self-attention mechanisms. This approach allows models to better capture global dependencies in images, improving performance in complex tasks like object segmentation and scene understanding. Vision transformers have set new benchmarks in computer vision, demonstrating the versatility of DL in handling large datasets and unstructured data.

1.3.3: The Evolution of AI Through ML and DL Technologies

The evolution of artificial intelligence (AI) has been marked by distinct phases, beginning with early rule-based systems, progressing through machine learning (ML), and culminating in deep learning (DL). Initially, AI systems were rule-based, relying on predefined logic to make decisions. While effective for simple tasks, these systems lacked the flexibility needed for complex real-world problems. The 1980s and 1990s saw the rise of ML, which enabled computers to learn from structured data using models like decision trees, support vector machines (SVMs), and ensemble methods. However, the advent of DL in the 2010s marked a turning point in AI, allowing machines to process unstructured data and extract hierarchical patterns through multi-layer neural networks. This section explores key milestones in AI's progression from ML to DL and how each phase has contributed to AI's expanding capabilities.

The evolution of AI can be divided into two major phases: early ML development and the deep learning revolution.

Early AI and ML (1980s-1990s) The development of machine learning brought significant advancements to AI. ML introduced algorithms that could learn from data, reducing the need for manual rule-coding. Key ML models from this era include:

> **Decision Trees**: These models gained popularity for their intuitive structure, breaking down decisions into simpler, interpretable steps. For example, a decision tree for predicting loan approvals might start by evaluating an applicant's income, followed by factors like credit history and employment status.
>
> **Support Vector Machines (SVMs)**: SVMs were developed to handle both linear and non-linear classification tasks by finding the optimal hyperplane that separates classes. They became especially useful for tasks like text categorization and image classification, where distinct class boundaries needed to be established.
>
> **Ensemble Methods**: Techniques like random forests and boosting algorithms improved predictive accuracy by combining the outputs of multiple models. For instance, a random forest model might use several decision trees to improve predictions, reducing variance and bias in the process.

Despite these advancements, early ML models were constrained by their reliance on structured data and manual feature engineering. For example, predicting heart disease risk required explicit input features like blood pressure, cholesterol levels, and age, making it difficult to incorporate more complex or unstructured data, such as medical images or free-form text.

Deep Learning Revolution (2010s-Present) The 2010s marked a significant shift with the emergence of deep learning, fueled by breakthroughs in algorithms, hardware, and data availability. Several factors contributed to DL's rapid adoption and effectiveness:

Backpropagation: The introduction of backpropagation allowed neural networks to adjust weights more efficiently during training. By propagating errors backward through the network, this technique enabled models to learn from complex patterns across multiple layers, making DL feasible for more sophisticated applications.

Increased Computational Power: The widespread use of Graphics Processing Units (GPUs) and the later introduction of Tensor Processing Units (TPUs) enabled faster training of DL models. GPUs' ability to handle parallel computations allowed models like CNNs and RNNs to process large datasets more efficiently.

Development of New Architectures:
Convolutional Neural Networks (CNNs) became the standard for computer vision, excelling at tasks like image classification, object detection, and medical imaging analysis.

Recurrent Neural Networks (RNNs) and their variants (e.g., LSTMs, GRUs) improved sequential data processing, making DL effective in NLP tasks such as language translation and speech recognition.

Transformers further revolutionized NLP by using self-attention mechanisms to understand context across long sequences, leading to breakthroughs in text generation, language understanding, and machine translation.

The transition from ML to DL has reshaped AI applications across industries, demonstrating clear advancements in performance, accuracy, and versatility:

Computer Vision: Early ML models in computer vision relied on manually extracted features like edges and textures, which were fed into SVMs or decision trees. For example, early facial recognition systems used these features to identify faces but struggled with variations in lighting, angles, and occlusions. With the rise of DL, CNNs replaced these models, enabling automated feature extraction from raw pixel data. This shift allowed for real-time object detection, which is now integral to applications like autonomous vehicles and medical imaging, where precision and speed are crucial.

Natural Language Processing (NLP): In the initial stages of NLP, ML models such as Naive Bayes or logistic regression relied on bag-of-words or TF-IDF features for text analysis. While effective for basic tasks like spam detection or sentiment analysis, these models often missed the nuances of language, such as sarcasm or context-specific meanings. DL models, particularly transformers, revolutionized NLP by capturing word relationships and context more effectively. This advancement enabled applications like virtual assistants, real-time language translation, and text generation, which require a deeper understanding of language.

Healthcare Diagnostics: In early AI healthcare applications, ML models analyzed structured data like patient demographics or lab results to predict disease risk. For instance, decision trees could predict heart disease risk based on factors like blood pressure and cholesterol. However, analyzing medical images required more advanced techniques. CNNs transformed medical imaging analysis by learning from raw image data, enabling the detection of tumors, fractures, and other anomalies with higher accuracy. This shift has significantly improved diagnostic capabilities, leading to better patient outcomes.

AI's evolution continues, marked by recent innovations that blend traditional ML techniques with DL advancements:

Hybrid Models: There is a growing interest in developing hybrid models that integrate symbolic reasoning with neural networks. These models aim to combine the pattern recognition capabilities of DL with the logical reasoning strengths of rule-based systems. For example, in automated medical diagnosis, hybrid models can use DL to identify visual patterns in scans while also applying logical rules based on clinical guidelines.

Transfer Learning: Transfer learning has become a critical tool in both ML and DL. By reusing pre-trained models on new tasks, transfer learning allows models to adapt quickly, even with limited labeled data. This approach has been particularly useful in applications like rare disease identification, where training data is scarce.

Self-Supervised Learning: Self-supervised learning, which enables models to learn from unlabeled data, has further enhanced DL's ability to generalize across various tasks. This approach generates pseudo-labels from the data itself, allowing models to train on vast amounts of raw data without manual labeling.

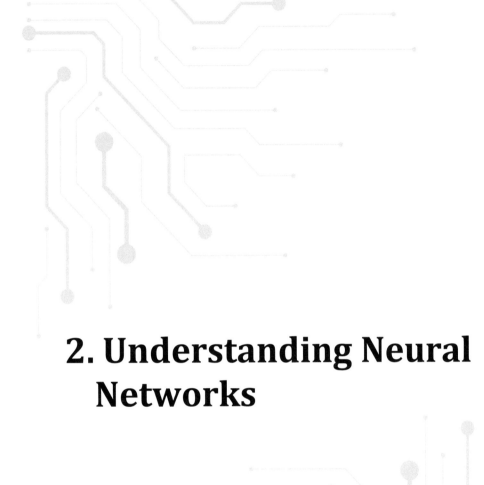

2. Understanding Neural Networks

2.1 Neural Network Basics

2.1.1: Introduction to Neurons and Activation Functions

Neurons are the fundamental units of neural networks, serving as the building blocks for artificial intelligence models. In many ways, they function similarly to biological neurons, which transmit signals based on stimuli received from the environment. In neural networks, each artificial neuron receives inputs, processes them, and determines whether to "fire" (i.e., activate), passing the signal forward. This decision-making process is controlled by activation functions, which play a critical role in determining how neural networks process and learn from data. Activation functions introduce non-linearity, enabling the network to learn complex patterns and relationships that linear models cannot capture.

Neurons process inputs by performing a weighted summation of the incoming signals, followed by the addition of a bias term. This operation helps the network adjust its outputs beyond purely linear relationships. Each input is associated with a weight that indicates its importance in the learning process. The weighted sum is then passed through an activation function, which decides whether the neuron should activate. If the output exceeds a certain threshold, the neuron becomes active, transmitting signals to the next layer. This chain reaction is what enables neural networks to model intricate relationships and improve predictions over time.

Activation functions are crucial in shaping the learning process of neural networks. Among the most commonly used activation functions are **Sigmoid**, **ReLU** (Rectified Linear Unit), and **Tanh**:

> **Sigmoid** maps input values to a range between 0 and 1, making it suitable for binary classification tasks. However, its outputs can be close to zero, especially for large negative inputs, leading to the vanishing gradient problem that slows down learning in deep networks.

> **ReLU**, in contrast, outputs the input value if it's positive and zero if it's not. This simplicity makes ReLU computationally efficient and popular in modern neural networks. By avoiding negative outputs, ReLU helps mitigate the vanishing gradient problem, speeding up training. However, it can suffer from the "dying ReLU" issue, where neurons stop activating altogether.

Tanh outputs values between -1 and 1, making it more effective than Sigmoid for capturing both positive and negative relationships. It provides stronger gradients, especially for negative inputs, enhancing learning in deeper layers.

Neurons and activation functions play vital roles in tasks such as image recognition and natural language processing (NLP). In **image recognition**, for example, neurons in the initial layers of a convolutional neural network (CNN) detect simple patterns like edges and textures. As the signal passes through deeper layers, activation functions enable the network to recognize more complex features, such as shapes and entire objects. In **NLP tasks**, activation functions allow models to understand sequential relationships between words, enabling tasks like sentiment analysis, where neurons activate based on the presence of positive or negative terms.

Recent advancements in activation functions have addressed some of the limitations of earlier functions. **Leaky ReLU**, for example, allows a small gradient for negative inputs, preventing neurons from becoming permanently inactive. Another innovation, **Swish**, provides smooth gradients and has demonstrated better performance than ReLU in certain tasks, particularly in deeper networks. These developments reflect ongoing efforts to enhance neural network performance by improving the mechanisms that govern neuron activation.

The interaction between neurons and activation functions is fundamental to how neural networks learn from data. By controlling the activation of neurons and enabling complex signal transformations across layers, activation functions shape the network's ability to capture both simple and intricate patterns in the input data. This capability is crucial for the success of neural networks in a wide range of applications, from identifying objects in images to understanding context in natural language.

2.1.2: Structure of a Neural Network (Input, Hidden, and Output Layers)

A neural network comprises three main layers: **input layer**, **hidden layers**, and **output layer**. Each of these layers plays a distinct role in processing data, working together to transform raw inputs into meaningful outputs. This layered structure allows the network to learn patterns and make predictions, from simple classifications to complex recognitions.

The **input layer** is the entry point of the network, receiving raw data from the input source. This data could be anything from pixel values in an image, numerical values in a dataset, or word embeddings from text. The input layer simply passes this data to the next set of layers without altering it. For example, in an image recognition task, the input layer receives pixel values representing colors and intensities, setting the stage for further processing.

Moving forward, the **hidden layers** form the core of the neural network, responsible for transforming the input data into more abstract representations. These layers contain neurons that perform weighted summations, apply activation functions, and pass the processed information forward. In simple neural networks, there might be only one hidden layer, but in **deep neural networks**, multiple hidden layers work together, enabling the model to learn hierarchical patterns. For instance, in a **convolutional neural network (CNN)**:

> **Early hidden layers** detect basic features like edges and textures.

> **Middle layers** capture intermediate features, such as shapes and patterns.

> **Deeper layers** identify complex combinations, recognizing entire objects or scenes.

This hierarchical learning is crucial in deep learning, as it allows the model to represent complex patterns that simpler models cannot capture.

The **output layer** is the final component, generating the model's prediction or classification. It takes the processed information from the last hidden layer and produces an output, such as a class label (e.g., "cat" or "dog" in image classification) or a numerical value (e.g., predicted stock price). In classification tasks, the output layer often uses the **Softmax** activation function to convert outputs into probabilities, selecting the most likely category.

Real-world applications demonstrate the power of this layered structure. For example, in a CNN used for image classification:

> The **input layer** receives raw pixel values.

> The **hidden layers** sequentially detect features, from simple edges to complex shapes.

The **output layer** generates a prediction, identifying the object in the image.

In a **facial recognition system**, the initial hidden layers might detect individual facial features (e.g., eyes, nose, mouth), while the deeper layers integrate these features to recognize an entire face.

As data flows through the **input**, **hidden**, and **output layers**, each layer's role becomes clearer. The network transforms raw data step-by-step, making neural networks highly effective for a variety of tasks—ranging from image recognition and speech synthesis to natural language processing.

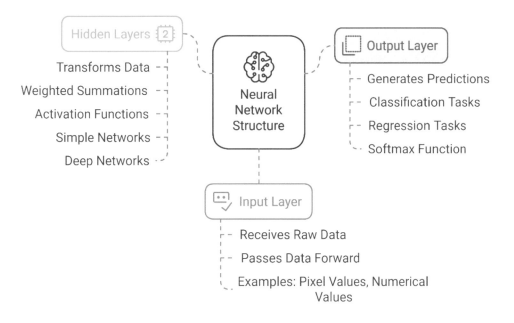

2.1.3: The Role of Weights and Biases in Learning

Weights and biases are the core components that enable neural networks to learn from data. In simple terms:

Weights determine the influence of each input on the output, reflecting the importance of different features in making predictions.

Biases allow the network to adjust outputs, helping the model fit patterns that aren't directly tied to the input values alone.

When an input enters a neuron, it is multiplied by a corresponding weight, which scales the input's impact. This weighted sum is then adjusted by adding a bias before passing it through an activation function. The combination of weights and biases enables the network to capture complex relationships in the data, allowing it to learn non-linear patterns. For example, in an image recognition task, the initial layers might assign higher weights to pixels representing edges, while deeper layers might focus more on shapes or patterns.

The learning process in neural networks revolves around continuously adjusting these weights and biases to minimize prediction errors. This adjustment is achieved through an optimization technique known as **gradient descent**:

1. **Calculate the gradient** of the loss function with respect to each parameter (weights and biases).
2. **Update weights and biases** by moving them in the opposite direction of the gradient, effectively reducing the error.
3. **Iterate this process** over multiple training cycles, gradually refining the parameters to improve prediction accuracy.

For instance, in **sentiment analysis** within natural language processing (NLP), the network aims to determine whether a given text has a positive, negative, or neutral sentiment. During training:

> Words with positive connotations (e.g., "good," "happy") are assigned higher weights, enhancing their influence on positive sentiment classification.

> Biases are adjusted to account for different sentence structures, helping the model maintain accuracy across varying contexts.

This fine-tuning of weights and biases enables the model to learn complex word associations, ultimately improving sentiment prediction accuracy.

Weights and biases are critical to how neural networks interpret and learn from data. By controlling the strength of inputs and adjusting the network's response, these parameters play a central role in shaping the learning process. This makes them indispensable in applications ranging from image recognition and speech processing to NLP and beyond.

2.2 Backpropagation and Gradient Descent

2.2.1: How Backpropagation Works in Adjusting Network Weights

Backpropagation is a fundamental algorithm that enables neural networks to learn from their mistakes and improve over time. It serves as the backbone of the training process, allowing the model to adjust its weights in response to errors in its predictions. By minimizing the difference between predicted outcomes and actual results, backpropagation guides the network toward more accurate predictions.

To understand backpropagation, it's important to first grasp the concept of how neural networks process data. When an input passes through the network, each layer transforms it by applying weights, biases, and activation functions. The network then produces an output, which is compared to the actual label (or target) using a **loss function**. The loss function quantifies the error, measuring how far off the network's prediction is from the expected outcome. This error becomes the focal point for backpropagation, which aims to reduce it.

How Backpropagation Adjusts Weights

The core mechanism of backpropagation involves calculating the **gradient** of the error with respect to each weight in the network. This process unfolds in three main steps:

1. **Forward Pass**: The input data is fed through the network, layer by layer, to generate an initial prediction. The output is then compared to the actual target, and the error is calculated using the loss function.
2. **Backward Pass**: Starting from the output layer, backpropagation propagates the error backward through the network. It calculates the gradient of the error with respect to each weight using the **chain rule** of calculus. This gradient indicates the direction and magnitude of change needed to reduce the error.
3. **Weight Adjustment**: The weights are updated in the opposite direction of the gradient (using techniques like **gradient descent**), ensuring that the error decreases. The size of the weight adjustment is influenced by the learning rate, which controls how quickly the model learns. A larger learning rate results in bigger adjustments, while a smaller one makes more gradual changes.

This iterative process continues until the model reaches an acceptable level of accuracy or the error converges to a minimal value. By adjusting the weights based on the gradient of the error, backpropagation allows the network to learn from its mistakes and improve its predictions.

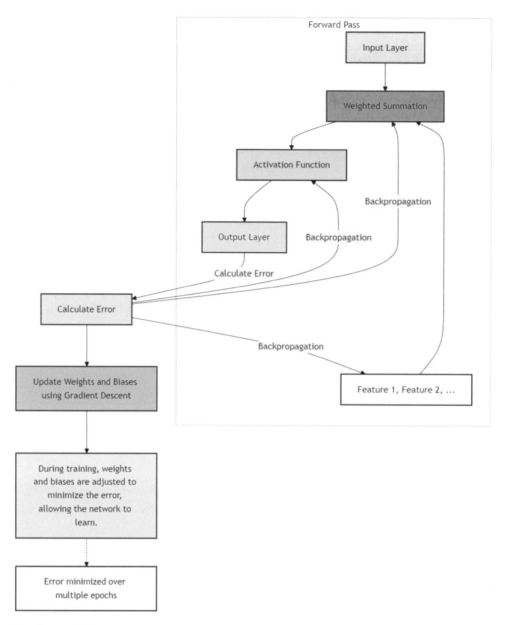

This diagram illustrates the forward and backward passes in the process of backpropagation within a neural network. In the forward pass, input features flow through layers of weighted summations, activation functions, and an output layer, generating initial predictions. The error, calculated by comparing predictions to actual values, is then propagated backward, adjusting the network's weights and biases through gradient descent. This iterative process, repeated over multiple epochs, enables the network to minimize errors and improve its predictive accuracy, making backpropagation essential for neural network training and optimization.

Example: Image Classification

Consider a **convolutional neural network (CNN)** trained to classify images as either "cat" or "dog." During the forward pass, the network analyzes features like edges, fur patterns, and shapes to generate a prediction. If the model incorrectly classifies a cat image as a dog, the loss function calculates the error based on the difference between the predicted and actual labels.

During the backward pass, backpropagation identifies which neurons and weights contributed most to the error. For instance:

- Early convolutional layers might have missed detecting specific fur patterns due to incorrect weight settings.
- Deeper layers might have misinterpreted the overall shape of the animal.

Backpropagation adjusts the weights associated with these features, increasing or decreasing their influence to minimize future errors. As the network continues training, it becomes better at distinguishing between cats and dogs, refining its understanding of image features through weight adjustments.

The Broader Impact of Backpropagation

Backpropagation is more than just an error-correction algorithm; it is the foundation of how neural networks learn from data. By systematically adjusting weights in response to errors, backpropagation enables the network to discover complex patterns, relationships, and dependencies in the data. This iterative refinement is what makes neural networks capable of achieving high accuracy in diverse tasks, from image recognition to natural language processing.

Moreover, backpropagation's influence extends beyond neural networks, as it is also a critical component in the training of advanced models like transformers and recurrent neural networks (RNNs). These models use backpropagation to handle sequential data, capturing dependencies across time steps or sentence structures, making it essential in applications like language translation, speech recognition, and text generation.

2.2.2: Gradient Descent as an Optimization Method for Training

Gradient descent is a foundational optimization technique used in training neural networks. Its primary purpose is to minimize the error in predictions by finding the optimal set of weights that reduce the **loss function**, which measures how far off the model's predictions are from the actual targets. By iteratively updating weights, gradient descent guides the neural network toward making more accurate predictions.

The core idea of gradient descent is to adjust weights by taking steps proportional to the **negative gradient** of the error. In this context:

- The **gradient** represents the slope of the error with respect to each weight, indicating the direction and rate of change needed to minimize the error.
- The **negative gradient** determines the direction of steepest descent, guiding the model to reduce the error.
- The **step size**, known as the learning rate, controls how much the weights are adjusted in each iteration.

The process begins with a forward pass, where the input data is passed through the network to generate a prediction. The error is then calculated using the loss function, and the gradients are computed using **backpropagation**. During the backward pass, the weights are updated based on the negative gradient, gradually reducing the error over multiple training cycles. The size of each step is determined by the learning rate, which plays a crucial role in balancing training speed and accuracy—large learning rates can lead to overshooting the minimum, while small rates can make the training process slow and potentially stuck in local minima.

Key Variations of Gradient Descent

There are three main variations of gradient descent, each differing in terms of speed, accuracy, and computational efficiency:

Batch Gradient Descent: Batch gradient descent calculates the gradient of the error for the entire training dataset before updating the weights. While this approach can provide a stable estimate of the gradient, it requires processing the entire dataset at once, making it computationally intensive, especially for large datasets. It is generally more accurate but slower, as updates occur less frequently.

Stochastic Gradient Descent (SGD): In contrast, SGD updates weights after processing each individual training example. This approach allows for faster updates and can escape local minima more effectively, making it suitable for large-scale training. However, the frequent updates can introduce more noise into the training process, leading to less stable convergence and oscillations in the loss function.

Mini-Batch Gradient Descent: Mini-batch gradient descent combines the benefits of both batch and stochastic approaches. It splits the training dataset into small batches and updates the weights after processing each batch. This variation balances computational efficiency and gradient accuracy, offering faster convergence and reduced noise compared to SGD, while still being more efficient than batch gradient descent.

Example: Language Translation

In natural language processing (NLP), gradient descent is widely used to train models for language translation tasks. For example, a neural network tasked with translating English to French might start with random weights and generate incorrect translations initially. However, by applying gradient descent, the model iteratively adjusts the weights based on the error between the predicted translations and the actual target sentences. As training progresses, the model becomes better at capturing nuances in word usage, sentence structure, and grammar, resulting in more accurate translations.

During training:

- **Batch gradient descent** might be used if computational resources are ample, ensuring stable convergence but slower updates.
- **SGD** could be employed for real-time translation systems, allowing the model to update quickly after processing individual sentences.
- **Mini-batch gradient descent** is often the preferred choice for training language models, as it strikes a balance between speed and accuracy, allowing the model to process text in chunks while maintaining a stable learning trajectory.

Gradient descent is not only a fundamental optimization technique but also an adaptable one, capable of supporting different training needs across various models and applications. By continuously adjusting weights in the direction that minimizes error, gradient descent enables neural networks to learn complex patterns, making it an essential part of the deep learning toolkit.

2.2.3: Common Challenges (Vanishing/Exploding Gradients)

Training deep neural networks often encounters two significant challenges: **vanishing gradients** and **exploding gradients**. Both issues arise during the backpropagation process, particularly in deep networks with many layers. These challenges affect how weights are adjusted, ultimately impacting the network's ability to learn effectively.

The **vanishing gradient** problem occurs when the gradients of the loss function become very small as they are propagated backward through the network. As a result, the weight updates in earlier layers are minimal, making it difficult for the network to learn long-range dependencies. This issue is especially common in deep networks with activation functions like Sigmoid or Tanh, which squash outputs to a narrow range, further diminishing gradients as they move through the layers. Consequently, the neurons in the initial layers may barely adjust during training, limiting the model's capacity to learn hierarchical patterns or dependencies that span longer sequences. This can be particularly problematic in tasks like natural language processing (NLP) or time-series analysis, where understanding context over longer sequences is crucial.

On the other hand, the **exploding gradient** problem is the opposite scenario. Here, the gradients become excessively large during backpropagation, causing massive weight updates. This often destabilizes the network, leading to oscillating loss values or even NaN (not a number) errors during training. Exploding gradients are more likely to occur when using activation functions that allow for large outputs (e.g., ReLU), or in deep networks without proper initialization. When the gradients explode, the network fails to converge, making it unable to learn meaningful patterns from the data.

Methods for Addressing Gradient Challenges

To mitigate these gradient-related issues, researchers have developed several techniques:

Gradient Clipping: This method is primarily used to combat exploding gradients. It works by setting a predefined threshold, such that any gradient exceeding this value is scaled back to the threshold. This prevents excessively large updates, stabilizing the training process and helping the model converge more effectively. Gradient clipping is particularly useful in training recurrent neural networks (RNNs), where long sequences can exacerbate gradient instability.

Specialized Architectures: Networks like Long Short-Term Memory (LSTM) and Gated Recurrent Units (GRUs) are designed to handle vanishing gradients in sequential data. These architectures have internal mechanisms, such as gating functions, that help retain information over long sequences, making them well-suited for tasks like language modeling, speech recognition, and machine translation.

Batch Normalization: Another technique for addressing vanishing gradients is batch normalization, which normalizes the inputs to each layer during training. By maintaining consistent input distributions, batch normalization prevents gradients from becoming too small, enabling more efficient weight updates. It also accelerates training and improves overall model performance by reducing internal covariate shifts.

Practical Example: Training Recurrent Neural Networks (RNNs)

Consider a recurrent neural network (RNN) trained for **speech recognition**. In this task, the model needs to learn dependencies across long sequences of audio data to accurately convert speech to text. However, the vanishing gradient problem can hinder the RNN's ability to learn these long-term dependencies. As gradients shrink while backpropagating through time (BPTT), the network struggles to adjust weights in the initial layers, leading to poor performance.

To address this, an LSTM-based model can be used instead. LSTMs have built-in memory cells that retain information over longer time steps, helping the model overcome the limitations of vanishing gradients. This enables it to maintain context across longer audio sequences, significantly improving speech recognition accuracy.

Gradient-related challenges are critical considerations when training deep neural networks, as they directly impact the model's ability to learn effectively. By implementing techniques like gradient clipping, specialized architectures, and batch normalization, these challenges can be mitigated, enabling more stable training and improved performance across a range of tasks.

2.3 Types of Neural Networks

2.3.1: Shallow vs. Deep Neural Networks

Neural networks are classified into **shallow** and **deep** networks based on their architecture and the number of hidden layers. This distinction not only affects their structure but also their ability to process data and capture complex patterns.

Shallow Neural Networks

Shallow neural networks typically have one or two hidden layers. They are simpler in design, often used for problems involving structured data with well-defined relationships. These networks are best suited for tasks where data patterns are relatively straightforward and can be captured by a limited number of transformations.

For example, consider a **linear regression task** for predicting sales based on a few variables, such as advertising spend, product price, and market reach. In this case, a shallow neural network with one hidden layer can model the relationships between these features and the target outcome (e.g., sales figures). The hidden layer learns to combine the input features linearly, allowing it to fit simple data patterns effectively. The relatively low number of parameters in shallow networks makes them computationally efficient and easy to train. Additionally, the simplicity of shallow networks ensures faster convergence, making them suitable for smaller datasets or scenarios where interpretability is crucial.

Shallow networks are also used in:

- **Logistic regression tasks**, where they classify binary outcomes (e.g., spam vs. not spam).
- **Basic clustering**, where they group data points into predefined categories.

However, the main limitation of shallow networks is their inability to model complex, non-linear relationships, making them less suitable for unstructured data like images, audio, or text.

Deep Neural Networks

In contrast, **deep neural networks (DNNs)** consist of multiple hidden layers stacked one after another. This architecture enables them to capture hierarchical relationships, making them adept at handling complex, high-dimensional data. As information flows through the layers of a DNN, each layer transforms the input data into progressively more abstract representations, allowing the network to extract features at different levels of granularity.

Take the example of **image classification** using a convolutional neural network (CNN), a type of deep neural network:

- **Early layers** might detect basic patterns like edges and textures.
- **Intermediate layers** capture more complex features like shapes and contours.
- **Deeper layers** integrate these features to recognize complete objects or scenes (e.g., detecting a dog or cat in an image).

This hierarchical learning is crucial for understanding intricate relationships, as it allows the network to build upon simpler patterns to recognize more complex structures. The depth of a neural network enables it to represent non-linear relationships, making it effective for tasks where patterns are deeply embedded within the data.

Deep neural networks excel in tasks like:

Natural Language Processing (NLP): For tasks like machine translation, DNNs (often with transformer architectures) capture syntactic and semantic nuances, handling complex sentence structures and long-range dependencies.

Speech Recognition: Deep networks can model audio signals over time, allowing for accurate transcription of speech into text by learning the dependencies across sequential data.

Object Detection: In addition to recognizing objects, DNNs can identify multiple objects within a single image and even predict their locations and boundaries.

Comparison

To illustrate the difference between shallow and deep networks, consider **sentiment analysis** versus **machine translation**:

In sentiment analysis, a **shallow network** can be trained to detect basic sentiment indicators (e.g., presence of positive or negative words) within short text reviews. The network might perform well in determining whether a review is positive or negative based on keywords, but it may struggle with more nuanced language or longer texts.

For machine translation, a **deep network** is necessary to capture complex linguistic rules, grammar, and context. Transformer-based models, which are deep networks, can process entire sentences and understand the relationships between words, making them capable of translating languages more accurately. The depth of the network allows it to maintain context and meaning across long sequences, resulting in more coherent translations.

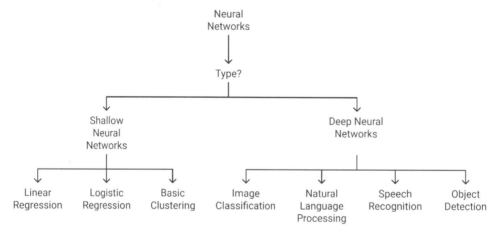

Implications for Learning Capacity

The depth of a neural network directly impacts its learning capacity:

Shallow networks are suitable for simpler tasks where relationships are linear or can be approximated with a small number of transformations. They require fewer computational resources and are more interpretable, making them ideal for structured data and straightforward tasks.

Deep networks are designed to handle complex, non-linear patterns, making them better suited for tasks involving high-dimensional or unstructured data. They require more computational resources and longer training times, but their ability to capture hierarchical patterns enables them to excel in tasks that require deep feature extraction.

2.3.2: Understanding Feedforward Networks and Multilayer Perceptrons (MLPs)

Feedforward neural networks represent the simplest form of neural network architecture. As the name suggests, information flows in a single direction—from the input layer, through the hidden layers, to the output layer—without any feedback loops. This straightforward, one-way flow of data makes feedforward networks foundational in neural network design, particularly in tasks that require straightforward mappings between inputs and outputs.

A specific type of feedforward network is the **Multilayer Perceptron (MLP)**, which consists of multiple layers, including one or more hidden layers between the input and output layers. Each of these hidden layers contains neurons that transform the input data using weights, biases, and activation functions. This layered architecture allows MLPs to handle complex, non-linear relationships, making them versatile for a variety of tasks, from classification and regression to pattern recognition. By stacking multiple hidden layers, MLPs can capture non-linear patterns, enabling them to extract more sophisticated features from both structured and unstructured data.

MLPs operate through a series of transformations as data passes through each layer. When input data is fed into the network, it undergoes the following processes:

Weighted Summation: Each input is multiplied by a weight that represents the importance of that feature. These weighted inputs are then summed together.

Adding Bias: A bias term is added to the weighted sum, allowing the model to shift the activation threshold, enabling more flexible learning.

Activation Function: The combined sum is passed through an activation function, which introduces non-linearity into the network, making it capable of learning complex patterns. Common activation functions used in MLPs include ReLU (Rectified Linear Unit), Sigmoid, and Tanh, each with its strengths depending on the task.

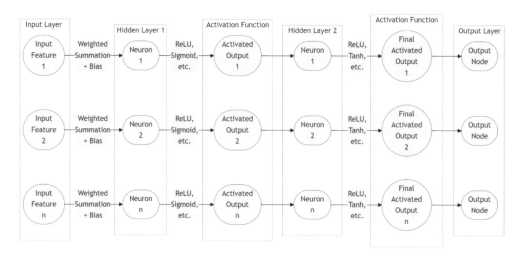

MLPs are widely used in various applications due to their versatility. One prominent example is **credit scoring** in the financial sector. In this context, an MLP can be trained to predict the likelihood of loan default based on features like income, age, credit history, and employment status. During training, the network learns the relationships between these features and the target variable (e.g., default or no default), adjusting weights and biases to minimize prediction errors. The hidden layers capture non-linear relationships, such as how a combination of low income and poor credit history might indicate a higher risk of default, even if one of these features alone does not.

MLPs are also used in:

Image Recognition: They can identify patterns in structured image data, such as distinguishing between different digits in handwritten digit recognition tasks.

Text Classification: MLPs can categorize documents based on the presence of specific words or phrases, making them useful for spam detection, sentiment analysis, or topic classification.

Regression Analysis: In tasks like predicting housing prices, MLPs can model non-linear relationships between features such as location, square footage, and number of bedrooms to accurately predict house prices.

2.3.3: Applications of Different Network Structures

Neural networks come in various structures, each designed to address specific types of data and learning challenges. Among the most prominent are **Convolutional Neural Networks (CNNs)**, **Recurrent Neural Networks (RNNs)**, and **Transformers**. Each of these structures has unique capabilities that make them well-suited for handling particular tasks, ranging from image recognition to language translation.

Convolutional Neural Networks (CNNs)

Convolutional Neural Networks (CNNs) are specialized for analyzing visual data, making them the backbone of computer vision applications. CNNs use **convolutional layers**, where filters (kernels) scan the input data in small chunks, identifying visual patterns like edges, textures, and shapes. These filters slide across the input in a process known as convolution, producing feature maps that highlight specific characteristics of the data. The ability to detect patterns hierarchically enables CNNs to capture both low-level and high-level features as the data moves deeper into the network.

Layer Types in CNNs:

Convolutional Layers: These layers apply filters that focus on small regions of the input, detecting localized features. Early layers typically capture basic features like edges, corners, and gradients, while deeper layers identify more complex patterns like shapes, textures, or even specific objects.

Pooling Layers: Pooling reduces the spatial dimensions of the feature maps by aggregating information, making the network more computationally efficient while retaining essential features. Common types include **Max Pooling**, which selects the maximum value within a region, and **Average Pooling**, which computes the average value.

Fully Connected Layers: At the end of the network, fully connected layers take the high-level features extracted by the convolutional layers and combine them to produce a final output, such as a class label in image classification tasks.

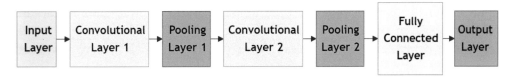

Applications of CNNs:

Medical Imaging: CNNs are widely used to detect anomalies in X-rays, MRIs, and CT scans. For example, in **cancer detection**, CNNs can identify tumors in mammograms by learning subtle patterns in the images that distinguish healthy tissue from abnormal growths. The hierarchical feature extraction in CNNs allows for high sensitivity, making them invaluable in early diagnosis.

Autonomous Vehicles: CNNs play a critical role in self-driving cars, where they identify lane markings, detect pedestrians, recognize road signs, and track other vehicles. The ability to process complex visual information in real time makes CNNs essential for the safety and decision-making of autonomous systems.

Facial Recognition: CNNs are used in facial recognition systems to identify individuals based on facial features. By learning from large datasets of faces, CNNs can accurately match input images to known profiles, even under varying lighting, angles, or facial expressions.

CNNs excel in tasks where spatial relationships are crucial, enabling them to capture intricate patterns within images and videos. Their layered structure allows for the extraction of increasingly abstract features, making them effective for a broad range of computer vision applications.

Recurrent Neural Networks (RNNs)

Recurrent Neural Networks (RNNs) are designed to handle sequential data, making them ideal for tasks where the order of inputs matters. Unlike feedforward networks, RNNs have connections that loop back, allowing them to retain information from previous time steps and maintain context over sequences. This capability enables RNNs to understand temporal dependencies, making them effective for tasks like language modeling, time-series forecasting, and speech recognition.

Layer Types in RNNs:

Recurrent Layers: The core of RNNs consists of recurrent layers that process input sequences one element at a time, updating their internal state to capture information from previous inputs. However, traditional RNNs struggle with long-range dependencies due to vanishing gradients, which is why advanced variants like **Long Short-Term Memory (LSTM)** networks and **Gated Recurrent Units (GRUs)** were developed.

LSTMs: LSTMs introduce memory cells that can store and retrieve information over long sequences, using gates to control the flow of information. This makes them well-suited for tasks like machine translation, where context needs to be maintained over multiple sentences.

GRUs: GRUs are similar to LSTMs but have fewer gates, making them computationally lighter while still retaining the ability to capture long-term dependencies. They are often used in real-time applications where speed is crucial.

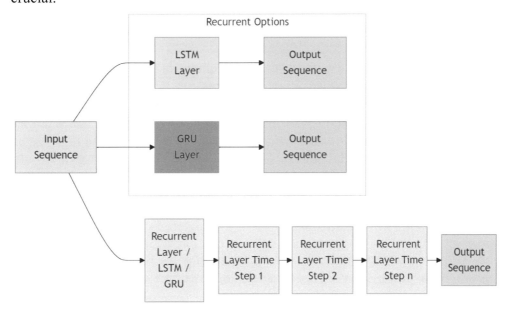

Applications of RNNs:

Speech Recognition: In speech recognition, RNNs convert spoken language into text by processing audio signals over time. For instance, an LSTM-based RNN can retain information from earlier audio frames, allowing it to understand words and phrases more accurately. This sequential processing is crucial for capturing the flow and rhythm of speech, enabling the model to transcribe spoken words into coherent text.

Time-Series Analysis: RNNs are used in finance for predicting stock prices, where the network analyzes historical data to forecast future trends. By maintaining context over long time horizons, RNNs can model complex dependencies between financial indicators, helping traders make informed decisions.

Language Modeling: In NLP, RNNs are employed to predict the next word in a sentence based on the preceding words. This capability is foundational for tasks like autocomplete, text generation, and language translation, where maintaining context is key to generating coherent outputs.

RNNs' ability to process sequences makes them indispensable for tasks where time or order is critical. Despite challenges with long-range dependencies, their variants like LSTMs and GRUs have made them effective in tasks involving sequential patterns.

Transformers

Transformers represent a significant advancement in neural network design, excelling at processing sequences while addressing the limitations of RNNs. Unlike RNNs, which process inputs sequentially, transformers use **self-attention mechanisms** to process entire sequences in parallel. This allows transformers to capture global dependencies, as they can weigh the importance of different parts of the input sequence simultaneously. As a result, transformers are more efficient and better suited for handling complex relationships across long sequences.

Key Components in Transformers:

Self-Attention Mechanism: This mechanism enables the model to focus on relevant parts of the input sequence, assigning attention scores to each word or token. For example, in a sentence, the word "it" may need to refer back to a specific noun, and the self-attention mechanism ensures the model pays more attention to the relevant context.

Multi-Head Attention: Transformers use multiple self-attention layers (or "heads") that operate in parallel, allowing the model to capture different types of relationships simultaneously. This parallel processing is critical for complex tasks like text generation and translation, where multiple contextual relationships need to be understood.

Position Embeddings: Because transformers process sequences in parallel, they use position embeddings to encode the order of inputs, helping the model maintain sequence information even when processing in parallel.

Applications of Transformers:

Language Translation: Transformers have revolutionized machine translation by enabling models to generate high-quality translations. For example, **Google Translate** uses transformers to translate sentences by understanding context across the entire input text, capturing nuances like idioms and grammatical structure.

Text Generation: Models like **GPT (Generative Pre-trained Transformer)** use transformers to generate coherent and contextually relevant text. GPT can generate anything from short responses in chatbots to entire articles, demonstrating an advanced understanding of language patterns and context.

Summarization and Question Answering: Transformers excel at tasks like text summarization, where they condense long documents into concise summaries while retaining key information. They are also used in question-answering systems, where they can retrieve relevant information from large documents and generate precise answers.

Transformers' ability to process sequences in parallel while capturing global dependencies makes them highly effective for natural language processing tasks. Their scalability and versatility have made them the architecture of choice for state-of-the-art language models, outperforming previous network structures in both accuracy and efficiency.

Choosing the Right Network Structure

Each of these network structures—CNNs, RNNs, and transformers—offers unique strengths tailored to different types of data and tasks:

CNNs are best for tasks involving spatial relationships, making them ideal for image and video analysis.

RNNs excel at capturing temporal patterns, making them suitable for sequential data like audio, time series, and text.

Transformers are versatile for handling complex language tasks, where global dependencies and parallel processing are critical.

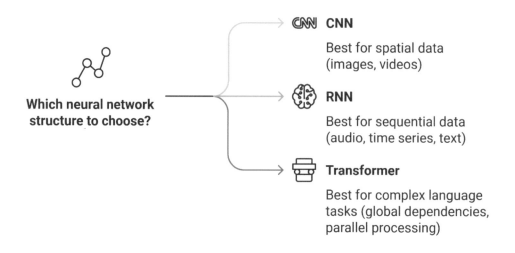

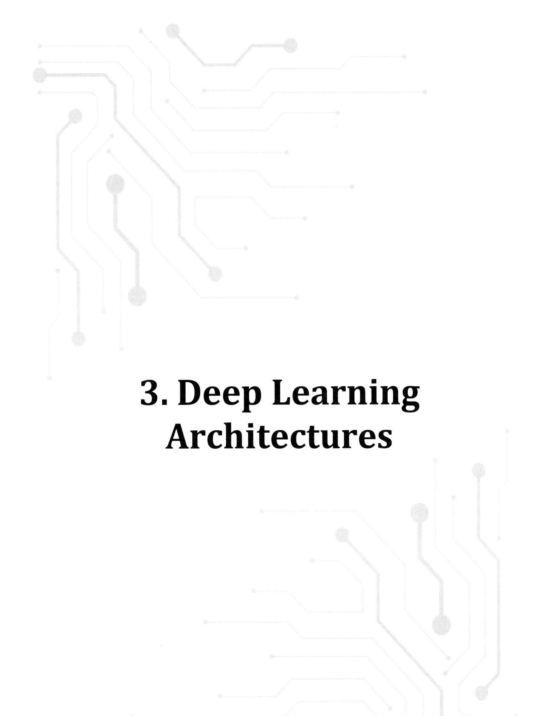

3. Deep Learning Architectures

3.1 Convolutional Neural Networks (CNNs)

3.1.1: The Structure of Convolutional Neural Networks (CNNs) and Their Role in Image Processing

Convolutional Neural Networks (CNNs) represent a significant evolution in neural network design, especially suited for processing grid-like data structures, such as images. Unlike traditional neural networks, which treat each input feature independently, CNNs can exploit the spatial structure of images, capturing relationships between neighboring pixels. This makes CNNs particularly effective for tasks that require pattern recognition in visual data, such as object detection, image classification, and facial recognition.

The architecture of CNNs is built around a series of specialized layers, each designed to progressively extract and refine features from the input image. The basic components of CNNs include **convolutional layers**, **activation functions**, **pooling layers**, and **fully connected layers**, all of which play distinct roles in the image processing workflow.

Convolutional Layers

The **convolutional layers** are the core building blocks of CNNs. These layers use filters (or kernels) that slide over the input image, performing convolution operations to detect patterns. During this process, the filter scans small regions of the input data and generates **feature maps**, which highlight important patterns, such as edges, textures, or corners. In the early layers, the filters typically detect simple features like edges or color gradients, while deeper convolutional layers capture more abstract patterns, such as shapes or specific objects within the image.

The ability to detect spatial hierarchies of features is what sets CNNs apart from traditional feedforward networks. For example, in a facial recognition system, the early convolutional layers might detect basic edges and contours of a face, while subsequent layers focus on more detailed facial features like eyes, nose, and mouth. This hierarchical approach enables CNNs to build complex representations of images, making them highly effective for visual recognition tasks.

Activation Functions

After the convolutional layers perform their operations, the output feature maps are passed through **activation functions**. Activation functions introduce non-linearity into the network, allowing CNNs to capture complex patterns that linear transformations alone cannot. Common activation functions used in CNNs include **ReLU (Rectified Linear Unit)**, which sets negative values to zero and keeps positive values unchanged, enabling faster training and reducing the likelihood of vanishing gradients. In some cases, more advanced activation functions like **Leaky ReLU** or **Swish** are used to improve performance, especially in deeper layers.

Pooling Layers

To further process the output from the convolutional layers, CNNs use **pooling layers**, which reduce the spatial dimensions of the feature maps while preserving the most important information. Pooling helps decrease the computational load, making the network more efficient and less prone to overfitting. Two common types of pooling are:

1. **Max Pooling**, which selects the maximum value from a region of the feature map, capturing the most prominent features.
2. **Average Pooling**, which computes the average value within a region, providing a smoother representation of the feature map.

Pooling layers contribute to the network's ability to maintain the spatial hierarchy of features, allowing CNNs to focus on the most important parts of an image while ignoring irrelevant details.

Fully Connected Layers

At the end of the network, the **fully connected layers** take the high-level features extracted by the convolutional and pooling layers and transform them into a final output, such as a probability distribution over classes in image classification tasks. These layers operate like traditional neural networks, using weights and biases to combine the features learned by the preceding layers and make predictions.

For example, in an image classification task involving handwritten digit recognition, the fully connected layers analyze the high-level features and generate an output that represents the probability of each digit (0-9). The digit with the highest probability is chosen as the final prediction.

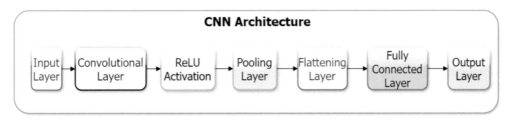

Applications of CNNs in Image Processing

CNNs have revolutionized the field of image processing, finding applications across diverse domains:

Facial Recognition: In security systems, CNNs identify and verify individuals by analyzing facial features. The network learns to recognize specific patterns in the input images, such as the distance between eyes or the shape of the nose, achieving high accuracy even under varying lighting and angles.

Medical Imaging: In healthcare, CNNs play a crucial role in detecting anomalies in medical images, such as identifying tumors in MRI scans or lesions in chest X-rays. By training on large datasets of labeled medical images, CNNs learn to differentiate between healthy and abnormal tissues, aiding in early diagnosis and treatment planning.

Autonomous Vehicles: CNNs are integral to self-driving cars, where they are used for object detection, lane tracking, and traffic sign recognition. The network processes visual input from cameras mounted on the vehicle, allowing it to understand and respond to its surroundings in real-time.

3.1.2: How Convolution Layers Work (Filters, Feature Maps, Pooling)

Convolution layers are the fundamental building blocks of Convolutional Neural Networks (CNNs), enabling them to process visual information effectively. These layers use **filters** (also called **kernels**) to scan input images, identifying patterns like edges, textures, and shapes that are critical for image recognition tasks. Unlike traditional neural networks that treat input data as a flat vector, convolution layers preserve the spatial relationships within the data, making them highly effective for analyzing grid-like structures, such as images.

The process begins with filters sliding over the input image, applying the convolution operation. Each filter is essentially a small matrix of weights that performs element-wise multiplication with the pixel values of the input image, producing an output known as a **feature map**. The feature map highlights the presence of specific patterns detected by the filter across different regions of the image. For example, in early layers, filters may focus on simple features like edges or corners, while filters in deeper layers detect more complex patterns, such as textures, shapes, or even objects like faces or cars. As training progresses, the filters learn to recognize features that are most important for the task at hand, adjusting their weights through backpropagation.

Once the feature maps are generated, they are passed through **activation functions** to introduce non-linearity. This is crucial because many patterns in images are non-linear in nature, and linear transformations alone would not be able to capture such complexities. The most commonly used activation function in CNNs is the **ReLU (Rectified Linear Unit)**, which replaces all negative values in the feature map with zeros. ReLU is computationally efficient and helps mitigate the vanishing gradient problem during training, making it suitable for deeper networks. However, other activation functions like **Leaky ReLU** and **Swish** may be used in certain cases to further improve performance, particularly in handling more complex visual patterns.

As feature maps progress through the network, they are subjected to **pooling layers**. Pooling layers play a critical role in reducing the spatial dimensions of the feature maps, making the network more computationally efficient while preserving the most important information. This process, known as **downsampling**, helps to focus on the most prominent features while ignoring less relevant details, reducing the computational burden and the likelihood of overfitting.

There are two main types of pooling used in CNNs:

1. **Max Pooling**: This operation divides the feature map into smaller regions and selects the maximum value from each region. Max pooling is particularly effective at preserving the strongest features, such as edges or textures, making it the most commonly used pooling method in CNNs. For instance, in **facial recognition**, max pooling helps the network retain sharp features like the shape of the eyes or nose, which are critical for identifying individuals.

2. **Average Pooling**: This operation computes the average value within each region of the feature map, providing a smoother representation. Average pooling is often used when capturing subtle patterns is more important than preserving the strongest features. It is useful in tasks like **object tracking** in surveillance systems, where smoother representations can help the network maintain context over time.

The combination of convolution, activation, and pooling layers enables CNNs to extract hierarchical features from images. Early layers capture basic visual elements, while deeper layers focus on more abstract features, such as specific objects or scenes. For example, in **autonomous vehicle systems**, convolution layers detect lane markings, road signs, and other vehicles, while pooling layers help reduce the complexity of the visual data, making it easier for the network to make real-time decisions.

In **medical imaging**, convolution layers are used to detect abnormalities in X-rays or MRI scans by identifying irregular patterns that suggest potential issues, such as tumors or lesions. Pooling layers help the network generalize these features, allowing it to detect anomalies across different scans and varying conditions. The hierarchical feature extraction process enables CNNs to provide accurate diagnoses, aiding healthcare professionals in early detection and treatment planning.

3.1.3: Use Cases in Image Classification and Object Detection

Convolutional Neural Networks (CNNs) have become the gold standard for tasks like **image classification** and **object detection**, owing to their exceptional ability to recognize patterns and identify objects in images. CNNs excel in visual recognition tasks by extracting hierarchical features from raw image data, allowing them to distinguish between different objects, categories, and attributes within images. The ability to learn from labeled data and generalize to new images has made CNNs an indispensable tool in various industries, from healthcare to autonomous vehicles.

Image Classification

Image classification is one of the most common applications of CNNs. In this task, CNNs are trained to assign a label to an entire image, effectively categorizing it based on the objects or patterns detected. For example, in **facial recognition** systems, CNNs are used to analyze facial features, distinguishing between different individuals based on characteristics like eye shape, nose contours, and jawline structure. The network is trained on a large dataset of labeled images, learning to recognize subtle differences in facial features to achieve accurate identification.

In **medical imaging**, CNNs play a critical role in diagnosing diseases by analyzing images like X-rays, MRIs, and CT scans. For instance, a CNN trained to detect lung cancer can identify potential tumors in chest X-rays by recognizing patterns that differentiate healthy tissue from abnormal growths. The network's ability to handle large amounts of labeled medical data allows it to generalize well to new, unseen cases, providing reliable support for healthcare professionals.

A notable CNN architecture used in image classification is **ResNet (Residual Network)**. ResNet introduced the concept of **residual connections**, which help the network maintain performance even as it gets deeper. By addressing the problem of vanishing gradients in deep networks, ResNet has set new benchmarks in image classification tasks, achieving state-of-the-art results on datasets like ImageNet. It has been widely adopted in fields ranging from healthcare diagnostics to retail, where it's used to analyze product images for categorization.

Object Detection

While image classification assigns a single label to an entire image, **object detection** goes a step further by identifying and localizing multiple objects within an image. CNNs are the backbone of many object detection algorithms, allowing models to recognize various objects and mark their positions using bounding boxes.

In **autonomous driving**, object detection is critical for identifying road signs, pedestrians, and other vehicles in real-time. For example, when a self-driving car encounters a pedestrian crossing the road, the CNN-based detection system recognizes the person, calculates their position, and triggers the necessary response to avoid a collision. The ability of CNNs to process visual data quickly and accurately makes them ideal for such safety-critical applications, where detecting multiple objects simultaneously is essential.

One of the most successful CNN models for object detection is **YOLO (You Only Look Once)**. Unlike traditional object detection methods that involve sliding windows, YOLO treats object detection as a single regression problem, predicting bounding boxes and class probabilities directly from full images. This approach makes YOLO extremely fast, enabling real-time detection in applications like surveillance, traffic monitoring, and robotics. By analyzing entire images in a single pass, YOLO can identify multiple objects efficiently, from identifying faces in crowds to detecting traffic signs in varying lighting conditions.

Applications Across Various Fields

CNNs' capabilities extend beyond facial recognition and autonomous driving, finding applications in a range of other fields as well:

Retail: CNNs are used in visual search engines, where users upload images of products to find similar items in an online store's catalog. By learning the visual attributes of products, CNNs can effectively match images to categories, enhancing customer experience and increasing conversion rates.

Agriculture: CNNs are applied in crop disease detection, where they analyze images of crops to identify signs of disease. By training on labeled images of healthy and diseased plants, CNNs can detect early signs of disease, enabling timely interventions and improving crop yield.

Security and Surveillance: In security systems, CNNs are used for anomaly detection, such as spotting unusual movements or identifying unauthorized personnel in restricted areas. The network's ability to learn from labeled surveillance footage makes it an effective tool for real-time security monitoring.

3.2 Recurrent Neural Networks (RNNs)

3.2.1: Structure of Recurrent Neural Networks (RNNs) and Their Use in Sequence Data

Recurrent Neural Networks (RNNs) are uniquely designed to process sequential data, making them essential for tasks where the order of inputs is crucial. Unlike feedforward neural networks, which process inputs independently, RNNs have a distinct architecture that includes **recurrent connections**, enabling them to maintain a form of "memory" across time steps. This memory-like mechanism allows RNNs to retain information from previous inputs, making them effective at capturing **temporal dependencies**.

Basic Architecture of RNNs

The architecture of an RNN revolves around the concept of **hidden states**, which evolve as the network processes each element of the sequence. Each time step in the sequence involves three primary components:

1. **Input at Time t**: The input vector at the current time step, denoted as x_t, which represents the current element of the sequence (e.g., a word in a sentence or a price at a given time).
2. **Hidden State at Time t**: The hidden state vector, denoted as h_t, which acts as a summary of the sequence processed so far. It is updated at each time step using both the current input and the hidden state from the previous time step.
3. **Output at Time t**: The output vector, denoted as y_t, which represents the network's prediction or transformation at the current time step, based on the updated hidden state.

The recurrent nature of RNNs allows them to maintain context by recursively updating the hidden state:

$$h_t = f(W_x \cdot x_t + W_h \cdot h_{t-1} + b)$$

where:

- W_x and W_h are weight matrices applied to the input and hidden state, respectively.
- b is a bias term, and
- f is the activation function, commonly **Tanh** or **ReLU**, which introduces non-linearity.

This iterative update enables RNNs to retain information from previous time steps while processing new inputs. As each input is processed, the hidden state evolves, accumulating context from the sequence.

Handling Temporal Dependencies

RNNs are particularly well-suited for tasks that require understanding of temporal relationships within data. This makes them ideal for applications like **language modeling**, **speech recognition**, and **time-series prediction**:

Language Modeling: In natural language processing, RNNs excel at predicting the next word in a sequence by using information from previous words. For instance, given the input sequence "The cat sat on the," the RNN processes each word sequentially, updating its hidden state to maintain context. By the time the network processes the word "the," it has accumulated enough context to predict that the next word is likely "mat," "couch," or another related word. This capability makes RNNs effective in tasks like **text generation**, **machine translation**, and **sentiment analysis**.

Speech Recognition: RNNs are also widely used in speech-to-text systems, where they convert audio signals into textual representations. As the audio signal is processed frame by frame, the RNN updates its hidden state at each time step, capturing phonetic information from earlier frames to understand the context of spoken words. For example, when transcribing the phrase "machine learning is fascinating," the RNN retains context from earlier words like "machine" and "learning," enabling it to generate coherent text. This sequential processing is crucial for handling variations in speech patterns, such as pauses, accents, or rapid speech.

Time-Series Prediction: In finance, RNNs analyze historical price trends to forecast future values, such as stock prices, interest rates, or currency exchange rates. As the network receives each new data point, it updates its hidden state to incorporate the latest information while retaining prior context. For example, if an RNN is trained to predict the closing price of a stock, it considers the sequence of previous prices, volume, and other features to forecast the next value. This makes RNNs particularly useful for detecting patterns, trends, and anomalies in sequential data.

Challenges and Solutions in RNNs

Despite their effectiveness, standard RNNs face limitations, particularly in handling **long-term dependencies**. As the sequence length increases, the influence of earlier inputs diminishes, leading to the **vanishing gradient problem**. This challenge arises when the gradients used to update the weights during training become extremely small, making it difficult for the network to retain information over long sequences.

To address this limitation, advanced variants of RNNs, such as **Long Short-Term Memory (LSTM)** networks and **Gated Recurrent Units (GRUs)**, have been developed:

LSTMs introduce memory cells that store information across time steps, using gating mechanisms (input, forget, and output gates) to control the flow of information. This enables LSTMs to maintain relevant information for longer sequences, making them more effective in tasks like **document summarization**, **machine translation**, and **video analysis**, where understanding context over extended periods is essential.

GRUs simplify the LSTM architecture by using fewer gates, making them computationally more efficient while still retaining the ability to capture long-range dependencies. GRUs are often preferred in real-time applications, such as **financial trading systems** or **real-time sentiment analysis**, where quick processing and decision-making are critical.

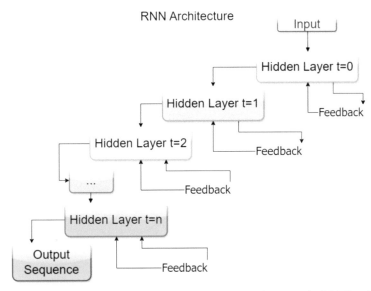

This diagram illustrates the architecture of a Recurrent Neural Network (RNN), which processes sequences step-by-step while maintaining context through feedback loops. Each hidden layer corresponds to a time step, using information from previous layers to build temporal dependencies. The final output sequence reflects the network's interpretation of the entire input, making RNNs effective for tasks like language modeling, time-series analysis, and sequential data processing.

Applications

RNNs are widely used across various fields due to their capacity to process sequential data effectively:

Chatbots and **Virtual Assistants**: RNNs power conversational AI, enabling chatbots to maintain context across interactions and generate coherent responses. For instance, a customer service chatbot might use an RNN to understand customer queries, retain context from previous interactions, and provide accurate responses.

Predictive Maintenance: In industrial applications, RNNs analyze sensor data from machinery to predict failures before they occur. By maintaining context across sequences of sensor readings, RNNs can detect anomalies and trends that indicate potential breakdowns, allowing for timely maintenance and reducing downtime.

Healthcare: RNNs are used to analyze patient records, monitor vital signs, and predict health outcomes. For example, in critical care units, RNNs process sequences of heart rate, blood pressure, and oxygen levels to predict complications and recommend interventions.

3.2.2: The Challenge of Long-Term Dependencies and Solutions (LSTMs, GRUs)

Recurrent Neural Networks (RNNs) are powerful for processing sequential data, but they encounter significant challenges when tasked with learning **long-term dependencies**—patterns or relationships that span across longer sequences. This limitation is primarily due to the **vanishing gradient problem**, a phenomenon that occurs during the training of deep neural networks, including RNNs. In the context of RNNs, as information from earlier time steps flows through multiple layers of the network, the gradients (which indicate how much the weights should be updated) can become extremely small. This makes it difficult for the network to retain relevant information from earlier parts of the sequence, effectively causing the "memory" of the network to fade over time.

The vanishing gradient problem significantly restricts the RNN's ability to learn dependencies that require context from distant past inputs. For instance, in language modeling, predicting the next word based on a subject introduced several sentences earlier can be challenging for a standard RNN, as it tends to "forget" information about the subject as the sequence length increases. This makes standard RNNs less effective for tasks that require maintaining context over extended sequences, such as **machine translation**, **document summarization**, and **long-form text generation**.

To address these challenges, specialized architectures like **Long Short-Term Memory (LSTM)** networks and **Gated Recurrent Units (GRUs)** have been developed. These models are designed to retain relevant information over longer sequences by using gating mechanisms that control the flow of information within the network.

Long Short-Term Memory (LSTM) Networks

LSTM networks are an advanced type of RNN that introduce **memory cells** capable of storing information over long time periods. Unlike standard RNNs, LSTMs use three key gates to regulate the flow of information:

Forget Gate: This gate determines how much of the past information should be "forgotten" at each time step. It takes the previous hidden state and current input as inputs, using a sigmoid activation function to produce a value between 0 and 1 for each element in the hidden state. A value of 0 means complete forgetting, while a value of 1 means complete retention.

$$f_t = \sigma\left(W_f \cdot [h_{t-1}, x_t] + b_f\right)$$

Input Gate: The input gate decides how much of the new input information should be added to the memory cell. It works in conjunction with a candidate value that is generated from the current input and previous hidden state.

$$i_t = \sigma\left(W_i \cdot [h_{t-1}, x_t] + b_i\right)$$

Output Gate: The output gate determines how much of the information stored in the memory cell should be passed to the next hidden state, allowing the network to decide what information is relevant for the current prediction.

$$o_t = \sigma\left(W_o \cdot [h_{t-1}, x_t] + b_o\right)$$

By using these gates, LSTMs can effectively retain or discard information, making them highly suitable for tasks that require learning long-term dependencies. For example, in **speech-to-text systems**, LSTMs can maintain context over an entire spoken sentence, allowing the network to generate accurate transcriptions by considering long-range dependencies. This makes LSTMs particularly effective in handling complex sentence structures, where the meaning of a word can depend on information several words or sentences earlier.

Gated Recurrent Units (GRUs)

GRUs are a simplified version of LSTMs that retain many of the benefits of learning long-term dependencies while reducing computational complexity. Unlike LSTMs, which use three gates, GRUs use only two: the **update gate** and the **reset gate**. This makes GRUs more efficient in terms of training time and memory usage, while still being able to retain important information over longer sequences.

Update Gate: This gate controls how much of the past information should be carried forward to the next time step. It combines the functions of the forget and input gates in LSTMs, determining what information to retain and what new information to add.

$$z_t = \sigma\left(W_z \cdot [h_{t-1}, x_t] + b_z\right)$$

Reset Gate: The reset gate decides how much of the past information should be ignored when computing the candidate hidden state, allowing the network to focus on more recent inputs when necessary.

$$r_t = \sigma\left(W_r \cdot [h_{t-1}, x_t] + b_r\right)$$

The simplified gating mechanism of GRUs makes them well-suited for tasks where computational efficiency is a priority. For example, in **time-series forecasting**, GRUs are used to predict future values based on historical data, such as stock prices or energy consumption. By retaining long-term dependencies while minimizing computation, GRUs can efficiently capture trends and patterns in sequential data, making them ideal for real-time prediction tasks.

Applications

Both LSTMs and GRUs have become the standard choice for tasks involving long-term dependencies in sequential data:

Machine Translation: In translation systems, LSTMs maintain the context of entire sentences, allowing the network to produce accurate translations by considering dependencies that span across multiple clauses. For instance, translating a sentence from English to French often requires retaining context over long sequences to ensure grammatical and semantic accuracy.

Document Summarization: In natural language processing, LSTMs are used to generate summaries of long documents by retaining critical information across paragraphs. The model learns to focus on the most relevant information, effectively summarizing the content while maintaining coherence.

Financial Time-Series Prediction: GRUs are commonly used in financial markets to analyze historical data and predict future trends. For example, a GRU model can be trained to forecast stock prices by retaining relevant features from past trading days, helping traders make informed decisions based on long-term patterns.

By addressing the vanishing gradient problem and introducing memory cells or gates, LSTMs and GRUs significantly improve the ability of neural networks to learn long-term dependencies. Their specialized architectures enable them to maintain context across longer sequences, making them indispensable tools for a wide range of applications, from speech recognition and machine translation to financial forecasting and document analysis.

3.2.3: Applications in Natural Language Processing and Time Series

Recurrent Neural Networks (RNNs) have proven highly effective in handling a wide range of applications within **natural language processing (NLP)** and **time-series analysis**. RNNs' ability to process sequential data makes them particularly well-suited for tasks where understanding the order and context of data points is critical. By updating hidden states at each time step, RNNs capture temporal dependencies, enabling them to maintain context throughout sequences.

RNNs in Natural Language Processing

In NLP, RNNs are extensively used for tasks like **language modeling**, **sentiment analysis**, **machine translation**, and **text generation**. These tasks rely on understanding and generating coherent sequences of words, making RNNs a natural fit.

Language Modeling: RNNs are fundamental to language modeling, where the goal is to predict the next word in a sentence based on the preceding words. For example, if given the input sequence "The sun is shining and the sky is," an RNN predicts the next word based on the context provided by the entire phrase. This capability is crucial for applications like **autocomplete** in search engines and messaging apps, where the model learns from vast amounts of text data to generate relevant predictions.

Sentiment Analysis: In sentiment analysis, RNNs analyze sequences of words to determine whether a given text conveys positive, negative, or neutral sentiment. For instance, when analyzing a product review, an RNN processes the sequence of words, updating its hidden state at each step to understand the overall tone of the review. By retaining context throughout the sequence, RNNs can accurately identify expressions of sentiment, even in longer reviews where meaning depends on multiple sentences.

Machine Translation: RNNs are widely used in machine translation systems, where they convert text from one language to another by processing words sequentially. For example, translating the English phrase "The cat sat on the mat" to French involves maintaining the grammatical structure and meaning throughout the sequence. RNNs handle this by generating the translation word-by-word, considering the relationships between words in both the source and target languages. Although transformers have largely replaced RNNs in modern translation systems due to their ability to handle long-range dependencies more efficiently, early versions of translation models like Google Translate were based on RNNs.

Text Generation: In text generation tasks, RNNs create new text sequences by predicting one word at a time, using previous outputs as inputs for generating the next word. For example, RNNs have been used in early versions of OpenAI's **GPT (Generative Pre-trained Transformer)**, where RNN-like architectures were employed to generate coherent text based on prompts. GPT-1, the initial version of the model, used a stacked RNN-like structure to generate paragraphs of text that maintained context across long sequences. While GPT models have since transitioned to transformer-based architectures, the foundational principles of sequential text generation were established with RNNs.

RNNs in Time-Series Analysis

RNNs are also widely applied in **time-series analysis**, where they analyze sequential data points to identify patterns, predict trends, and detect anomalies. Time-series data is prevalent across industries, making RNNs an essential tool for forecasting and decision-making.

Trend Prediction: In financial markets, RNNs predict stock prices, exchange rates, and other financial indicators by analyzing historical data. For instance, an RNN trained on historical stock prices uses the sequence of past prices to forecast the next day's closing price. By updating its hidden state with each new data point, the RNN learns to recognize patterns like upward or downward trends, helping traders make informed decisions. This capability is also applicable in other fields, such as energy demand forecasting, where RNNs predict future electricity consumption based on past usage patterns.

Anomaly Detection: RNNs are effective in detecting anomalies in time-series data, such as identifying unusual spikes in sensor readings or unexpected changes in network traffic. In **predictive maintenance**, for example, RNNs monitor sequences of sensor data from industrial equipment, learning the normal operational patterns. When the network detects deviations from these patterns, it signals potential equipment failures, allowing for timely maintenance and reducing downtime.

Sales Forecasting: RNNs are used in retail and e-commerce to forecast sales based on historical transaction data, seasonal trends, and other variables. By processing sequences of past sales figures, RNNs can predict future sales volumes, helping businesses manage inventory, optimize marketing strategies, and plan production.

RNNs' strengths in modeling sequential dependencies and retaining context make them versatile for a wide range of real-world applications. In NLP, their ability to process sequences of words makes them effective in tasks that require understanding language structure, tone, and meaning. In time-series analysis, RNNs' capacity to recognize patterns and trends across sequences enables accurate forecasting and anomaly detection, making them valuable tools for finance, healthcare, and industry.

Despite their effectiveness, RNNs face limitations when dealing with very long sequences, as discussed in the previous section. Variants like **LSTMs** and **GRUs** have addressed some of these limitations by introducing gating mechanisms that enhance the retention of long-range dependencies. While transformers now dominate many NLP tasks due to their parallel processing capabilities and improved handling of long-term dependencies, RNNs continue to be widely used in time-series analysis and other applications where sequence processing is essential.

3.3 Advanced Architectures

3.3.1: Introduction to Transformer Networks and Attention Mechanisms

Transformer networks have revolutionized deep learning, particularly in handling sequential data for natural language processing (NLP). Unlike Recurrent Neural Networks (RNNs), which process inputs sequentially, transformers can analyze entire sequences simultaneously using a mechanism called **self-attention**. This parallel processing capability, combined with the ability to capture both local and global dependencies, has made transformers the architecture of choice for tasks like text generation, translation, summarization, and more.

Self-Attention: The Core Mechanism

The **self-attention mechanism** is the cornerstone of transformer architecture, enabling the model to focus on different parts of the input sequence with varying degrees of importance. This allows transformers to capture complex dependencies and relationships, even across long sequences. Self-attention operates by computing attention scores that represent how much each input element should "attend" to the other elements in the sequence.

Here's how the self-attention mechanism works step-by-step:

1. **Encoding Inputs**: Each input token (e.g., a word or sub-word in a sentence) is first embedded into a vector representation. These embeddings capture semantic information about the tokens, such as their meanings and relationships with other tokens.

2. **Creating Query, Key, and Value Vectors**: For each input token, three vectors are generated:

   1. **Query (Q) Vector**: Represents the token that is seeking context from other tokens.
   2. **Key (K) Vector**: Represents the potential relevance of other tokens in the sequence.
   3. **Value (V) Vector**: Contains the actual information that will be passed along to the next layer. These vectors are obtained through linear transformations of the input embeddings, using learned weight matrices. If the input embedding is represented as x_i, then the Q, K, and V vectors are computed as:

$$Q_i = W_Q \cdot x_i, \quad K_i = W_K \cdot x_i, \quad V_i = W_V \cdot x_i$$

where W_Q, W_K, and W_V are weight matrices specific to the query, key, and value vectors, respectively.

3. **Calculating Attention Scores**: The attention scores between tokens are calculated by taking the dot product of the query vector with the key vector of every other token in the sequence. This dot product measures the similarity between the tokens:

$$\text{Attention Score} = Q_i \cdot K_j$$

To ensure stability during training, these scores are scaled by dividing by the square root of the dimensionality of the key vectors, $\sqrt{d_k}$, where d_k is the dimensionality of the key vectors:

$$\text{Scaled Attention Score} = \frac{Q_i \cdot K_j}{\sqrt{d_k}}$$

4. **Applying Softmax for Normalization**: The scaled attention scores are passed through a **softmax** function to convert them into probabilities, ensuring that they sum to 1. This normalization step determines how much attention each token should pay to the others, effectively weighting the contributions of other tokens.

5. **Generating Weighted Sums**: The final step involves generating the output vector by taking a weighted sum of the value vectors, where the weights are the attention probabilities obtained from the softmax step:

$$\text{Output}_i = \sum_j \left(\text{Attention Probability}_{ij} \cdot V_j \right)$$

This output represents the contextually refined embedding of the input token, capturing both local and global dependencies in the sequence.

Multi-Head Attention

One of the key innovations of transformers is the **multi-head attention** mechanism, which extends the self-attention process by allowing the model to focus on different aspects of relationships simultaneously. Instead of computing a single set of attention scores, multi-head attention involves multiple parallel attention heads, each learning a different representation of the relationships within the sequence. Each head computes its own set of Q, K, and V vectors, performs self-attention, and generates an output. These outputs are then concatenated and linearly transformed to form the final output of the multi-head attention layer.

Mathematically, if there are h heads, the multi-head attention output is given by:

$$\text{MultiHead}(Q,K,V) = \text{Concat}\left(\text{Head}_1, \text{Head}_2, ..., \text{Head}_h\right) \cdot W_O$$

where W_O is a learned weight matrix that combines the outputs of the different heads into a single vector. This approach allows transformers to capture diverse patterns and relationships, making them highly flexible and effective in processing complex inputs.

Positional Encoding

Unlike RNNs, transformers do not inherently capture the order of tokens because they process sequences in parallel. To address this, transformers use **positional encodings**, which are added to the input embeddings to provide information about the position of each token in the sequence. Positional encodings can be fixed or learned, with fixed encodings often based on sinusoidal functions that provide unique position vectors. The inclusion of positional information enables the model to distinguish between sequences like "The cat sat on the mat" and "The mat sat on the cat," preserving the semantic differences that depend on word order.

Feedforward Layers and Residual Connections

After the multi-head attention layer, transformers use **feedforward neural networks** to further refine the representations of the tokens. These layers introduce non-linearity and help the model learn complex patterns. Each feedforward layer operates independently on each token, without considering the relationships between tokens, making it an efficient step that focuses on individual token transformations.

Transformers also employ **residual connections** around both the multi-head attention and feedforward layers. These connections help stabilize training and prevent issues like vanishing gradients by allowing gradients to flow directly through the network. Combined with **layer normalization**, which normalizes the outputs within each layer, these mechanisms enhance the training efficiency and performance of transformers, enabling them to be trained on massive datasets.

Applications of Transformers

Transformers have transformed NLP by enabling more accurate and scalable models across various tasks:

Language Translation: Transformers are the core of modern translation models, such as Google's Transformer and OpenAI's **GPT**. These models translate entire sentences simultaneously by capturing global dependencies. For example, translating the English sentence "The cat sat on the mat" to French as "Le chat s'est assis sur le tapis" involves understanding word relationships across the entire sequence. Transformers' ability to model long-range dependencies and maintain context improves the grammatical accuracy and fluency of translations compared to RNN-based models.

Text Classification: **BERT (Bidirectional Encoder Representations from Transformers)**, one of the most widely used transformer models, excels in text classification tasks. By using a bidirectional attention mechanism, BERT can understand the full context of a word by looking at both its left and right neighbors simultaneously. This enables it to handle tasks like sentiment analysis and named entity recognition with high accuracy. For instance, in sentiment analysis, BERT can differentiate between subtle expressions of sentiment, such as "I really liked the movie" versus "I liked the movie, but the ending was disappointing," capturing nuanced opinions.

Text Generation: Generative models like **GPT (Generative Pre-trained Transformer)** are built on the transformer architecture. GPT models, particularly GPT-3 and GPT-4, have demonstrated remarkable capabilities in generating coherent and contextually relevant text. GPT models generate text word-by-word, using self-attention to maintain consistency in topics, tone, and style across long passages. For example, GPT can write entire articles, compose poetry, or even engage in dialogue, making it a powerful tool for creative writing, customer service, and virtual assistants.

Text Summarization: Models like **T5 (Text-to-Text Transfer Transformer)** use transformers to condense long documents into concise summaries while retaining essential information. In tasks like summarizing research papers or news articles, transformers can process the entire text simultaneously, extracting the most relevant information without losing coherence. This parallel processing makes summarization faster and more effective, as transformers can consider all parts of the document simultaneously, ensuring a holistic understanding.

Impact on NLP

Transformers have redefined NLP by enabling models to achieve state-of-the-art results in a range of complex tasks, from language understanding to generation. Their ability to capture both local and global dependencies, combined with parallel processing, makes them not only faster but also more accurate than traditional models. As a result, transformers have become the foundation of modern NLP, powering applications from chatbots and virtual assistants to content recommendation systems and advanced search engines.

3.3.2: Graph Neural Networks (GNNs) and Their Real-World Applications

Graph Neural Networks (GNNs) represent a fundamental shift in deep learning architecture, specifically designed to process **graph-structured data**. Unlike regular grid-based data (e.g., images, text), graphs represent irregular, non-Euclidean data with complex relational structures, where nodes represent entities and edges represent relationships between these entities. Graph data is prevalent in various domains, such as **social networks**, **biological networks**, **knowledge graphs**, and **transportation systems**, where understanding the relationships between nodes is as crucial as understanding the nodes themselves.

Traditional neural networks are inadequate for graph data due to the irregular connectivity and variable sizes of graphs. GNNs overcome these limitations by employing **message-passing algorithms**, which iteratively propagate information across nodes and edges, enabling the network to learn rich and dynamic representations of both individual nodes and the overall graph structure.

Detailed Operation of GNNs

The operation of GNNs revolves around a multi-step process that iteratively updates node embeddings based on information aggregated from neighboring nodes. This iterative updating captures the dependencies and relationships in graph data, enabling GNNs to recognize both **local patterns** (e.g., direct connections between nodes) and **global patterns** (e.g., community structures, graph-level features).

Initialization of Node Embeddings

Each node v in the graph G is initialized with a **feature vector** $h_v^{(0)}$, which captures the node's intrinsic properties. These initial features can vary depending on the application:

> In **social networks**, node features may include user attributes like age, location, and interests.

> In **molecular graphs**, node features might represent atom types, bond strengths, or charge distributions.

> In **knowledge graphs**, node features can be embeddings derived from pre-trained models, such as word embeddings or entity embeddings.

Message Passing and Aggregation

The core mechanism of GNNs is **message passing**, an iterative process where nodes exchange information with their neighbors to update their embeddings. This process involves three key steps: message generation, message aggregation, and embedding update.

1. **Message Generation**: In each iteration (or "layer") k, a node v generates messages to its neighbors u using a message function M:

$$m_{v \to u}^{(k)} = M\left(h_v^{(k)}, h_u^{(k)}, e_{(v,u)}\right)$$

> where:

- $h_v^{(k)}$ and $h_u^{(k)}$ are the embeddings of nodes v and u at iteration k.
- $e_{(v,u)}$ represents the edge features between nodes v and u, if available.
- M is a learnable function, often implemented using a neural network, which determines the content of the message based on the node and edge features.

2. **Message Aggregation**: After generating messages, each node aggregates incoming messages from its neighbors using an aggregation function Agg:

$$m_v^{(k)} = \mathrm{Agg}\left(\{m_{u \to v}^{(k)} : u \in N(v)\}\right)$$

where $N(v)$ denotes the set of neighbors of node v, and Agg can be various operations, such as:

Summation: Captures the total influence from neighbors.
Mean: Provides an average influence from neighbors.
Max-pooling: Focuses on the strongest signal received from neighbors.

The choice of aggregation function is critical, as it determines how information is combined and propagated across the graph. Advanced GNNs use more sophisticated aggregation functions, such as **attention mechanisms** that assign different weights to messages from different neighbors. The **Graph Attention Network (GAT)**, for example, computes attention scores between nodes based on their embeddings, allowing it to focus on more important connections.

3. **Node Embedding Update**: After aggregating messages, each node updates its embedding using an update function U:

$$h^{(k+1)}_v = U\left(h^{(k)}_v, m^{(k)}_v\right)$$

The update function U is typically implemented as a neural network layer, such as a feedforward neural network with non-linear activation functions (e.g., ReLU or Tanh). The updated embedding $h^{(k+1)}_v$ incorporates both the node's original features and the aggregated information from its neighbors, capturing local and global patterns in the graph.

This message-passing process continues for a specified number of layers (or iterations), with each layer expanding the range of information captured in the node embeddings. As more layers are added, nodes can aggregate information from increasingly distant neighbors, allowing GNNs to learn higher-order dependencies and relationships.

Advanced Variants of GNNs

Several advanced GNN architectures have been developed to handle different types of graph data and tasks more effectively:

Graph Convolutional Networks (GCNs): GCNs generalize the concept of convolution to graph data. They use a layer-wise propagation rule that aggregates information from neighbors and scales it by the degree of each node, ensuring that the contribution of neighbors is normalized:

$$h^{(k+1)}_v = \sigma\left(\sum_{u \in N(v)} \frac{1}{\sqrt{d_v d_u}} W^{(k)} h^{(k)}_u\right)$$

where:

- d_v and d_u are the degrees of nodes v and u, respectively.
- $W^{(k)}$ is a learnable weight matrix.
- σ is a non-linear activation function. GCNs are particularly effective in semi-supervised node classification tasks, such as identifying communities in social networks or classifying nodes in knowledge graphs.

GraphSAGE (Graph Sample and Aggregation): GraphSAGE extends the scalability of GNNs by sampling a fixed number of neighbors during message passing, rather than aggregating information from all neighbors. This makes it more efficient for large graphs, such as recommendation systems and citation networks. GraphSAGE uses neighborhood sampling followed by aggregation, enabling it to generalize to unseen nodes by learning inductive representations.

Graph Attention Networks (GATs): GATs introduce attention mechanisms to GNNs, allowing the model to learn which neighbors are more relevant for a given node. By computing attention scores between nodes, GATs can prioritize important relationships, making them effective in tasks where the significance of edges varies widely, such as predicting links in citation networks or interactions in social networks.

Message Passing Neural Networks (MPNNs): MPNNs are a general framework for GNNs that supports flexible message-passing strategies, incorporating both node and edge features. MPNNs are commonly used in molecular graph analysis, where edge features represent bond types or distances, enabling the network to capture detailed chemical interactions.

Applications of GNNs

The flexibility and versatility of GNNs make them applicable in a wide range of fields, each leveraging the network's ability to capture both local and global dependencies:

Social Network Analysis: In social networks, GNNs are used for tasks like **community detection**, **node classification**, and **link prediction**. For instance, by aggregating information from users' connections, GNNs can predict whether a user belongs to a specific community or group based on shared interests, interactions, and behaviors. Platforms like Facebook and LinkedIn use GNNs to recommend new connections by analyzing user-item interactions and clustering users with similar features.

Recommendation Systems: In recommendation systems, user-item interactions can be represented as bipartite graphs, where GNNs predict future interactions based on historical data. For example, e-commerce platforms like Amazon use GNNs to suggest products by analyzing past purchases, ratings, and browsing behaviors. By capturing the hierarchical structure of user-item interactions, GNNs can generate personalized recommendations that adapt to changing user preferences.

Drug Discovery and Molecular Analysis: In drug discovery, GNNs analyze **molecular graphs**, where nodes represent atoms and edges represent chemical bonds. GNNs model the interactions between atoms to predict properties like **binding affinity**, **toxicity**, and **solubility**. In a common use case, GNNs are used to predict whether a given drug molecule will interact effectively with a target protein. The model aggregates information from atom embeddings and bond features, enabling it to learn complex chemical patterns that are crucial for identifying potential drug candidates.

Transportation Networks: In transportation networks, GNNs optimize routes, predict traffic patterns, and manage logistics by analyzing the relationships between nodes (e.g., intersections, stations) and edges (e.g., roads, rails). For instance, in urban traffic management, GNNs can predict congestion points by learning from historical traffic data, weather conditions, and event schedules. By incorporating both local traffic patterns and global network structures, GNNs help improve the efficiency and reliability of transportation systems.

Financial Fraud Detection: In the financial sector, GNNs model transaction networks to identify fraudulent behavior. By representing transactions as edges and entities (e.g., accounts, users) as nodes, GNNs can detect anomalies that indicate potential fraud. For example, GNNs can flag unusual transaction patterns by analyzing relationships between entities, such as sudden spikes in transaction volume or connections to known fraudulent nodes.

3.3.3: Neural Architecture Search (NAS) and Automated Model Design

Neural Architecture Search (NAS) is a pivotal innovation in deep learning, designed to automate the creation of neural network architectures. Traditionally, designing neural networks has been a labor-intensive process, relying heavily on manual experimentation to determine the optimal arrangement of layers, neurons, and activation functions. NAS changes this by automating the search for optimal architectures, exploring various configurations to maximize model performance and efficiency. This approach not only reduces human effort but often results in architectures that are more effective and resource-efficient than manually crafted models.

The central idea behind NAS is to use a search algorithm to navigate a predefined space of possible architectures. The algorithm generates different architectures, trains each one on a given task, and evaluates its performance. The goal is to identify the architecture that achieves the best accuracy while considering constraints like computation time, memory usage, or latency. This process has been highly successful in designing models tailored for specific tasks or hardware environments, such as models optimized for image classification on mobile devices or natural language processing (NLP) in cloud environments.

Methods of Neural Architecture Search

Three primary methods drive the NAS process: **reinforcement learning-based NAS**, **evolutionary algorithms**, and **gradient-based approaches** like DARTS (Differentiable Architecture Search). Each method adopts a distinct strategy to explore the architecture space, balancing exploration depth, computational cost, and model accuracy.

Reinforcement Learning-Based NAS

In **Reinforcement Learning (RL)-based NAS**, the architecture search is framed as a sequential decision-making process, where an agent learns to generate effective neural architectures. The agent uses an evolving policy that selects architectural components such as the number of layers, filter sizes, and activation functions. The agent receives a reward based on the performance of the generated architecture, usually measured by validation accuracy or loss. The search process continues iteratively, with the agent refining its policy based on the cumulative rewards, aiming to discover high-performing configurations.

An example of RL-based NAS is **NASNet**, developed by Google Brain. NASNet was able to outperform hand-crafted models like ResNet and Inception in image classification tasks. However, while effective, RL-based NAS is computationally expensive. Training and evaluating each generated architecture can require significant resources, often involving multiple GPUs or TPUs over extended periods. This limitation has spurred the development of more efficient search strategies that aim to reduce the computational burden.

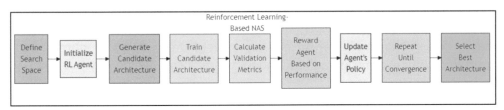

Evolutionary Algorithms for NAS

Evolutionary algorithms (EAs) in NAS are inspired by natural selection, where a population of neural architectures evolves over generations. The process begins with an initial population of randomly generated architectures, each represented as a "genome" encoding its structural features. Each architecture is trained and evaluated to determine its "fitness," typically based on model accuracy.

The fittest architectures are then selected for the next generation, with variations introduced through **mutation** (e.g., changing the number of neurons in a layer) and **crossover** (e.g., combining parts of two architectures). Over successive generations, the population evolves toward more optimal configurations, refining model performance and efficiency.

Evolutionary NAS has been particularly successful in designing architectures for resource-constrained environments. For instance, **MobileNetV3**, discovered through evolutionary search, is optimized for mobile deployment, achieving high accuracy with low latency and memory usage. By focusing on the survival of the fittest architectures, evolutionary NAS effectively balances exploration and exploitation, often generating models that are robust and well-suited for real-world applications.

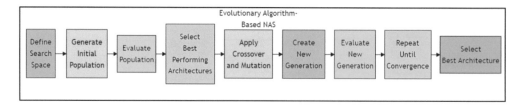

Gradient-Based NAS (e.g., DARTS)

Gradient-based NAS, particularly **Differentiable Architecture Search (DARTS)**, introduces a more efficient approach by making the search space continuous. Instead of selecting discrete architectural components, DARTS assigns continuous parameters to different options within the architecture space. This approach allows for the use of gradient descent to optimize both the architecture parameters and the model weights simultaneously.

During the search phase, DARTS leverages backpropagation to update architecture choices, making the process faster and more computationally feasible. For example, instead of selecting a specific convolutional layer type, DARTS learns a combination of possible layers, assigning weights to each option. After training, the most promising components are selected, yielding a final discrete architecture.

DARTS has been successfully applied in tasks like image classification, achieving results comparable to more computationally intensive methods like RL-based NAS but with significantly reduced computational cost. The main advantage of DARTS is its scalability, making it a popular choice for scenarios where computational resources are limited.

Applications of NAS

The applications of NAS span various fields, demonstrating its versatility and effectiveness in optimizing neural network architectures across different tasks:

Image Classification: NAS has been instrumental in designing state-of-the-art convolutional neural networks (CNNs), such as **EfficientNet**. EfficientNet utilizes a compound scaling method, adjusting the network's width, depth, and resolution in a balanced manner. Discovered through NAS, EfficientNet models achieve superior accuracy on benchmarks like ImageNet while using fewer parameters and less computational power compared to traditional models like ResNet and VGG. This makes EfficientNet an ideal choice for deployment on mobile devices and embedded systems, where resource constraints are a significant factor.

Optimized RNNs for NLP: NAS has been used to enhance Recurrent Neural Network (RNN) architectures for NLP tasks, such as language modeling, text classification, and machine translation. By searching for optimized RNN cell structures, NAS has improved the performance of language models, making them better suited for capturing long-term dependencies in text. For example, models like **GPT-2** and **T5** have integrated NAS to refine their architectures, resulting in more effective language understanding and generation.

Neural Machine Translation: In neural machine translation (NMT), NAS has helped optimize transformer architectures by exploring different configurations of attention heads, feedforward dimensions, and the depth of encoder/decoder layers. This approach has led to the creation of models like **T5 (Text-to-Text Transfer Transformer)**, which are more efficient in processing large-scale text data. By automating the architectural design, NAS reduces the time and effort required to develop high-performance NMT models, enabling faster deployment in real-world applications.

Model Compression and Edge Deployment: One of the most significant impacts of NAS is its ability to generate models tailored for specific hardware constraints. NAS has been used to design models for edge devices, such as smartphones and IoT devices, where memory and processing power are limited. By optimizing models for latency, inference speed, and memory usage, NAS enables efficient deployment in applications like real-time object detection, speech recognition, and face recognition on mobile devices.

Benefits and Implications of NAS

The adoption of NAS in neural network design offers several key advantages. First, by automating the search for optimal architectures, NAS reduces the reliance on manual trial-and-error, freeing researchers to focus on data preprocessing, fine-tuning, and other critical aspects of model development. Second, NAS often discovers novel architectures that outperform traditional models in both accuracy and efficiency, as evidenced by models like EfficientNet and NASNet. Finally, NAS accelerates the development cycle, enabling faster iteration and deployment of neural networks in production environments.

4. Data Collection and Preprocessing

4.1 Data Preparation for Deep Learning

4.1.1: Collecting Large-Scale Datasets for Deep Learning

In deep learning, the availability of large-scale datasets is crucial for model performance, generalization, and robustness. The complex architectures of deep learning models, such as Convolutional Neural Networks (CNNs), Recurrent Neural Networks (RNNs), and Transformers, are designed to learn intricate patterns from data. To do so effectively, these models need access to massive amounts of labeled data. Large datasets help reduce overfitting by enabling models to capture a diverse range of variations in the data, making them better equipped to generalize to new, unseen examples. As the quantity of data increases, the model's ability to discern meaningful patterns improves, leading to more accurate predictions and more reliable performance across different tasks.

Types of Data Sources in Deep Learning

To build robust and efficient deep learning models, various sources of data are employed, each with its own characteristics, benefits, and limitations. Below, we explore the most common sources of large-scale data in deep learning.

Public Datasets

Public datasets are a foundational resource for deep learning research and development. They are openly accessible, often pre-labeled, and have been used to benchmark many state-of-the-art models.

ImageNet: This dataset is widely used for image classification tasks and contains over 14 million labeled images across more than 20,000 categories. ImageNet has been critical in training models like ResNet and EfficientNet, where preprocessing involves resizing images, converting them to arrays, and normalizing pixel values.

COCO (Common Objects in Context): COCO is popular for object detection, segmentation, and captioning tasks. It contains over 330,000 images, with more than 1.5 million object instances annotated. Models trained on COCO require detailed preprocessing, including bounding box extraction and data augmentation.

Wikipedia Dumps for NLP: For natural language processing (NLP), Wikipedia dumps offer a wealth of unstructured text data. They are used to train language models like GPT and BERT. Preprocessing involves tokenization, lowercasing, removing special characters, and creating word embeddings for model inputs.

These public datasets provide a baseline for training deep learning models, allowing researchers to focus more on model architecture and optimization rather than data acquisition.

Synthetic Data Generation

When real-world data is scarce, synthetic data generation becomes a vital alternative. This approach is particularly useful in fields like medical imaging, where data privacy and availability constraints limit the amount of data that can be collected.

Data Augmentation: One of the simplest forms of synthetic data generation, data augmentation involves modifying existing data to create new variations. For image data, common augmentation techniques include:

- **Rotations** (e.g., rotating an image by 15 degrees)
- **Scaling** (e.g., zooming in/out by a factor of 1.2)
- **Flipping** (e.g., horizontal or vertical flips)
- **Color Jittering** (e.g., random changes in brightness, contrast, or saturation)

Here's a sample Python code snippet using **TensorFlow** for image augmentation:

```python
import tensorflow as tf

def augment_image(image):
    image = tf.image.random_flip_left_right(image)
    image = tf.image.random_brightness(image, max_delta=0.2)
    image = tf.image.random_contrast(image, lower=0.8,
upper=1.2)
    return image
```

Generative Adversarial Networks (GANs): GANs are used to generate synthetic examples that mimic real data distribution. In healthcare, GANs have been used to generate synthetic MRI images to augment training datasets while preserving patient privacy. The generator in a GAN learns to create realistic data samples, while the discriminator learns to distinguish between real and synthetic samples. Over time, this adversarial training leads to high-quality synthetic data that can enhance model training.

Web Scraping and APIs

Web scraping and APIs are other common methods for collecting large-scale datasets, particularly when real-world data is not publicly available in structured formats.

Web Scraping: This technique involves extracting data from web pages using tools like Beautiful Soup and Scrapy in Python. Web scraping can be used to gather diverse datasets, such as product reviews, news articles, or social media posts. However, it is essential to comply with ethical guidelines and legal restrictions (e.g., terms of service, GDPR compliance) when using this method.

Here's a sample Python code snippet using Beautiful Soup:

```python
from bs4 import BeautifulSoup
import requests

url = 'https://example.com'
response = requests.get(url)
soup = BeautifulSoup(response.text, 'html.parser')

data = soup.find_all('p')   # Extract all paragraph texts
paragraphs = [p.text for p in data]
```

APIs: APIs allow developers to access structured data from platforms like Twitter (Twitter API) or Kaggle (Kaggle API). For instance, the Twitter API can be used to collect tweets for sentiment analysis, while the Kaggle API provides datasets for tasks ranging from computer vision to NLP.

Example code using the Twitter API:

```python
import tweepy

consumer_key = 'your_consumer_key'
consumer_secret = 'your_consumer_secret'
access_token = 'your_access_token'
access_token_secret = 'your_access_token_secret'

auth = tweepy.OAuthHandler(consumer_key, consumer_secret)
auth.set_access_token(access_token, access_token_secret)
api = tweepy.API(auth)

tweets = api.search(q='deep learning', lang='en', count=100)
```

Technical Considerations for Collecting and Handling Large Datasets

Collecting large-scale datasets is not just about obtaining raw data but also involves various technical considerations to ensure data quality, consistency, and storage efficiency.

Data Quality Management: The first step in handling large datasets is to ensure data quality. This involves removing duplicates, correcting corrupt records, and validating that samples are representative of different classes or categories. Failure to maintain data quality can lead to biased models and unreliable predictions.

Scalable Data Storage Solutions: As datasets grow, scalable storage solutions become essential. Common storage systems include:

> **HDFS (Hadoop Distributed File System)**: Suitable for managing and processing large datasets in distributed environments.
>
> **AWS S3 (Amazon Simple Storage Service)**: Offers secure, scalable cloud storage, with features like versioning and access control for managing large datasets.
>
> **Google Cloud Storage**: Provides seamless integration with Google's AI tools, enabling efficient storage and processing of datasets used in model training.

Data Annotation and Labeling: For supervised learning tasks, labeled data is crucial. Common annotation methods include:

> **Manual Labeling**: Performed by human annotators who label data based on predefined criteria, often used for complex tasks like image segmentation.
>
> **Crowdsourcing**: Platforms like Amazon Mechanical Turk allow large-scale labeling through crowdsourcing, which can be cost-effective for simple tasks.
>
> **Automated Labeling Tools**: Tools like Labelbox and Prodigy use active learning to assist with labeling, improving speed and accuracy.

Examples of Large-Scale Data Collection

Major tech organizations like **Google**, **OpenAI**, and **Facebook** have developed sophisticated data pipelines to collect and manage massive datasets for training state-of-the-art models like BERT, GPT, and ResNet. For instance:

Google collects vast amounts of data for its NLP models, using publicly available datasets as well as web-scraped text data from the internet. The data collection process involves tokenization, deduplication, and quality checks to ensure diverse and representative samples.

OpenAI uses data from Wikipedia, book collections, and web pages to train models like GPT. The data is preprocessed using tokenizers to convert raw text into a format suitable for training transformers.

Facebook gathers image and video data from its platform to train models for facial recognition, content moderation, and object detection, using both public datasets and user-generated content (with privacy controls in place).

4.1.2: Understanding Structured vs. Unstructured Data

The success of deep learning models hinges not only on the quantity of data but also on the nature of the data itself. Data used in training can be broadly categorized into **structured** and **unstructured data**, each requiring different preprocessing and management techniques to be suitable for deep learning tasks.

Structured vs. Unstructured Data: Definitions and Differences

Structured data refers to data that is highly organized and easily represented in tabular formats, such as databases, spreadsheets, and CSV files. It typically consists of rows and columns, where each column corresponds to a variable and each row represents an observation. Examples include sales transactions, customer demographics, and sensor readings. Because of its clear and consistent format, structured data can be readily queried, filtered, and analyzed using SQL databases or data analysis libraries like Pandas.

On the other hand, **unstructured data** lacks a predefined format and is often stored as raw files or documents. This type of data includes text, images, audio, and video files, which are more complex to process. For instance, an article on a news website, an image uploaded to social media, or an audio recording of a conversation all constitute unstructured data. While unstructured data is more challenging to manage and analyze, it often contains rich, valuable information that deep learning models can leverage once it's properly preprocessed.

Characteristics of Structured Data

Structured data is composed of well-defined attributes organized into rows and columns, making it suitable for tasks that rely on numerical and categorical information. Below, we explore the properties and handling of structured data in more detail:

Organization and Storage: Structured data is typically stored in relational databases (e.g., SQL databases) or tabular files (e.g., CSV, Excel), which allow for straightforward queries and analysis. Each attribute (or column) in the dataset has a specific data type, such as integers, floats, or strings, enabling effective storage, indexing, and querying.

Let's consider a sample **financial transactions dataset** that records details like transaction ID, customer ID, transaction amount, date, and transaction type:

Transaction ID	Customer ID	Amount	Date	Transaction Type
001	123	250.00	2024-01-05	Debit
002	124	150.75	2024-01-06	Credit
003	125	320.20	2024-01-07	Debit

This tabular structure makes it easy to perform SQL queries or use Python's Pandas for data manipulation. For instance, filtering transactions over $200 can be done using the following code:

```python
import pandas as pd

# Load data into a DataFrame
data = pd.read_csv('transactions.csv')

# Filter transactions greater than $200
filtered_data = data[data['Amount'] > 200]
print(filtered_data)
```

Tools and Frameworks: Common tools for managing structured data include:

- **SQL Databases**: MySQL, PostgreSQL, and SQLite are used for querying and managing structured data.

- **Pandas (Python)**: Widely used for data manipulation, cleaning, and preprocessing in deep learning pipelines.
- **BigQuery (Google Cloud)**: A scalable solution for handling large-scale structured data in cloud environments.

  For example, here's a simple SQL query to select credit transactions from the dataset above:

```
SELECT * FROM transactions WHERE "Transaction Type" = 'Credit';
```

Structured data, while easier to handle, is generally limited to fixed fields and predefined relationships, making it less versatile than unstructured data for certain complex deep learning tasks.

Characteristics of Unstructured Data

Unstructured data, due to its raw and free-form nature, presents unique challenges in preprocessing but also offers opportunities for deep learning models to learn more complex patterns and relationships.

Types of Unstructured Data:

Text: This includes documents, social media posts, chat logs, and other forms of natural language data. Text data often requires preprocessing steps like tokenization, stemming, lemmatization, and conversion into embeddings before it can be fed into neural networks.

Images: Images are represented as pixel arrays, where each pixel has values corresponding to color intensity. Image data requires preprocessing steps such as resizing, normalization, and converting images to RGB arrays.

Audio and Video: Audio data needs to be converted into spectrograms, which are 2D visual representations of sound waves over time. Video data, being a combination of images and audio, is even more complex to process, requiring frame extraction, audio isolation, and possibly annotation.

Preprocessing Unstructured Data for Deep Learning

Text Data Preprocessing (NLP):

Tokenization: Splitting sentences into individual words or sub-words (tokens).

Stemming and Lemmatization: Reducing words to their base or root forms (e.g., "running" becomes "run").

Embedding Techniques: Transforming words into vectors that capture semantic meaning. Common embedding techniques include **Word2Vec**, **GloVe**, and modern transformer-based models like **BERT**. For instance, BERT converts words into high-dimensional vectors, capturing context and meaning through self-attention mechanisms.

Here's a code snippet using the **NLTK** library in Python for tokenization:

```python
from nltk.tokenize import word_tokenize

text = "Deep learning models require a lot of data to be
effective."
tokens = word_tokenize(text)
print(tokens)  # Output: ['Deep', 'learning', 'models',
'require', 'a', 'lot', 'of', 'data', 'to', 'be',
'effective']
```

Image Data Preprocessing (Computer Vision):

Resizing: Standardizes image dimensions to a fixed size (e.g., 224x224 pixels for models like ResNet).

Normalization: Scales pixel values to a range of [0, 1] or standardizes them to have zero mean and unit variance.

Converting to RGB Arrays: Transforms images into 3D arrays with dimensions corresponding to height, width, and color channels.

An example code snippet using **OpenCV** to preprocess images:

```python
import cv2

image = cv2.imread('image.jpg')
resized_image = cv2.resize(image, (224, 224))
normalized_image = resized_image / 255.0  # Normalize pixel
values
```

Audio Data Preprocessing (Speech Recognition):

Spectrogram Conversion: Converts audio waveforms into spectrograms, which are then fed into models like RNNs or CNNs. Spectrograms capture the frequency and amplitude of sound signals over time, making them suitable for neural network inputs.

Here's a code snippet using **librosa** for converting an audio file to a spectrogram:

```
import librosa
import librosa.display
import matplotlib.pyplot as plt

y, sr = librosa.load('audio.wav')
spectrogram = librosa.feature.melspectrogram(y, sr=sr)
librosa.display.specshow(librosa.power_to_db(spectrogram,
ref=np.max))
plt.colorbar(format='%+2.0f dB')
plt.show()
```

Use Cases of Structured and Unstructured Data in Deep Learning

The distinction between structured and unstructured data is critical in understanding their roles in different deep learning applications:

Structured Data Applications:

> **Customer Churn Prediction**: Using structured data from CRM databases, models can predict the likelihood of a customer leaving a service, relying on features like account age, transaction history, and support interactions.
>
> **Financial Forecasting**: Models can predict stock prices or economic trends based on structured financial indicators like historical prices, economic indicators, and transaction volumes.

Unstructured Data Applications:

> **Image Classification with CNNs**: CNNs process pixel arrays to classify objects in images, handling tasks like facial recognition, medical imaging analysis, and object detection.
>
> **Text Generation with Transformers**: Models like GPT-3 generate coherent text by processing large volumes of unstructured text data, learning from diverse language patterns and contexts.
>
> **Speech Recognition with RNNs and LSTMs**: RNNs and LSTMs handle sequential audio data to transcribe spoken language into text, enabling applications like virtual assistants and real-time transcription services.

4.1.3: *Ethical Considerations in Data Collection*

Ethical considerations are fundamental to data collection for deep learning, affecting model fairness, trustworthiness, and overall data quality. Adhering to ethical guidelines not only protects users' privacy and rights but also improves model performance by ensuring a representative and unbiased dataset. Failure to follow ethical practices can lead to significant risks, including biased model predictions, privacy breaches, and legal violations, potentially causing harm to individuals or groups and damaging an organization's reputation. Given the increasing role of AI in critical sectors like healthcare, finance, and law enforcement, ethical data collection is not just a technical concern—it's a societal obligation.

Key Ethical Issues in Data Collection

Ethics in data collection encompasses multiple dimensions, including bias, privacy, and data ownership. Below, we explore these aspects in depth, highlighting their implications for deep learning models and practical strategies to address them.

Bias and Fairness

Bias in data can lead to biased models, resulting in skewed predictions that unfairly affect certain groups. Bias can manifest in various forms, including:

> **Selection Bias**: Occurs when the dataset is not representative of the target population. For example, a facial recognition model trained primarily on lighter-skinned faces may perform poorly on darker-skinned individuals, as was the case with early versions of some commercial facial recognition systems.
>
> **Confirmation Bias**: Arises when the data collection process reinforces pre-existing beliefs. For instance, using historical hiring data to train an HR algorithm can perpetuate biases against minority candidates if the original hiring practices were biased.

Consider the case of **COMPAS**, an algorithm used in the U.S. to predict recidivism. Studies revealed that it was biased against Black defendants, often predicting higher risk scores for them compared to white defendants with similar profiles. This example demonstrates how biased data can result in unfair decisions with serious consequences. To mitigate such biases, data collection should focus on ensuring diverse and representative samples across different demographic groups. Techniques like **re-sampling, re-weighting,** and using **fairness-aware algorithms** can also help reduce bias during model training.

Data Privacy and Consent

Respecting user privacy and obtaining informed consent are vital when collecting personal data, especially in sensitive domains like healthcare, finance, or social media. Ethical data collection should comply with data protection laws such as the **General Data Protection Regulation (GDPR)** in Europe or the **California Consumer Privacy Act (CCPA)** in the United States.

Privacy-preserving techniques can help ensure compliance and protect user information:

Anonymization: Removing personally identifiable information (PII) from datasets to prevent re-identification of individuals.

Differential Privacy: Adding statistical noise to datasets or model outputs to obscure individual data points while preserving aggregate patterns. This technique has been employed by companies like Apple and Google to collect user data for improving services without compromising individual privacy.

Federated Learning: Involves training models directly on users' devices rather than centralizing data. It allows models to learn from decentralized data while keeping sensitive information on local devices. For example, Google uses federated learning to improve its keyboard prediction model without uploading user data to central servers.

Data Ownership and Security

Data ownership defines who has the rights to access, use, and control collected data. Ethical data collection requires clear agreements on data ownership, especially when data is collected from third-party sources or through partnerships. Key aspects of ethical data ownership and security include:

Data Usage Agreements: Establish clear terms that outline how data can be used, who has access, and the duration of use. This ensures transparency and prevents unauthorized use.

Data Encryption: Protects sensitive data both in transit and at rest by using encryption algorithms like **AES (Advanced Encryption Standard)** or **RSA**

(Rivest-Shamir-Adleman). This prevents unauthorized access, even in the event of a data breach.

Access Controls: Implement role-based access controls (RBAC) to restrict data access to authorized users only. This minimizes the risk of data misuse and ensures that sensitive information is accessed only by those who need it.

An example of ethical failure in data ownership is the **Cambridge Analytica scandal**, where data from millions of Facebook users was harvested without consent and used for political advertising. The incident highlights the critical importance of maintaining strict data ownership controls and enforcing ethical standards in AI development.

Examples of Ethical Challenges in Data Collection

Ethical lapses in data collection have led to significant legal and reputational consequences for companies and organizations, underscoring the need for robust ethical guidelines. Below are some notable cases:

Facial Recognition in Law Enforcement: Several law enforcement agencies faced backlash for using facial recognition systems that were shown to be biased against certain racial groups. Studies by organizations like MIT Media Lab revealed that facial recognition models trained on biased datasets had error rates of up to 35% for darker-skinned women, compared to less than 1% for lighter-skinned men. This led to calls for stricter ethical guidelines and even moratoriums on the use of facial recognition technology in public spaces.

Health Data Breaches: In healthcare, data privacy violations can have severe consequences, as seen in the **Anthem Inc. data breach** of 2015, where hackers accessed the personal information of 78.8 million individuals. This breach led to massive lawsuits and a $16 million settlement with the U.S. Department of Health and Human Services (HHS).

Successful Ethical Data Practices

Despite these challenges, some organizations have established robust ethical frameworks for AI development:

Google's AI Principles: Google has committed to developing AI systems that are socially beneficial, avoid creating or reinforcing unfair bias, and are built and tested for safety. The company's AI research teams use techniques like differential privacy and federated learning to ensure ethical data practices in model training.

Microsoft's AI Ethics Guidelines: Microsoft has developed comprehensive AI ethics guidelines that emphasize transparency, accountability, and fairness in AI development. The company has also created the **AI Fairness Checklist**, a set of guidelines for researchers and engineers to follow when collecting, processing, and using data for model training.

4.2 Feature Scaling and Normalization

4.2.1: Why Feature Scaling is Critical for Neural Networks

Feature scaling is a preprocessing technique that adjusts the scale of input data to fit within a specified range or distribution. It is an essential step in preparing data for neural networks, as these models are sensitive to the scale of their input features. When the input data is not scaled, neural networks often face issues such as slower convergence, suboptimal performance, or even complete training failures. This section explores why feature scaling is critical, how it affects neural network performance, and its impact on optimization algorithms like gradient descent.

The Importance of Feature Scaling in Neural Networks

Neural networks process inputs through a series of weight transformations, and these transformations are highly influenced by the scale of the input data. For instance, consider a dataset where one feature has values ranging from 1 to 10, while another ranges from 1,000 to 10,000. Without scaling, the gradient updates during backpropagation can become uneven, leading to inefficient learning. The gradients for features with larger values tend to dominate, which can distort the learning process and affect convergence.

From a mathematical perspective, the loss function L is minimized by adjusting weights w based on the gradient ∇L. In backpropagation, the weight update for each neuron is given by:

$$w_{new} = w_{old} - \eta \cdot \nabla L$$

where η is the learning rate. When input features have significantly different scales, the gradient ∇L becomes imbalanced, leading to unstable training dynamics such as **gradient explosions** or **vanishing gradients**:

- **Gradient Explosions**: Occur when gradients become excessively large, causing weights to update too rapidly, which destabilizes the network. This often happens when unscaled input features have large values, leading to inflated gradient calculations during backpropagation.
- **Vanishing Gradients**: Arise when gradients become very small, causing slow or halted learning in deeper layers of the network. This issue is more common in networks with unscaled inputs, as the gradient diminishes across multiple layers.

Feature scaling mitigates these issues by ensuring that all input features have a similar scale, allowing neural networks to learn more efficiently and consistently.

Impact of Feature Scaling on Optimization Algorithms

Feature scaling significantly improves the performance of optimization algorithms like **gradient descent** by promoting faster and more stable convergence. Optimization in neural networks involves navigating a complex, multidimensional loss landscape to find the global minimum. When input features have different scales, the loss landscape becomes highly irregular, making it challenging for gradient descent to converge efficiently.

Example: Gradient Descent with and without Feature Scaling

Consider a simple neural network with two input features: one ranging from 1 to 10 and the other from 1,000 to 10,000. Without scaling, the loss landscape is skewed, as shown in the graph below:

- **Unscaled Data**: The gradients are steep in one direction (due to the larger feature values) and flat in the other, causing the gradient descent algorithm to oscillate or take a zigzag path toward the minimum. This results in slower convergence and higher computational cost.
- **Scaled Data**: When features are scaled to a similar range, the loss landscape becomes smoother and more symmetric. This allows gradient descent to take more direct steps toward the minimum, improving convergence speed and stability.

Scaling techniques like **Min-Max Scaling** (scaling data to the range [0, 1]) or **Z-Score Normalization** (standardizing data to have a mean of 0 and standard deviation of 1) ensure that gradients are balanced and well-aligned, facilitating smoother learning.

Code Example: Feature Scaling with Min-Max Scaling

The following Python code demonstrates how to implement Min-Max scaling using **scikit-learn**:

```python
from sklearn.preprocessing import MinMaxScaler
import numpy as np

# Sample data
data = np.array([[500, 2000], [1000, 3000], [1500, 4000]])

# Apply Min-Max Scaling
```

```
scaler = MinMaxScaler()
scaled_data = scaler.fit_transform(data)

print(scaled_data)
```

In this example, the Min-Max scaling technique transforms all features to the range [0, 1], ensuring that gradients are more balanced during backpropagation.

How Feature Scaling Affects Different Types of Neural Networks

The benefits of feature scaling extend across various types of neural networks, each of which relies on scaled inputs to achieve optimal performance:

Feedforward Neural Networks (FNNs)

In feedforward neural networks, feature scaling enhances weight initialization and reduces the risk of getting stuck in local minima. By scaling inputs, the initial weight distribution becomes more balanced, leading to faster convergence and better generalization. For example, when predicting house prices using numerical features like square footage or number of rooms, scaling these features improves the network's ability to learn relationships between them.

Recurrent Neural Networks (RNNs)

RNNs, which process sequential data, are particularly sensitive to the scale of time-series inputs. When inputs like stock prices or temperature readings vary greatly in magnitude, unscaled data can exacerbate issues like vanishing gradients, hindering the model's ability to learn long-term dependencies. Scaling time-series data ensures that the RNN can maintain stable gradients over time, improving its capacity to model temporal dependencies.

Consider an RNN that predicts future sales based on past sales data. Without scaling, the network may struggle to learn patterns effectively, especially if the sales figures range from tens to thousands. Scaling the data to a standardized range improves the network's performance by maintaining consistent gradients across time steps.

Convolutional Neural Networks (CNNs)

In CNNs, feature scaling is typically applied to image pixel values. For instance, images are often normalized to a range of [0, 1] or standardized to have zero mean and unit variance. This scaling improves the network's ability to learn hierarchical features, such as edges, textures, and objects, without being biased toward specific pixel intensity ranges.

The following code snippet demonstrates how to normalize pixel values in an image using **TensorFlow**:

```
import tensorflow as tf

# Load and normalize an image
image = tf.io.read_file('image.jpg')
image = tf.image.decode_jpeg(image, channels=3)
image = tf.image.convert_image_dtype(image, tf.float32)  #
Normalize to [0, 1]
```

Scaling pixel values ensures that CNNs learn uniformly across all layers, enhancing their performance in tasks like object detection or facial recognition.

Applications of Feature Scaling in Neural Networks

Feature scaling is widely applied across industries to improve neural network performance:

Finance: In credit scoring models, scaling features like income, debt, and transaction amounts ensures that the model can accurately predict credit risk without being biased toward features with larger magnitudes.

Healthcare: In medical imaging, normalizing pixel intensities allows CNNs to focus on detecting anomalies (e.g., tumors) without being influenced by variations in image brightness.

Retail: In sales forecasting models, scaling historical sales data enables RNNs to predict future sales trends more accurately, regardless of the absolute scale of past sales figures.

Connecting Feature Scaling to Neural Network Efficiency

Feature scaling is a critical preprocessing step that impacts the efficiency of optimization algorithms, convergence speed, and overall model performance. By transforming input data to a uniform scale, feature scaling helps neural networks learn faster, converge more stably, and generalize better to new data. As neural network architectures become more complex and datasets grow larger, the role of feature scaling in achieving optimal performance cannot be overstated.

4.2.2: Techniques for Normalization (Min-Max, Z-Score)

Normalization is a crucial preprocessing technique that transforms data into a specific scale, facilitating efficient learning in neural networks. By adjusting the scale of features, normalization ensures that models treat all features equally, preventing those with larger magnitudes from dominating the learning process. Unlike feature scaling, which typically brings values to a specific range, normalization often aims to center the data around a mean or within a defined range, making it more suitable for certain types of neural network architectures and optimization algorithms. This section will explore two popular normalization techniques: **Min-Max Normalization** and **Z-Score Normalization**, explaining their formulas, applications, and implementation.

Min-Max Normalization

Min-Max Normalization scales data to a fixed range, usually [0, 1], making it one of the most widely used normalization techniques in deep learning. It's particularly useful for models that rely on distance metrics, such as k-Nearest Neighbors (k-NN), and for neural networks where consistent scaling aids in gradient-based learning.

Mathematical Formula

Min-Max Normalization is defined by the following formula:

$$X_{scaled} = \frac{X - X_{min}}{X_{max} - X_{min}}$$

Here:

- X is the original feature value.
- X_{min} is the minimum value in the dataset for that feature.
- X_{max} is the maximum value in the dataset for that feature.
- X_{scaled} is the transformed feature value, scaled between 0 and 1.

This transformation helps ensure that all feature values are proportional, preventing any single feature from dominating the model's learning process. For example, in a dataset where age ranges from 20 to 70 and income ranges from 30,000 to 150,000, Min-Max normalization scales both features to a comparable range, making the training process smoother.

Code Example: Implementing Min-Max Normalization in Python

Using Python's **scikit-learn**, Min-Max normalization can be easily applied:

```python
from sklearn.preprocessing import MinMaxScaler
import numpy as np

# Sample data
data = np.array([[25, 50000], [35, 70000], [45, 120000]])

# Min-Max Normalization
scaler = MinMaxScaler()
scaled_data = scaler.fit_transform(data)

print("Scaled Data:\n", scaled_data)
```

This code snippet demonstrates how to transform raw feature values into the [0, 1] range, making it easier for neural networks to process the input data effectively. Min-Max normalization is especially effective in cases where the data is uniformly distributed or when the neural network uses activation functions like Sigmoid, which output values between 0 and 1.

Applications of Min-Max Normalization

Image Preprocessing: In computer vision, pixel values are often scaled to [0, 1] to ensure that gradients are balanced during backpropagation. This is especially useful in convolutional neural networks (CNNs), where scaled pixel intensities lead to faster convergence and more accurate learning of visual patterns.

Finance: Min-Max normalization is used to scale features like stock prices or transaction amounts, making it easier for neural networks to predict future trends without being biased toward larger numerical values.

NLP (Natural Language Processing): In text-based models, Min-Max normalization is applied to word embedding vectors to ensure that vector magnitudes are comparable across different words, improving the model's ability to learn semantic relationships.

Z-Score Normalization

Z-Score Normalization, also known as **standardization**, transforms data to have a mean of 0 and a standard deviation of 1. This approach is particularly useful when the input features have different scales and distributions, making it effective for neural networks that benefit from zero-centered data.

Mathematical Formula

Z-Score Normalization is defined by the following formula:

$$X_{standardized} = \frac{X - \mu}{\sigma}$$

Here:

- X is the original feature value.
- μ is the mean of the dataset for that feature.
- σ is the standard deviation of the dataset for that feature.
- $X_{standardized}$ is the transformed feature value, centered around 0 with unit variance.

Z-Score normalization is particularly beneficial in models where gradients oscillate around zero, as it stabilizes the learning process by keeping feature values within a more predictable range.

Code Example: Implementing Z-Score Normalization in Python

Using Python's **scikit-learn**, Z-Score normalization can be applied as follows:

```python
from sklearn.preprocessing import StandardScaler
import numpy as np

# Sample data
data = np.array([[25, 50000], [35, 70000], [45, 120000]])

# Z-Score Normalization
scaler = StandardScaler()
standardized_data = scaler.fit_transform(data)

print("Standardized Data:\n", standardized_data)
```

In this code snippet, the features are transformed to have a mean of 0 and a standard deviation of 1. This normalization technique is well-suited for models that use activation functions like ReLU or Tanh, which perform better when inputs are centered around zero.

Applications of Z-Score Normalization

Image Preprocessing: Standardization is often used in advanced CNN architectures like ResNet or VGG, where pixel intensities are transformed to have zero mean and unit variance. This approach helps the model learn more effectively by keeping input distributions consistent.

Finance: In time-series forecasting models, Z-Score normalization is applied to financial indicators like returns or trading volumes, making it easier for models to identify trends and anomalies without being influenced by scale differences across features.

NLP (Natural Language Processing): In NLP tasks, Z-Score normalization is used to standardize word embedding vectors, ensuring that their distributions are consistent across different features. This normalization step improves the performance of models like RNNs or Transformers, which benefit from zero-centered input distributions.

Connecting Normalization Techniques to Neural Network Performance

Both Min-Max and Z-Score normalization play critical roles in improving neural network performance by aligning feature scales and ensuring balanced gradients. By transforming features to comparable ranges or distributions, normalization techniques prevent model biases and facilitate faster convergence, making training more efficient and reliable. In addition, normalization reduces the likelihood of getting stuck in local minima, as consistent input scales promote smoother loss landscapes during optimization.

The choice between Min-Max and Z-Score normalization depends on the specific characteristics of the dataset and the neural network architecture in use. While Min-Max normalization is more suitable for uniformly distributed data and models with Sigmoid or softmax activations, Z-Score normalization is ideal for zero-centered data distributions and models with ReLU or Tanh activations.

4.2.3: *Handling Categorical and Continuous Data Types*

Neural networks can handle a variety of data types, but the preprocessing steps required for effective training differ significantly between **categorical** and **continuous data**. Proper handling of these data types ensures that neural networks can learn meaningful patterns without biases or performance issues caused by data scale or representation. In this section, we will explore how to preprocess categorical and continuous data, discussing common techniques, their implementations, and real-world applications.

Categorical vs. Continuous Data

Categorical and continuous data represent distinct forms of information that require tailored preprocessing techniques:

- **Categorical Data**: Refers to discrete values that represent categories or labels, such as color (red, blue, green), gender (male, female), or product type (electronics, clothing, food). Categorical data is non-numeric, making it incompatible with neural networks in its raw form.
- **Continuous Data**: Refers to numeric values that can take an infinite range within a defined scope, such as age, temperature, or stock price. Continuous data is inherently numeric and can be directly fed into neural networks after normalization or standardization.

Preprocessing Techniques for Categorical Data

Categorical data must be transformed into numerical representations that neural networks can understand. Below are some of the most common preprocessing techniques for categorical data:

One-Hot Encoding

One-Hot Encoding converts categorical values into binary vectors. Each category is represented as a vector of 0s and 1s, where the position of 1 corresponds to the presence of a specific category. This technique is widely used because it eliminates any ordinal relationship between categories, ensuring that the neural network treats each category as distinct.

For example, consider a categorical feature representing colors: **red**, **blue**, and **green**. After one-hot encoding, the feature is transformed as follows:

Color	One-Hot Encoding
Red	[1, 0, 0]
Blue	[0, 1, 0]
Green	[0, 0, 1]

Code Example: Implementing One-Hot Encoding in Python

Using **pandas** and **scikit-learn**, one-hot encoding can be implemented as follows:

```
import pandas as pd
from sklearn.preprocessing import OneHotEncoder
```

```
# Sample data
data = pd.DataFrame({'Color': ['Red', 'Blue', 'Green', 'Blue',
'Red']})

# One-hot encoding using pandas
one_hot_encoded_data = pd.get_dummies(data['Color'])
print("One-Hot Encoded Data (pandas):\n", one_hot_encoded_data)

# One-hot encoding using scikit-learn
encoder = OneHotEncoder(sparse=False)
encoded_data = encoder.fit_transform(data[['Color']])
print("One-Hot Encoded Data (scikit-learn):\n", encoded_data)
```

One-hot encoding is simple and effective for low-cardinality categorical features but can lead to high-dimensional input data when applied to features with many categories, increasing computational complexity.

Label Encoding

Label Encoding assigns integer values to categories, making it a straightforward method to convert categorical data into numerical form. However, it introduces an unintended ordinal relationship between categories, which can mislead neural networks into interpreting a ranking or hierarchy where none exists.

For example, if label encoding is applied to the colors **red**, **blue**, and **green**, the encoded values might be 0, 1, and 2, respectively. The neural network could incorrectly assume that "green" is greater than "blue," which is not the intended outcome.

Code Example: Implementing Label Encoding in Python

```
from sklearn.preprocessing import LabelEncoder

# Sample data
data = pd.DataFrame({'Color': ['Red', 'Blue', 'Green', 'Blue',
'Red']})

# Label encoding
label_encoder = LabelEncoder()
encoded_labels = label_encoder.fit_transform(data['Color'])
print("Label Encoded Data:\n", encoded_labels)
```

Label encoding is best suited for ordinal categories, such as education level (e.g., high school, college, graduate) or survey responses (e.g., disagree, neutral, agree).

Categorical Embeddings for High-Cardinality Features

For features with a large number of categories (high-cardinality features), **categorical embeddings** are more efficient than one-hot encoding or label encoding. Categorical embeddings represent categories as dense vectors in a lower-dimensional space, preserving semantic relationships between categories. They are learned during training and are commonly used in models like word embeddings in NLP or user embeddings in recommendation systems.

The transformation of a categorical variable into embeddings can be represented mathematically as:

$$v_i = W \cdot x_i$$

where:

- v_i is the embedding vector for category i.
- W is the embedding matrix learned during training.
- x_i is the one-hot encoded vector representing the category.

Diagram: Categorical Embeddings

Here's a conceptual diagram illustrating how categorical embeddings map high-cardinality features to dense vectors:

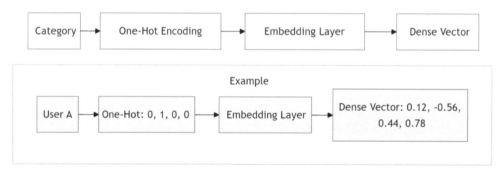

Categorical embeddings are effective in applications like recommendation systems, where user IDs or item IDs have high cardinality and one-hot encoding would be computationally expensive.

Preprocessing Techniques for Continuous Data

Continuous data, being numeric, can be directly fed into neural networks, but its scale often needs to be adjusted to ensure stable training dynamics.

Normalization for Continuous Data

Normalization techniques like **Min-Max Scaling** and **Z-Score Normalization** (discussed in 4.2.2) are commonly applied to continuous data. By scaling continuous variables to a specific range or standardizing them to have zero mean and unit variance, neural networks can learn more efficiently. For example, normalizing temperature readings to a [0, 1] range or standardizing stock price returns to a normal distribution helps models converge faster.

Binning for Continuous Variables

In some cases, continuous variables can be transformed into categorical-like bins, making them easier for certain models to handle. Binning involves dividing continuous values into intervals or bins, effectively converting them into ordinal categories. For example, age can be binned into categories like **0-18** (youth), **19-35** (adult), **36-60** (middle-aged), and **60+** (senior).

Code Example: Implementing Binning in Python

```python
# Sample data
data = pd.DataFrame({'Age': [15, 25, 45, 70, 55]})

# Binning age into categories
bins = [0, 18, 35, 60, 100]
labels = ['Youth', 'Adult', 'Middle-Aged', 'Senior']
data['Age_Group'] = pd.cut(data['Age'], bins=bins,
labels=labels)
print("Binned Data:\n", data)
```

Binning can be useful in simplifying model complexity or making the model more interpretable, though it comes at the cost of reducing granularity.

Applications of Handling Categorical and Continuous Data

Handling both categorical and continuous data types effectively is essential in various deep learning applications:

Categorical Data Applications:

Natural Language Processing (NLP): Word tokens in NLP are treated as categorical data, requiring techniques like one-hot encoding or word embeddings to transform them into numerical vectors for model input.

E-commerce: In customer segmentation tasks, categories like user demographics (e.g., age group, gender) and browsing history (e.g., product category) are encoded using categorical embeddings to improve recommendation accuracy.

Continuous Data Applications:

Financial Modeling: Continuous variables like stock prices, trading volumes, or economic indicators are normalized to improve neural network performance in predicting trends or identifying anomalies.

IoT (Internet of Things): Sensor data collected in IoT applications, such as temperature, humidity, or pressure readings, are treated as continuous variables that are often normalized or standardized for efficient processing by neural networks.

Connecting Categorical and Continuous Data Handling to Neural Network Training

Effective handling of both categorical and continuous data types is critical for neural network training. By transforming categorical data into meaningful numerical representations and scaling continuous data appropriately, neural networks can learn efficiently and generalize well to new data. Proper preprocessing not only improves model accuracy but also reduces training time and computational costs, making it an essential step in building robust deep learning models.

4.3 Handling Missing Data

4.3.1: Methods for Detecting and Addressing Missing Data

Missing data is a frequent challenge in datasets used for deep learning, affecting model training, accuracy, and fairness. Models trained on incomplete data may learn biased patterns, leading to poor generalization and flawed predictions. Understanding and addressing missing data is crucial for building robust deep learning models. There are different types of missing data, each of which affects data handling strategies:

> **Missing Completely at Random (MCAR)**: The missingness has no relationship with any variable in the dataset.
>
> **Missing at Random (MAR)**: The missingness is related to observed variables but not the missing value itself.
>
> **Missing Not at Random (MNAR)**: The missingness is related to the unobserved value.

These distinctions guide the choice of detection and handling techniques, as MCAR, MAR, and MNAR require different strategies for effective preprocessing.

Methods for Detecting Missing Data

Detecting missing data is the first step in handling it, as it helps identify patterns and informs appropriate handling strategies.

Visual Inspection

Visual tools can reveal patterns of missing data, helping researchers determine if missing values are random or related to specific variables. Common visualization techniques include:

- **Heatmaps**: Display missing values as a matrix of colors, making it easy to spot patterns.
- **Bar Plots**: Show the count of missing values for each variable, offering a quick overview of which features have the most missing data.

Code Example: Visualizing Missing Data in Python

Using **seaborn** and **pandas**, we can create a heatmap to visualize missing data:

```
import pandas as pd
```

```python
import seaborn as sns
import matplotlib.pyplot as plt

# Sample dataset with missing values
data = pd.DataFrame({
    'Age': [25, 30, None, 22, 28],
    'Income': [50000, None, 45000, 52000, None],
    'Gender': ['M', 'F', None, 'F', 'M']
})

# Visualizing missing data using a heatmap
sns.heatmap(data.isnull(), cbar=False, cmap='viridis')
plt.title('Missing Data Heatmap')
plt.show()
```

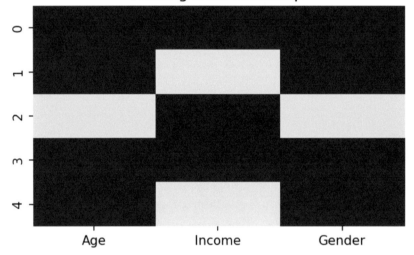

In the heatmap, missing values are highlighted, making it clear which variables have missing data and their distribution across observations.

Statistical Analysis

Statistical techniques help quantify missing data and understand its extent:

Checking for NaN Values: The simplest approach is to count the number of NaN values in each column.

Little's MCAR Test: A statistical test used to determine if missing data is MCAR. It is useful for deciding whether listwise deletion can be applied without introducing bias.

Code Example: Detecting Missing Values in Python

Using **pandas**, we can identify missing values and their proportions:

```
# Checking for missing values
missing_counts = data.isnull().sum()
print("Missing Values Count:\n", missing_counts)

# Calculating the proportion of missing values
missing_proportion = data.isnull().mean()
print("Proportion of Missing Values:\n", missing_proportion)
```

This analysis helps determine which variables have significant amounts of missing data, guiding decisions about how to handle them.

Advanced Detection Techniques

Advanced techniques provide deeper insights into the nature of missing data:

- **Correlation Analysis**: Determines if missing values in one variable correlate with other variables, indicating whether the missing data is MAR or MNAR.
- **Imputation Modeling**: Uses predictive models to estimate missing values based on observed data, helping identify patterns that could suggest MAR or MNAR.

Methods for Addressing Missing Data

Once missing data is detected, it's essential to address it using appropriate techniques that minimize bias and preserve data integrity.

Listwise Deletion

Listwise deletion removes all rows with missing values, making it a simple but aggressive approach. It's suitable when the missing data is MCAR and the proportion of missingness is low. However, it can lead to data loss and potential bias if the data is MAR or MNAR.

Code Example: Implementing Listwise Deletion in Python

```
# Dropping rows with missing values
cleaned_data = data.dropna()
print("Data after Listwise Deletion:\n", cleaned_data)
```

While listwise deletion is easy to implement, it's not recommended for datasets with high levels of missing data or when the missingness is related to other variables.

Pairwise Deletion

Pairwise deletion retains more data by using available values for analysis rather than removing entire rows. It's more effective than listwise deletion when missing data is MAR, but it can still lead to biased estimates, especially in complex models.

Indicator Variable for Missingness

Creating an **indicator variable** is a technique where a new binary variable is added to indicate whether a value is missing. This approach allows neural networks to learn from the patterns of missingness, providing valuable information that can improve predictions.

For instance, if the "Income" variable has missing values, we can create an indicator variable called "Income_Missing" that marks whether the income value is missing (1) or not (0).

Code Example: Creating an Indicator Variable for Missingness

```
# Creating an indicator variable for missing income values
data['Income_Missing'] = data['Income'].isnull().astype(int)
print("Data with Indicator Variable:\n", data)
```

This technique is useful for models like decision trees or neural networks, which can learn relationships between missingness and target variables.

Practical Examples of Handling Missing Data

Addressing missing data effectively is critical across various domains:

Healthcare: In medical records, missing values can arise from incomplete patient data or lost records. Imputation techniques, like mean imputation for continuous variables or using domain-specific models, help maintain data integrity and improve predictive accuracy in patient outcome models

Finance: In financial datasets, missing data in features like transaction amounts or account balances can introduce bias in credit risk models. Creating indicator variables for missing values or using predictive imputation helps maintain model fairness.

E-commerce: In customer segmentation tasks, missing demographic information (e.g., age, income) can skew segmentation results. Advanced imputation methods like KNN imputation or model-based imputation help fill in gaps without introducing significant bias.

Connecting Missing Data Detection and Handling to Model Performance

Effective detection and handling of missing data are crucial for building accurate and fair deep learning models. By understanding the nature of missingness (MCAR, MAR, or MNAR), researchers can select the most suitable techniques to address it, minimizing biases and improving model robustness. Proper handling of missing data not only enhances model performance but also ensures that the results are interpretable and reliable in real-world applications.

4.3.2: Imputation Techniques for Neural Networks

Data imputation involves filling in missing values to create complete datasets, a critical step for training neural networks effectively. Incomplete data can hinder model performance, introduce bias, and reduce generalization. Imputation helps maintain data consistency, allowing neural networks to learn from a comprehensive dataset and achieve better predictive accuracy.

Common Imputation Techniques

Imputation methods range from simple statistical approaches to advanced deep learning techniques. Below, we detail several imputation techniques, their implementations, and their use cases.

Mean, Median, and Mode Imputation

Mean, Median, and Mode Imputation are basic yet widely used methods that replace missing values with the average (mean), the middle value (median), or the most frequent value (mode) of the observed data. These techniques are effective for datasets with a low percentage of missing values and for features where the missing data is not related to other variables.

> **Mean Imputation**: Suitable for continuous variables with a roughly normal distribution.
> **Median Imputation**: Effective for skewed distributions, reducing the influence of outliers.

Mode Imputation: Best for categorical variables, filling in missing categories with the most common label.

Code Example: Mean, Median, and Mode Imputation in Python

Using **pandas** and **scikit-learn**, these imputation techniques can be implemented as follows:

```python
import pandas as pd
from sklearn.impute import SimpleImputer

# Sample data with missing values
data = pd.DataFrame({
    'Age': [25, 30, None, 22, 28],
    'Gender': ['M', 'F', None, 'F', 'M']
})

# Mean imputation for continuous data
mean_imputer = SimpleImputer(strategy='mean')
data['Age'] = mean_imputer.fit_transform(data[['Age']])

# Mode imputation for categorical data
mode_imputer = SimpleImputer(strategy='most_frequent')
data['Gender'] = mode_imputer.fit_transform(data[['Gender']])

print("Data after Imputation:\n", data)
```

While these methods are straightforward, they assume that the missing values are MCAR and may not be suitable for MAR or MNAR situations. They can also reduce variance, leading to biased estimates when applied extensively.

K-Nearest Neighbors (KNN) Imputation

K-Nearest Neighbors (KNN) Imputation estimates missing values by finding the k nearest neighbors of the missing value and using their average (for continuous variables) or most frequent category (for categorical variables). KNN imputation is more accurate than simple imputation methods, as it accounts for relationships between variables.

The mathematical approach involves identifying the k nearest neighbors based on a distance metric (e.g., Euclidean distance) and computing the mean or mode of the neighbors' values to fill in the missing data.

Code Example: KNN Imputation in Python

Using **scikit-learn**, KNN imputation can be applied as follows:

```python
from sklearn.impute import KNNImputer
```

```
# Sample data with missing values
data = pd.DataFrame({
    'Age': [25, 30, None, 22, 28],
    'Income': [50000, 60000, 45000, None, 70000]
})

# KNN Imputation
knn_imputer = KNNImputer(n_neighbors=2)
imputed_data = knn_imputer.fit_transform(data)

print("Data after KNN Imputation:\n", imputed_data)
```

KNN imputation is particularly useful for structured datasets where relationships between variables can be leveraged to provide more accurate estimates. However, it can be computationally intensive for large datasets, as the algorithm requires calculating distances for each missing value.

Multivariate Imputation by Chained Equations (MICE)

Multivariate Imputation by Chained Equations (MICE), also known as **Iterative Imputation**, models each feature with missing values as a function of other features. MICE iteratively imputes missing values by using regression models, making it suitable for complex datasets where variables have interdependencies.

The process involves multiple steps:

1. Initialize missing values with simple imputation (e.g., mean).
2. For each variable with missing data, create a regression model using the other variables as predictors.
3. Update the missing values with the predictions from the model.
4. Repeat steps 2 and 3 until convergence is reached or a predefined number of iterations is completed.

Mathematical Representation of MICE

Let X be the dataset with missing values, and let X_i be a feature with missing values. The imputation process can be represented as:

$$X^{(t)}_i = f\left(X^{(t-1)}_{-i}\right) + \epsilon_i$$

where:

- $X^{(t)}_i$ is the imputed value at iteration t.
- f is the predictive model for feature i.
- $X^{(t-1)}_{-i}$ represents all other variables used as predictors.

129

- ϵ_i is a random error term to introduce variability.

Code Example: MICE Imputation in Python

Using **statsmodels**, MICE imputation can be implemented as follows:

```
from statsmodels.imputation.mice import MICEData

# Sample data with missing values
data = pd.DataFrame({
    'Age': [25, 30, None, 22, 28],
    'Income': [50000, 60000, 45000, None, 70000]
})

# MICE Imputation
mice_data = MICEData(data)
imputed_data = mice_data.data
print("Data after MICE Imputation:\n", imputed_data)
```

MICE is particularly effective for datasets with complex relationships between variables, as it iteratively updates imputed values based on multiple predictors, leading to more accurate imputations.

Deep Learning-Based Imputation: Autoencoders

Autoencoders, a type of neural network architecture, can be used to perform deep learning-based imputation. An autoencoder learns to reconstruct input data by encoding it into a latent representation and then decoding it back to its original form. For imputation, the autoencoder is trained on the dataset with missing values masked, and the reconstruction error is minimized.

An autoencoder consists of:

Encoder: Compresses the input into a lower-dimensional latent representation.
Decoder: Reconstructs the input from the latent representation.

The autoencoder's objective function is to minimize the reconstruction error:

$$L(x,\hat{x}) = \| x - \hat{x} \|^2$$

where:

- x is the original input.
- $\hat{x}$ is the reconstructed input.

Code Example: Autoencoder for Imputation in TensorFlow

Here's a simplified example of using an autoencoder for imputation:

```python
import tensorflow as tf
from tensorflow.keras import layers

# Sample dataset with missing values (replace None with NaN for
imputation)
import numpy as np
data = np.array([[25, 50000], [30, 60000], [np.nan, 45000],
[22, np.nan], [28, 70000]])

# Define an autoencoder model
input_dim = data.shape[1]
autoencoder = tf.keras.Sequential([
    layers.InputLayer(input_shape=(input_dim,)),
    layers.Dense(64, activation='relu'),
    layers.Dense(input_dim, activation='linear')
])

# Compile and train the autoencoder
autoencoder.compile(optimizer='adam', loss='mse')
autoencoder.fit(data, data, epochs=50, batch_size=2, verbose=0)

# Impute missing values with the autoencoder
imputed_data = autoencoder.predict(data)
print("Data after Autoencoder Imputation:\n", imputed_data)
```

Autoencoder-based imputation captures complex relationships in the data, making it suitable for high-dimensional datasets with intricate patterns.

Applications of Imputation

Imputation techniques are widely used across various domains:

Healthcare: In medical datasets, imputation techniques fill in missing lab results, allowing models to make accurate predictions for patient outcomes.

Finance: In financial datasets, imputation helps estimate missing transaction values, maintaining data continuity for credit scoring models.

E-commerce: Imputation is applied to customer segmentation, where missing demographic information is filled to improve targeting accuracy.

Connecting Imputation Techniques to Neural Network Training

Effective imputation of missing values ensures that neural networks can learn from complete datasets, improving performance and generalization. The choice of imputation technique depends on the complexity of the data, the relationships between variables, and computational constraints. Simple methods like mean or mode imputation are suitable for small, simple datasets, while advanced methods like MICE or autoencoders are better suited for complex, high-dimensional data.

4.3.3: Dealing with Missing Data in Time Series

Handling missing data in time-series data presents unique challenges due to the temporal dependencies inherent in sequences. Missing values disrupt the continuity of sequences, which can significantly impact the training and accuracy of models like Recurrent Neural Networks (RNNs), Long Short-Term Memory Networks (LSTMs), and Gated Recurrent Units (GRUs). Effective imputation is crucial for maintaining sequence integrity and ensuring that time-series models can learn meaningful patterns.

Methods for Addressing Missing Data in Time Series

Different imputation techniques are tailored to address the sequential nature of time-series data, from basic forward-fill methods to advanced Kalman filtering.

Forward Fill and Backward Fill

Forward Fill and **Backward Fill** are simple imputation techniques that propagate the last known value forward or backward, respectively, to fill missing data. These methods help maintain sequence continuity, making them suitable for short gaps in time-series data where values are expected to be stable or slowly varying.

- **Forward Fill**: Replaces missing values with the most recent non-missing value.
- **Backward Fill**: Replaces missing values with the next observed value.

These techniques assume that the missing value is likely to be similar to the adjacent known values, which may not be accurate in cases of rapid changes or high variability in the data.

Code Example: Implementing Forward Fill and Backward Fill in Python

Using **pandas**, we can apply forward fill and backward fill as follows:

```python
import pandas as pd

# Sample time-series data with missing values
data = pd.Series([100, 110, None, None, 130, 140])

# Forward Fill
forward_filled_data = data.fillna(method='ffill')
print("Forward Filled Data:\n", forward_filled_data)

# Backward Fill
backward_filled_data = data.fillna(method='bfill')
print("Backward Filled Data:\n", backward_filled_data)
```

Forward fill and backward fill are best suited for short-term missing values in scenarios where the data tends to be stable over short intervals, such as temperature readings within a day or hourly sales data in retail.

Linear Interpolation

Linear Interpolation estimates missing values by fitting a straight line between two known data points, making it useful for smoothly varying time-series data. It assumes that the change between two points is linear, making it effective in cases where the time series exhibits gradual changes.

Mathematical Formula for Linear Interpolation

If a time series has two known values, y_1 at time t_1 and y_2 at time t_2, and a missing value at time t, the interpolated value $\hat{y}$ is given by:

$$\hat{y} = y_1 + \left(\frac{y_2 - y_1}{t_2 - t_1}\right) \cdot (t - t_1)$$

Code Example: Implementing Linear Interpolation in Python

Using **pandas**, we can perform linear interpolation as follows:

```python
# Sample time-series data with missing values
data = pd.Series([100, 110, None, 130, 140])

# Linear Interpolation
interpolated_data = data.interpolate(method='linear')
print("Linear Interpolated Data:\n", interpolated_data)
```

Linear interpolation is effective for continuous data where the underlying trend is relatively smooth, such as daily stock prices or monthly sales figures.

Seasonal Decomposition

Seasonal Decomposition is an advanced technique that breaks down a time series into its **trend**, **seasonal**, and **residual** components. This decomposition helps identify patterns that can be used to impute missing values based on the behavior of each component.

Seasonal decomposition uses methods like **classical decomposition** or **Seasonal and Trend decomposition using Loess (STL)** to separate the components. Missing values are then estimated by analyzing these decomposed components.

Code Example: Implementing Seasonal Decomposition in Python

Using **statsmodels**, we can perform seasonal decomposition and imputation as follows:

```python
import pandas as pd
from statsmodels.tsa.seasonal import seasonal_decompose

# Sample time-series data with missing values
data = pd.Series([100, 105, None, 115, 120, None, 130])

# Seasonal Decomposition
decomposition = seasonal_decompose(data.interpolate(),
model='additive', period=3)
trend = decomposition.trend
seasonal = decomposition.seasonal
residual = decomposition.resid

print("Trend Component:\n", trend)
print("Seasonal Component:\n", seasonal)
```

After decomposition, the missing values in the trend, seasonal, and residual components can be imputed independently, providing a more accurate representation of the missing values.

Kalman Filtering and State Space Models

Kalman Filtering is a statistical method used for modeling time-series data, particularly when the data is noisy or incomplete. It uses a series of measurements observed over time, containing noise and other inaccuracies, and produces estimates of unknown variables that tend to be more precise than those based on a single measurement alone.

The Kalman filter operates using a two-step process:

1. **Predict Step**: Generates estimates of the current state variables, along with their uncertainties.
2. **Update Step**: Adjusts the estimates based on new measurements, refining the predictions.

Mathematical Representation of Kalman Filtering

The Kalman filter's state-space model is defined by two equations:

State Equation:

$$x_t = F \cdot x_{t-1} + w_t$$

where:

- x_t is the state at time t.
- F is the state transition matrix.
- w_t is the process noise.

Observation Equation:

$$y_t = H \cdot x_t + v_t$$

where:

- y_t is the observation at time t.
- H is the observation matrix.
- v_t is the observation noise.

Code Example: Implementing Kalman Filtering in Python

Using **pykalman**, we can implement Kalman filtering for imputation as follows:

```python
from pykalman import KalmanFilter
import numpy as np

# Sample time-series data with missing values
data = np.array([100, 110, np.nan, 130, 140, np.nan, 160])

# Kalman Filter setup
kf = KalmanFilter(initial_state_mean=100, n_dim_obs=1)
data_imputed, _ = kf.em(data, n_iter=10).smooth(data)
```

```
print("Data after Kalman Filter Imputation:\n", data_imputed)
```

Kalman filtering is particularly useful in fields like finance, healthcare, and IoT, where time-series data can be noisy and incomplete, and accurate imputation is critical for model performance.

Applications of Handling Missing Time-Series Data

Addressing missing values in time-series data is essential in various domains:

Finance: Imputation techniques like linear interpolation or Kalman filtering are used to fill missing stock prices, maintaining the continuity of financial models.

Healthcare: In patient monitoring, forward fill or autoencoder-based imputation is used to fill missing vital signs, enabling accurate predictions of patient conditions.

Weather Forecasting: In climate models, techniques like seasonal decomposition help estimate missing temperature or precipitation data, improving forecast accuracy.

5. Training Deep Neural Networks

5.1 Setting Up a Deep Learning Environment

5.1.1: Installing TensorFlow, PyTorch, and Keras Frameworks

Deep learning frameworks like **TensorFlow**, **PyTorch**, and **Keras** form the backbone of modern neural network development. These frameworks provide a rich set of tools for building, training, and deploying neural networks across various tasks, from computer vision to natural language processing. Leveraging these frameworks is essential for exploiting the full potential of deep learning, particularly when paired with GPUs for accelerated computations. In this section, we will explore how to install each of these frameworks on different platforms and set up a comprehensive environment to facilitate deep learning development.

Important Note: At the time of publication, here are the compatible Python versions for TensorFlow, PyTorch, and Keras:

TensorFlow

> **Compatible Python Versions:** TensorFlow 2.12 and later support Python 3.10, 3.11, and recently added support for Python 3.12 in TensorFlow 2.16. Versions before 2.12 support Python up to 3.9.

> **Note:** TensorFlow 2.15 is the last version that includes Keras 2 by default. TensorFlow 2.16 switches to Keras 3, which also supports Python 3.12

PyTorch

> **Compatible Python Versions:** PyTorch 2.0 supports Python 3.8 to 3.11. For earlier PyTorch versions, Python compatibility starts from Python 3.6 but is typically limited to Python 3.9 in versions up to PyTorch 1.10.

> **Note:** Make sure to use the right PyTorch installation commands for specific CUDA versions, as this affects compatibility .

Keras

> **Python Versions:** Keras 3 supports Python 3.10 to 3.12, aligning with TensorFlow 2.16. Earlier Keras versions (e.g., Keras 2.x) are compatible with Python 3.6 to 3.9 and are maintained as part of TensorFlow 2.15 and earlier .

If you have a Python veer or lower than these, you can download a compatible version of Python from the *official Python website*. Adjust the installation command accordingly to ensure compatibility with your selected deep learning framework.

Setting Up TensorFlow

TensorFlow is one of the most popular frameworks in deep learning, known for its extensive library, scalability, and support for distributed training. It supports both CPU and GPU versions, allowing users to tailor installations based on available hardware.

Installing TensorFlow with pip

1. **CPU Version:**
   Install the CPU version of TensorFlow using pip:

```
pip install tensorflow
```

2. **GPU Version:**
   To enable GPU acceleration, ensure that CUDA and cuDNN are installed (compatible versions are crucial).
   Install the GPU version of TensorFlow with pip:

```
pip install tensorflow-gpu
```

3. **Verify TensorFlow Installation:**
   Once installed, verify the setup by importing TensorFlow in Python:

```
import tensorflow as tf
print(tf.__version__)
print("GPU Available:",
tf.config.list_physical_devices('GPU'))
```

Installing TensorFlow with Conda

1. **CPU Version:**
   Install TensorFlow using Conda for CPU support:

```
conda install tensorflow
```

2. **GPU Version:**
   For GPU support, use:

```
conda install tensorflow-gpu
```
   Verify the installation using the same Python code snippet provided earlier.

Setting Up PyTorch

PyTorch is a widely-used deep learning framework known for its dynamic computation graphs, which allow for flexible model development. It supports seamless integration with CUDA for accelerated training on GPUs.

Installing PyTorch with pip

1. Visit the official *PyTorch website* to find the appropriate installation command based on your OS, Python version, and CUDA version.
2. **Example Command:**
   Install the CPU version:

```
pip install torch torchvision torchaudio
```

   Install the GPU version (e.g., for CUDA 11.7):

```
pip install torch torchvision torchaudio --extra-index-url
https://download.pytorch.org/whl/cu117
```

3. **Verify PyTorch Installation:**
   Import PyTorch and check GPU availability:

```
import torch
print(torch.__version__)
print("CUDA Available:", torch.cuda.is_available())
```

Installing PyTorch with Conda

1. **CPU Version:**
   Install PyTorch for CPU support:

```
conda install pytorch torchvision torchaudio cpuonly -c
pytorch
```

2. **GPU Version:**
   Install PyTorch with GPU support (e.g., CUDA 11.7):

```
conda install pytorch torchvision torchaudio
cudatoolkit=11.7 -c pytorch
```

   Verify the installation using the Python code provided earlier.

Setting Up Keras

Keras is now tightly integrated with **TensorFlow 2.x** as its high-level API, simplifying the process of building neural networks. Therefore, installing TensorFlow automatically sets up Keras.

Installing Keras via TensorFlow

Since Keras is a part of TensorFlow, use:

```
pip install tensorflow
```

Verify Keras setup:

```
from tensorflow import keras
print(keras.__version__)
```

Troubleshooting Common Installation Issues

1. **Compatibility Errors:** Check Python and framework compatibility. For instance, TensorFlow 2.x requires Python 3.6-3.10. If errors persist, consider creating a separate virtual environment with the correct Python version.

2. **CUDA/CuDNN Issues:** Ensure that the installed CUDA version matches TensorFlow or PyTorch requirements. Check environment variables like *PATH* and *CUDA_HOME* to confirm CUDA visibility.

3. **Library Conflicts:** If conflicts occur, uninstall existing versions using:

```
pip uninstall tensorflow torch keras
```

Then, reinstall the frameworks with the appropriate commands.

Creating and Managing Virtual Environments

Setting up virtual environments is crucial for maintaining clean and isolated setups, particularly when working with multiple deep learning projects.

Using Conda

1. **Create a new environment:**

```
conda create -n deep_learning_env python=3.8
```

2. **Activate the environment:**

```
conda activate deep_learning_env
```

3. **Install frameworks:**
   Once the environment is activated, install TensorFlow, PyTorch, or other required libraries using pip or Conda, as described earlier.

Using venv

1. **Create a virtual environment:**

```
python -m venv deep_learning_env
```

2. **Activate the environment:**
   On Windows:

```
deep_learning_env\Scripts\activate
```

On macOS/Linux:

```
source deep_learning_env/bin/activate
```

3. **Install packages:**
   Use pip to install TensorFlow, PyTorch, or any other dependencies.

Visual Overview of Framework Architectures

To provide a clear understanding of how these frameworks interact with underlying hardware and dependencies, a flowchart is shown below:

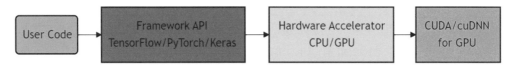

Example of Complete Deep Learning Environment Setup

The following code block sets up a complete environment with both TensorFlow and PyTorch:

```
# Create and activate a new environment
conda create -n dl_env python=3.8
conda activate dl_env

# Install TensorFlow and PyTorch
conda install tensorflow
conda install pytorch torchvision torchaudio cudatoolkit=11.7 -
c pytorch

# Verify installations
python -c "import tensorflow as tf; print(tf.__version__)"
python -c "import torch; print(torch.__version__)"
```

5.1.2: Using GPUs for Faster Training and Cloud Computing Options

In deep learning, **Graphics Processing Units (GPUs)** play a critical role in accelerating model training, particularly when handling large datasets or complex architectures like convolutional neural networks (CNNs) or transformers. Unlike **Central Processing Units (CPUs)**, which excel at sequential computations, GPUs are designed for parallel processing, making them highly efficient at performing the matrix operations fundamental to neural network training. This ability to parallelize computations significantly reduces training time, making it feasible to train models that would otherwise take days or even weeks on CPUs.

Leveraging GPU Acceleration in Deep Learning Frameworks

Deep learning frameworks like **TensorFlow** and **PyTorch** offer built-in support for GPU acceleration, making them highly suitable for both local and cloud-based training. Setting up GPU support requires configuring **CUDA** and **cuDNN**, which are essential for maximizing performance during training.

Configuring CUDA and cuDNN for GPU Acceleration

What Are CUDA and cuDNN?

CUDA (Compute Unified Device Architecture) is a parallel computing platform developed by NVIDIA, enabling developers to leverage the computing power of GPUs.

cuDNN (CUDA Deep Neural Network library) is a GPU-accelerated library for deep learning primitives, such as convolutions, which are heavily used in neural networks. It works alongside CUDA to optimize the performance of operations in TensorFlow and PyTorch.

Step-by-Step Installation Guide for CUDA and cuDNN

1. **Checking Compatibility:** Before installing CUDA, ensure that the CUDA version is compatible with your installed version of TensorFlow or PyTorch. This compatibility is crucial to avoid errors during training. You can check the compatibility on the *TensorFlow* or *PyTorch* websites.

2. **Installing CUDA with Conda:**
   Use Conda to install CUDA in a new environment:

   ```
   conda install cudatoolkit=<desired_version>
   ```

   For instance, to install CUDA 11.7, run:

   ```
   conda install cudatoolkit=11.7
   ```

3. **Installing cuDNN:**

After installing CUDA, download the corresponding cuDNN version from the *NVIDIA website* and extract it to the CUDA directory (e.g., `/usr/local/cuda` on Linux).

Set up environment variables to ensure that TensorFlow or PyTorch can access cuDNN:

```
export
LD_LIBRARY_PATH=/usr/local/cuda/lib64:$LD_LIBRARY_PATH
```

4. **Verifying GPU Setup:**

   Use Python code snippets to verify successful installation:

```
import torch
print("PyTorch CUDA Available:", torch.cuda.is_available())

import tensorflow as tf
print("TensorFlow CUDA Available:",
len(tf.config.list_physical_devices('GPU')) > 0)
```

Troubleshooting Common Issues

- **Compatibility Errors:** Ensure that both CUDA and cuDNN versions match your framework requirements.
- **Environment Variables:** If cuDNN is not detected, check whether the CUDA paths are correctly set in the environment variables.
- **Driver Issues:** Ensure that the NVIDIA driver is installed and compatible with your GPU model.

Exploring Cloud-Based GPU Options for Deep Learning

While local GPUs are useful, cloud-based solutions provide more scalability, allowing users to leverage powerful GPUs without investing in expensive hardware. Several cloud platforms offer GPU-enabled instances optimized for TensorFlow and PyTorch training.

Google Colab is a free cloud service that provides GPU access through Jupyter notebooks, making it ideal for rapid prototyping.

Enabling GPU Acceleration:
1. Open a new Colab notebook.
2. Go to *Runtime > Change runtime type*.
3. Select **GPU** under the Hardware Accelerator dropdown.

Verifying GPU Setup:

```
import torch
```

```
print("GPU Available:", torch.cuda.is_available())

import tensorflow as tf
print("GPU Available:",
len(tf.config.list_physical_devices('GPU')) > 0)
```

AWS EC2 with GPUs offers a variety of GPU-enabled instances, such as P2, P3, and the newer P4 instances, optimized for large-scale deep learning workloads.

Setting Up a GPU-Enabled Instance:

1. Select an instance type with GPU support (e.g., *p3.2xLarge*).
2. Configure the instance with a deep learning AMI (Amazon Machine Image), which includes pre-installed frameworks like TensorFlow and PyTorch.
3. Connect to the instance via SSH and verify GPU availability using the same code snippets mentioned earlier.

Scaling Training on Multiple GPUs: AWS EC2 supports distributed training across multiple GPUs, enabling faster training of large models like BERT or GPT.

Azure ML with GPUs offers GPU-powered virtual machines for deep learning, with support for both TensorFlow and PyTorch.

Setting Up an Azure ML Instance:

1. Create a new virtual machine with a GPU type like the **NC series**.
2. Install the necessary frameworks and configure CUDA and cuDNN as described earlier.
3. Use Jupyter notebooks or SSH for remote training and model development.

Comparing CPU vs. GPU Performance

To provide a clear understanding of the impact of GPU acceleration, the table below summarizes key metrics comparing CPU and GPU training:

Metric	CPU	GPU
Training Time	Slow	Fast (2x-10x speedup)
Parallel Processing	Limited	High (thousands of cores)
Cost (Cloud)	Lower	Higher (depends on instance)
Ideal For	Small datasets,	Large datasets, complex

	debugging		models

Additionally, the following graph showcases the reduction in training time when using GPUs compared to CPUs for training a CNN on the CIFAR-10 dataset:

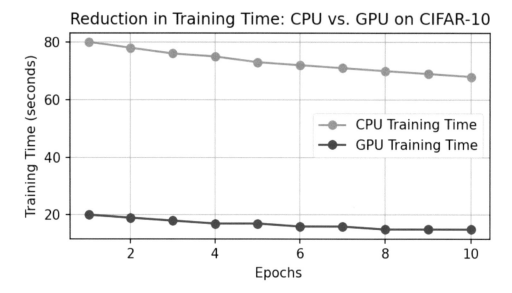

Examples of GPU Acceleration in Deep Learning

1. **Image Classification with CNNs:** Training a CNN for tasks like ImageNet classification on a CPU can take days, while using a GPU (e.g., NVIDIA V100) reduces training time to hours.

2. **NLP with Transformers:** Models like GPT or BERT benefit immensely from GPUs, which handle the massive matrix multiplications required during training. GPUs accelerate training by allowing for larger batch sizes and faster gradient computations.

3. **Reinforcement Learning:** GPUs enable faster simulations and policy updates, making them crucial for training agents in environments like OpenAI Gym.

Logical Flow and Practical Implications

Using GPUs is not just a convenience but a necessity in many deep learning scenarios. The speedups offered by GPUs make it feasible to train larger models, explore more hyperparameter combinations, and deploy models in production faster. The combination of local and cloud-based solutions provides flexibility and scalability, enabling researchers and practitioners to build cutting-edge models efficiently.

5.1.3: Setting Up Version Control for Experiments (Git, DVC)

Version control is essential in deep learning projects for managing not only code but also datasets, model checkpoints, and experimental results. Unlike traditional software development, deep learning projects involve large amounts of data, frequent model updates, and complex pipelines, all of which require robust tracking mechanisms to ensure reproducibility and collaboration. Tools like **Git** and **DVC (Data Version Control)** provide a comprehensive solution to these challenges, enabling efficient tracking of changes across the entire development cycle.

The Role of Version Control in Deep Learning

In deep learning workflows, version control serves several critical functions:

- **Reproducibility**: By tracking code, datasets, and model changes, researchers can reproduce results and understand which modifications led to performance improvements.
- **Collaboration**: Teams can work together seamlessly by branching, merging, and resolving conflicts, all while maintaining a clear history of changes.
- **Experiment Tracking**: Version control allows users to test different models, hyperparameters, and data processing pipelines in parallel, ensuring a streamlined workflow for experimentation.

Let's explore how Git and DVC can be used together to create a comprehensive version control setup for deep learning projects.

Setting Up Git for Deep Learning Projects

Git is the foundation of version control in software development, and it plays a vital role in managing the codebase of deep learning projects.

Step-by-Step Guide for Setting Up Git
1. **Install Git**:
   On Windows: Download the installer from *git-scm.com* and follow the installation instructions.
   On macOS: Use Homebrew:

```
brew install git
```

   On Linux: Use the package manager:

```
sudo apt-get install git
```

2. **Configure Git**:

   Set up user details for committing changes:

```
git config --global user.name "Your Name"
git config --global user.email "youremail@example.com"
```

3. **Basic Git Commands for Code Repositories**:

   Initialize a repository in your project directory:

```
git init
```

   Add files to the staging area and commit changes:

```
git add .
git commit -m "Initial commit"
```

   Create and switch to a new branch for experimenting with different model architectures or data preprocessing methods:

```
git branch new_experiment
git checkout new_experiment
```

4. **Remote Repository Management**:

   Use GitHub, GitLab, or Bitbucket to manage remote repositories, enabling collaboration and remote access.

   Set up a remote origin and push changes:

```
git remote add origin <repository_url>
git push -u origin main
```

   Pull changes from the remote repository to keep local code synchronized:

```
git pull origin main
```

Best Practices for Using Git in Deep Learning Projects

- **Branching and Merging**: Use branches to experiment with different models or data preprocessing steps. Merge changes carefully to maintain a clean and functional main branch.

- **Commit Messages**: Write clear commit messages that describe changes accurately, making it easier to track and review experiments.

- **Resolving Conflicts**: During merging, conflicts may occur if changes overlap. Use Git commands (*git merge*, *git rebase*) and visual tools (e.g., GitHub Desktop, Sourcetree) to resolve conflicts efficiently.

Introduction to DVC for Data and Model Versioning

While Git is ideal for managing code, **DVC** extends version control to data and models, addressing the specific needs of deep learning workflows. DVC is designed to handle large files, automate pipelines, and ensure consistent results across experiments, making it a vital tool for tracking datasets and models in deep learning projects.

Setting Up DVC in Deep Learning Projects

1. **Install DVC**:
   Install DVC using pip:

```
pip install dvc
```

2. **Initialize DVC in a Project**:
   Start DVC in the project directory to create configuration files:

```
dvc init
```

3. **Tracking Data and Model Files**:
   Add datasets or model checkpoints to DVC for versioning:

```
dvc add data/dataset.csv
dvc add models/model.pth
```

   Commit changes to the DVC configuration files using Git:

```
git add data.dvc models.dvc .gitignore
git commit -m "Track dataset and model with DVC"
```

Automating Pipelines with DVC

DVC allows for the automation of data preprocessing, training, and evaluation through pipelines defined in **YAML files**. Here's an example of a basic DVC pipeline:

```
stages:
  preprocess:
    cmd: python preprocess.py
    deps:
      - data/raw_data.csv
    outs:
      - data/preprocessed_data.csv
  train:
    cmd: python train.py
    deps:
      - data/preprocessed_data.csv
```

```
      - models/config.json
  outs:
      - models/trained_model.pth
evaluate:
  cmd: python evaluate.py
  deps:
      - models/trained_model.pth
  outs:
      - reports/metrics.json
```

Run the DVC pipeline:

dvc repro

Using DVC Remotes for Large File Management

DVC supports remotes (e.g., AWS S3, Google Cloud Storage) for storing large datasets and models efficiently:

1. **Set up a remote storage location**:

   ```
   dvc remote add -d myremote s3://bucket-name/path
   ```

2. **Push data to the remote**:

   dvc push

3. **Pull data from the remote when needed**:

   ```
   dvc pull
   ```

Visualizing Git and DVC in Deep Learning Workflows

The following diagram illustrates how Git and DVC work together in a typical deep learning project:

Git manages the codebase, tracking changes in scripts, configuration files, and experiment logs.

DVC manages data files, models, and pipelines, ensuring that all components of the experiment are reproducible and trackable.

Remote storage is used to store large datasets and models, enabling seamless access and collaboration across teams.

Examples of Git and DVC in Deep Learning Projects

NLP Projects: In natural language processing tasks, researchers use Git to manage code changes while using DVC to track versions of tokenized datasets and fine-tuned language models.

Computer Vision Projects: In computer vision applications, teams use Git to manage model scripts, while DVC tracks image datasets and model checkpoints, facilitating parallel development and reproducibility.

Collaboration Best Practices: Use **feature branches** in Git to experiment with different model architectures or preprocessing methods without affecting the main codebase. Use DVC's **pipelines** to automate the entire workflow, from data preprocessing to model evaluation, ensuring consistency across experiments.

5.2 Building Models with TensorFlow and PyTorch

5.2.1: Step-by-Step Guide to Creating Models with TensorFlow and PyTorch

Creating neural network models is a fundamental step in deep learning, and **TensorFlow** and **PyTorch** are two of the most powerful and widely used frameworks for this purpose. Each framework offers unique advantages, with TensorFlow's static computation graph (coupled with Keras for high-level abstraction) supporting efficient production deployment, and PyTorch's dynamic computation graph providing flexibility for research and experimentation. This section delves into the model creation process in both frameworks, covering the entire workflow—from importing libraries to implementing training loops, visualizing key differences along the way.

Overview of TensorFlow and PyTorch for Model Creation

TensorFlow and PyTorch are designed to facilitate neural network creation and training, but they differ in execution:

- **TensorFlow**: Uses a combination of static and dynamic computation graphs (via Keras or eager execution). It is optimized for production, offering tools like TensorFlow Serving and TensorFlow Lite.
- **PyTorch**: Relies on a dynamic computation graph, which builds the graph as operations are performed, making debugging and model modifications intuitive.

Let's explore step-by-step how to build a basic feedforward neural network model using each framework, focusing on differences in syntax, workflow, and implementation strategies.

Building a Basic Neural Network with TensorFlow

TensorFlow is well-suited for building neural networks with both high-level APIs (e.g., Keras) and low-level operations (e.g., $tf.GradientTape$). This example focuses on the **Keras Sequential API**, a user-friendly way to construct models.

1. Import Required Libraries

Begin by importing TensorFlow and Keras modules needed for model creation:

```
import tensorflow as tf
```

152

```
from tensorflow.keras.models import Sequential
from tensorflow.keras.layers import Dense, Dropout
from tensorflow.keras.optimizers import Adam
from tensorflow.keras.losses import CategoricalCrossentropy
from tensorflow.keras.datasets import mnist
from tensorflow.keras.utils import to_categorical
```

TensorFlow provides the core framework, while **Keras** simplifies model building.

Dense Layer: Implements a fully connected layer.

Dropout Layer: Adds regularization by randomly dropping neurons during training.

2. Define the Model Architecture

Use the **Sequential API** to build a feedforward neural network:

```
# Initialize the Sequential model
model = Sequential()

# Add input and hidden layers
model.add(Dense(128, input_shape=(784,), activation='relu'))  #
Input layer with ReLU activation
model.add(Dropout(0.2))  # Dropout layer for regularization
model.add(Dense(64, activation='relu'))  # Hidden layer

# Add the output layer
model.add(Dense(10, activation='softmax'))  # Output layer for
10 classes
```

Input Layer: Accepts 784 features (flattened 28x28 pixel images from the MNIST dataset).

Hidden Layers: Each hidden layer has a specific number of neurons and an activation function, often **ReLU**.

Output Layer: Uses **Softmax** activation to provide probabilities for each class in multi-class classification.

3. Compile the Model

Compiling prepares the model for training by setting optimization parameters:

```
# Compile the model with optimizer, loss, and metrics
model.compile(
    optimizer=Adam(learning_rate=0.001),
    loss=CategoricalCrossentropy(),
    metrics=['accuracy']
```

)

Adam Optimizer: Combines the advantages of **AdaGrad** and **RMSprop**, adjusting learning rates dynamically.

Categorical Crossentropy: Measures the difference between the predicted probabilities and actual labels.

Accuracy: Used as a metric to evaluate model performance.

4. Load and Preprocess Data

Load the **MNIST dataset**, normalize it, and one-hot encode labels:

```
# Load MNIST data
(X_train, y_train), (X_test, y_test) = mnist.load_data()

# Reshape and normalize input data
X_train = X_train.reshape(-1, 784).astype('float32') / 255.0
X_test = X_test.reshape(-1, 784).astype('float32') / 255.0

# One-hot encode labels
y_train = to_categorical(y_train, 10)
y_test = to_categorical(y_test, 10)
```

Reshaping: Converts each image from 28x28 to a 1D vector of size 784.

Normalization: Scales pixel values to [0, 1] to improve convergence.

One-Hot Encoding: Converts labels to binary vectors, making them compatible with categorical crossentropy.

5. Train the Model

Fit the model on the training data, monitoring performance:

```
# Train the model
history = model.fit(
    X_train, y_train,
    batch_size=32,
    epochs=5,
    validation_split=0.2
)
```

Batch Size: Defines the number of samples used per gradient update.

Epochs: Number of complete passes through the training dataset.

Validation Split: Allocates a portion of the training data for validation.

6. Evaluate Model Performance

Evaluate the model's accuracy on the test dataset:

```
test_loss, test_accuracy = model.evaluate(X_test, y_test)
print(f"Test Accuracy: {test_accuracy * 100:.2f}%")
```

Evaluation: Measures how well the trained model generalizes to unseen data.

Building a Basic Neural Network with PyTorch

PyTorch allows for more control and customization when defining models, making it particularly popular in research environments.

1. Import Required Libraries

Import PyTorch modules and utilities for model building:

```
import torch
import torch.nn as nn
import torch.nn.functional as F
import torch.optim as optim
from torchvision import datasets, transforms
from torch.utils.data import DataLoader
```

torch.nn: Provides building blocks for neural networks.
torch.optim: Offers optimization algorithms like SGD, Adam, etc.
torchvision: Contains datasets and transformation utilities.

2. Define the Model Architecture

Create a custom model by subclassing **nn.Module**:

```
class SimpleNN(nn.Module):
    def __init__(self):
        super(SimpleNN, self).__init__()
        self.fc1 = nn.Linear(784, 128)  # Input to hidden layer
        self.dropout = nn.Dropout(0.2)  # Dropout for
regularization
        self.fc2 = nn.Linear(128, 64)  # Second hidden layer
        self.fc3 = nn.Linear(64, 10)   # Output layer

    def forward(self, x):
        x = F.relu(self.fc1(x))  # ReLU activation
        x = self.dropout(x)  # Apply dropout
        x = F.relu(self.fc2(x))  # ReLU activation
        x = F.log_softmax(self.fc3(x), dim=1)  # Log-Softmax
for classification
        return x
```

nn.Linear: Defines fully connected layers.

forward(): Specifies the forward pass through the network.

3. Set Up Training Components

Initialize the model, define the loss function, and choose an optimizer:

```
model = SimpleNN()
criterion = nn.CrossEntropyLoss()  # Cross-entropy loss for
classification
optimizer = optim.Adam(model.parameters(), lr=0.001)
```

CrossEntropyLoss: Combines Log-Softmax and NLLLoss (Negative Log-Likelihood Loss).

Adam Optimizer: Adjusts learning rates based on the first and second moments of gradients.

4. Load and Preprocess Data

Load and preprocess the MNIST dataset using PyTorch utilities:

```
# Data transformations
transform = transforms.Compose([
    transforms.ToTensor(),
    transforms.Normalize((0.5,), (0.5,))
])

# Load the dataset
train_dataset = datasets.MNIST(root='data', train=True,
download=True, transform=transform)
train_loader = DataLoader(train_dataset, batch_size=32,
shuffle=True)
```

ToTensor: Converts images to PyTorch tensors.

Normalize: Scales images to have a mean of 0.5 and standard deviation of 0.5.

5. Implement the Training Loop

Define the training loop, iterating through batches and updating model weights:

```
epochs = 5
for epoch in range(epochs):
    running_loss = 0.0
    for images, labels in train_loader:
```

```
        images = images.view(images.size(0), -1)  # Flatten
images

        # Forward pass
        outputs = model(images)
        loss = criterion(outputs, labels)

        # Backward pass and optimization
        optimizer.zero_grad()
        loss.backward()
        optimizer.step()

        running_loss += loss.item()

    print(f'Epoch [{epoch+1}/{epochs}], Loss:
{running_loss/len(train_loader):.4f}')
```

zero_grad(): Clears previous gradients.

backward(): Computes gradients.

step(): Updates model parameters.

6. Evaluate Model Performance

Evaluate model accuracy on test data:

```
    test_loader = DataLoader(datasets.MNIST('data', train=False,
    transform=transform), batch_size=32, shuffle=False)

    correct = 0
    total = 0
    with torch.no_grad():
        for images, labels in

     test_loader:
            images = images.view(images.size(0), -1)
            outputs = model(images)
            _, predicted = torch.max(outputs.data, 1)
            total += labels.size(0)
            correct += (predicted == labels).sum().item()

    print(f"Test Accuracy: {100 * correct / total:.2f}%")
```

torch.max: Identifies the predicted class with the highest probability.

no_grad(): Disables gradient computation during evaluation.

Visualizing Differences: TensorFlow vs. PyTorch

The following diagram illustrates key differences between the two frameworks:

157

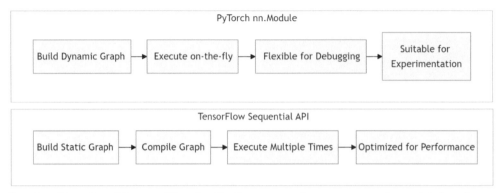

Static Graphs (TensorFlow): Built once, then executed multiple times, optimizing for performance.

Dynamic Graphs (PyTorch): Built on-the-fly, offering flexibility for debugging and experimentation.

Applications

Image Classification: Models built with TensorFlow or PyTorch can be used for recognizing handwritten digits in MNIST, classifying images in CIFAR-10, or even more complex tasks like object detection.

NLP: Both frameworks support RNNs, LSTMs, and transformers for tasks like sentiment analysis, text generation, and machine translation.

Research and Production: TensorFlow's deployment tools (e.g., TensorFlow Lite, TensorFlow Serving) make it ideal for production, while PyTorch's flexibility makes it popular in research environments.

5.2.2: Customizing Layers, Activations, and Optimizers

Customization is a cornerstone of deep learning, enabling practitioners to fine-tune models to improve performance across a wide range of tasks. By tailoring neural network layers, activation functions, and optimizers, models can achieve better convergence, higher accuracy, and improved generalization. In this section, we'll explore how to customize these components in **TensorFlow** and **PyTorch**, delving into their implementation, impacts, and use cases.

The Importance of Customization in Neural Networks

Deep learning models often require adjustments beyond predefined layers, activations, and optimizers to address specific challenges, such as learning complex patterns in data, improving gradient flow, or accelerating convergence. Customization allows developers to:

Improve Model Performance: Tailor layers to better extract relevant features from data, adjust activations to control non-linearity, and modify optimizers to enhance learning dynamics.

Adapt to Different Tasks: Use specialized layers, activations, or optimizers to meet the demands of diverse tasks like image segmentation, natural language processing, or reinforcement learning.

Experiment with New Architectures: Implement novel components to test new research ideas, leading to potential breakthroughs in model performance or efficiency.

Customizing Layers in TensorFlow and PyTorch

TensorFlow and **PyTorch** allow users to define custom layers, providing flexibility to implement unique operations or structures tailored to specific use cases.

1. Customizing Layers in TensorFlow

In TensorFlow, custom layers can be created using the **Keras API** by subclassing **tf.keras.layers.Layer**.

Example: Defining a Custom Convolution Layer in TensorFlow

```python
import tensorflow as tf

class CustomConvLayer(tf.keras.layers.Layer):
    def __init__(self, filters, kernel_size):
        super(CustomConvLayer, self).__init__()
        self.conv = tf.keras.layers.Conv2D(filters,
kernel_size, padding='same')
        self.bn = tf.keras.layers.BatchNormalization()

    def call(self, inputs, training=False):
        x = self.conv(inputs)
        x = self.bn(x, training=training)
        return tf.nn.relu(x)
```

Conv2D Layer: Applies 2D convolution, often used in image processing tasks.

BatchNormalization Layer: Normalizes activations to stabilize training.

call Method: Specifies the forward pass, which includes convolution, batch normalization, and ReLU activation.

2. Customizing Layers in PyTorch

In PyTorch, custom layers are defined by subclassing the **nn.Module** class.

Example: Defining a Custom Dropout Layer in PyTorch

```python
import torch
import torch.nn as nn

class CustomDropoutLayer(nn.Module):
    def __init__(self, dropout_rate=0.5):
        super(CustomDropoutLayer, self).__init__()
        self.dropout_rate = dropout_rate

    def forward(self, x):
        if self.training:  # Only apply dropout during training
            return x * torch.bernoulli(torch.full(x.shape, 1 - self.dropout_rate)) / (1 - self.dropout_rate)
        return x
```

nn.Module: Base class for all neural network modules in PyTorch.

forward Method: Specifies the operations to be performed during the forward pass, incorporating custom dropout behavior.

Exploring Activation Functions in TensorFlow and PyTorch

Activation functions introduce non-linearity into neural networks, allowing them to learn complex patterns in data. While common functions like **ReLU** (Rectified Linear Unit), **Sigmoid**, and **Tanh** are widely used, more advanced options like **Leaky ReLU**, **Swish**, and **GELU** can offer performance improvements in specific tasks.

1. Implementing Activation Functions in TensorFlow

ReLU, Leaky ReLU, and Swish Activation Functions:

```python
import tensorflow as tf

# Standard ReLU
x = tf.nn.relu(inputs)

# Leaky ReLU with alpha=0.2
x = tf.nn.leaky_relu(inputs, alpha=0.2)

# Swish activation
x = tf.nn.swish(inputs)
```

ReLU: Sets negative values to zero, commonly used in most layers.

Leaky ReLU: Allows a small gradient for negative values, helping avoid dead neurons.

Swish: Provides smoother activation, enhancing model performance in tasks like NLP and image classification.

2. Implementing Activation Functions in PyTorch

GELU Activation Function:

```
import torch
import torch.nn.functional as F

# GELU activation
x = F.gelu(inputs)
```

GELU (Gaussian Error Linear Unit): Smoothly approximates the ReLU activation, offering benefits in transformer models by better handling gradient flow.

Customizing Optimizers in TensorFlow and PyTorch

Optimizers play a critical role in adjusting model parameters based on computed gradients. Customizing optimizers and their hyperparameters (e.g., learning rate, momentum) can significantly impact convergence speed, stability, and model performance.

1. Customizing Optimizers in TensorFlow

TensorFlow's **tf.keras.optimizers** module provides a variety of built-in optimizers, allowing fine-tuning of hyperparameters.

Example: Using AdamW Optimizer in TensorFlow

```
from tensorflow.keras.optimizers import AdamW

# Initialize AdamW optimizer with weight decay
optimizer = AdamW(learning_rate=0.001, weight_decay=1e-4)
```

AdamW: An improved version of Adam with decoupled weight decay, reducing overfitting.

2. Customizing Optimizers in PyTorch

PyTorch's **torch.optim** module offers optimizers that can be configured with specific parameters.

Example: Using Lookahead Optimizer in PyTorch

```python
import torch
from torch.optim import Adam

class Lookahead:
    def __init__(self, base_optimizer, k=5, alpha=0.5):
        self.optimizer = base_optimizer
        self.k = k  # Number of "lookahead" steps
        self.alpha = alpha

    def step(self):
        # Implement lookahead logic here (simplified)
        pass

# Initialize base optimizer
base_optimizer = Adam(model.parameters(), lr=0.001)
optimizer = Lookahead(base_optimizer)
```

Lookahead Optimizer: Combines the base optimizer (e.g., Adam) with a lookahead mechanism, allowing for more stable convergence.

Performance Comparison of Activation Functions and Optimizers

Different activation functions and optimizers affect convergence speed, accuracy, and generalization. The following table compares their performance in image classification and NLP tasks:

Activation/Optimizer	Model Task	Impact on Performance	Typical Use Cases
ReLU	CNNs	Fast convergence, risk of dead neurons	Image classification
Leaky ReLU	RNNs, CNNs	Handles negative slopes better	Speech recognition, object detection
Swish	Transformers	Smoother gradient flow	Text classification, sentiment analysis
AdamW	All models	Reduces overfitting, good for NLP	Text generation, language models

Lookahead + Adam	NLP, Vision	Stabilizes training, improves robustness	Large-scale models, multi-modal tasks

Examples of Model Customization

Image Segmentation with CNNs: Custom layers (e.g., specialized convolution layers) are often used to refine feature extraction for detailed segmentation tasks, like medical image analysis.

Transformer Models in NLP: Using advanced activation functions like **GELU** in transformers helps achieve smoother training and better language representation in tasks like sentiment analysis, translation, or text generation.

Optimized Optimizers for GANs: In Generative Adversarial Networks (GANs), advanced optimizers like **RMSprop** and **Lookahead** stabilize the adversarial training process, improving convergence.

Implications of Customizing Layers, Activations, and Optimizers

Customizing components in deep learning models is crucial for achieving state-of-the-art performance. By understanding the impact of each modification on model behavior, practitioners can fine-tune neural networks to meet the demands of specific tasks, improve convergence rates, and enhance generalization across unseen data. This depth of customization empowers deep learning practitioners to push the boundaries of AI applications, creating models that are not only accurate but also robust and scalable.

5.2.3: Comparing TensorFlow and PyTorch Workflows

TensorFlow and **PyTorch** are two leading frameworks in deep learning, each offering unique approaches to model building, training, and deployment. Understanding the differences in their workflows is essential for choosing the right framework based on project requirements, development speed, and deployment needs. This section delves into how these frameworks differ in model definition, training loops, and deployment, using detailed examples, code snippets, and comparisons.

Overview: Static vs. Dynamic Computation Graphs

The most fundamental difference between TensorFlow and PyTorch lies in their approach to computation graphs:

- **TensorFlow** uses a **static computation graph**, also known as "Graph Mode." The entire graph is defined before execution, allowing for extensive optimizations. This is particularly useful for production deployment, as models can be optimized and serialized in advance.
- **PyTorch** uses a **dynamic computation graph**, meaning the graph is built as operations are performed. This dynamic nature allows for more flexibility and easier debugging, making it ideal for research and experimentation.

Model Building in TensorFlow and PyTorch

Model Building in TensorFlow

TensorFlow offers multiple APIs for defining models, with the **Sequential API** and **Functional API** being the most common.

1. Using the Sequential API in TensorFlow

The **Sequential API** is ideal for building simple models where layers are stacked sequentially.

```
import tensorflow as tf
from tensorflow.keras.models import Sequential
from tensorflow.keras.layers import Dense, Dropout

# Define a basic feedforward model using the Sequential API
model = Sequential([
    Dense(128, activation='relu', input_shape=(784,)),
    Dropout(0.2),
    Dense(64, activation='relu'),
    Dense(10, activation='softmax')
])
```

Sequential API: Provides a straightforward way to stack layers linearly.

Static Graph: The entire computation graph is defined before model execution, allowing TensorFlow to optimize it during training and deployment.

2. Using the Functional API in TensorFlow

The **Functional API** is more flexible, enabling the creation of complex models like multi-input, multi-output models or models with shared layers.

```python
from tensorflow.keras.layers import Input

inputs = Input(shape=(784,))
x = Dense(128, activation='relu')(inputs)
x = Dropout(0.2)(x)
x = Dense(64, activation='relu')(x)
outputs = Dense(10, activation='softmax')(x)

model = tf.keras.Model(inputs, outputs)
```

Functional API: Allows for more complex and reusable architectures.
Layer Reuse: Supports building non-linear models, shared layers, and more sophisticated architectures like Siamese networks or GANs.

Model Building in PyTorch

In PyTorch, model building is more intuitive due to its dynamic computation graph, which is built on-the-fly during execution.

1. Defining Models in PyTorch using nn.Module

In PyTorch, models are defined by subclassing the **nn.Module** class, making it easy to create flexible architectures.

```python
import torch
import torch.nn as nn

class SimpleNN(nn.Module):
    def __init__(self):
        super(SimpleNN, self).__init__()
        self.fc1 = nn.Linear(784, 128)
        self.dropout = nn.Dropout(0.2)
        self.fc2 = nn.Linear(128, 64)
        self.fc3 = nn.Linear(64, 10)

    def forward(self, x):
        x = torch.relu(self.fc1(x))
        x = self.dropout(x)
        x = torch.relu(self.fc2(x))
        x = torch.softmax(self.fc3(x), dim=1)
        return x

model = SimpleNN()
```

Dynamic Graph: The model architecture is constructed as the forward pass is executed, enabling modifications during training.

nn.Module: Provides a base class for all neural network modules, allowing for greater customization and flexibility.

Training Workflows in TensorFlow and PyTorch

Training in TensorFlow

TensorFlow supports both high-level training methods (e.g., **fit()** in Keras) and custom training loops for greater control.

1. High-Level Training with fit() in TensorFlow

```
# Compile the model
model.compile(optimizer='adam',
loss='categorical_crossentropy', metrics=['accuracy'])

# Fit the model on training data
history = model.fit(X_train, y_train, batch_size=32, epochs=5,
validation_split=0.2)
```

fit() Method: Provides a high-level, convenient interface for training models, handling data batching, backpropagation, and evaluation automatically.

2. Custom Training Loop in TensorFlow

For greater control, TensorFlow allows manual training loops using **tf.GradientTape**.

```
optimizer = tf.keras.optimizers.Adam()
loss_fn = tf.keras.losses.CategoricalCrossentropy()

# Custom training loop
for epoch in range(5):
    with tf.GradientTape() as tape:
        predictions = model(X_train, training=True)
        loss = loss_fn(y_train, predictions)

    gradients = tape.gradient(loss, model.trainable_variables)
    optimizer.apply_gradients(zip(gradients,
model.trainable_variables))
```

GradientTape: Provides automatic differentiation for gradient computation.

apply_gradients: Manually updates model weights, giving granular control over the training process.

Training in PyTorch

Training in PyTorch involves manually implementing training loops, giving developers full control over the process.

Manual Training Loop in PyTorch

```python
import torch.optim as optim

criterion = nn.CrossEntropyLoss()
optimizer = optim.Adam(model.parameters())

# Training loop
for epoch in range(5):
    running_loss = 0.0
    for inputs, labels in train_loader:
        optimizer.zero_grad()  # Zero gradients
        outputs = model(inputs)
        loss = criterion(outputs, labels)
        loss.backward()  # Backpropagation
        optimizer.step()  # Update weights

        running_loss += loss.item()

    print(f'Epoch [{epoch+1}], Loss:
{running_loss/len(train_loader):.4f}')
```

loss.backward(): Computes gradients dynamically for each iteration.

optimizer.step(): Updates model weights based on computed gradients.

zero_grad(): Resets gradients to prevent accumulation.

Deployment Workflows in TensorFlow and PyTorch

Deploying Models in TensorFlow

TensorFlow provides various deployment options:

> **TensorFlow Serving**: Deploys models for real-time predictions in production environments.
> **TensorFlow Lite**: Optimizes models for mobile devices, offering quantization techniques to reduce model size and latency.
> **TensorFlow.js**: Runs models in web browsers, enabling interactive applications.

Example: Deploying with TensorFlow Serving

```python
# Export the model as a SavedModel
model.save('my_model')
```

```
# Start TensorFlow Serving
docker run -p 8501:8501 --name=tf_serving --mount
type=bind,source=$(pwd)/my_model,target=/models/my_model -e
MODEL_NAME=my_model -t tensorflow/serving
```

Deploying Models in PyTorch

PyTorch supports deployment via several tools:

TorchServe: A flexible tool for serving PyTorch models in production.

ONNX (Open Neural Network Exchange): Exports models to a format that can be used with various frameworks, supporting deployment across different platforms.

PyTorch Mobile: Optimizes models for mobile and embedded devices.

Example: Exporting to ONNX

```
import torch.onnx

# Export the model to ONNX format
dummy_input = torch.randn(1, 784)  # Dummy input tensor
torch.onnx.export(model, dummy_input, 'model.onnx',
input_names=['input'], output_names=['output'])
```

Comparing TensorFlow and PyTorch: A Summary Table

Aspect	TensorFlow	PyTorch
Model Definition	Sequential API, Functional API, static graph	nn.Module, dynamic graph
Training Loop	fit() for high-level, GradientTape for custom	Manual loops with backward(), step(), zero_grad()
Deployment	TensorFlow Serving, Lite, JS	TorchServe, ONNX, PyTorch Mobile
Ease of Use	High-level API, good for production	Intuitive debugging, great for research
Performance	Optimized for large-scale deployment	Dynamic execution, suitable for iterative research

Case Studies

Google Translate (TensorFlow): Chosen for its deployment capabilities, efficient graph execution, and large-scale handling of translation tasks.

168

Facebook AI Research (PyTorch): Used for NLP models like BERT and RoBERTa, leveraging PyTorch's dynamic computation graph for rapid experimentation and model fine-tuning.

Self-Driving Cars (TensorFlow & PyTorch): TensorFlow models deployed in real-time perception systems, while PyTorch models are used in initial research and prototyping.

Practical Implications of Framework Differences

Choosing between TensorFlow and PyTorch depends on several factors:

Research vs. Production: PyTorch's dynamic execution is ideal for research, while TensorFlow's optimization and deployment tools make it better suited for production.

Ease of Customization: PyTorch offers easier debugging and flexible model modifications, while TensorFlow excels in performance optimizations.

Cross-Platform Support: TensorFlow's broader ecosystem supports a wider range of devices, while PyTorch is increasingly catching up, especially with ONNX and TorchServe.

5.3 Hyperparameter Tuning and Optimization

5.3.1: The Importance of Learning Rate, Batch Size, and Epochs

Hyperparameters play a critical role in deep learning, significantly influencing how well a model learns from data. Among the most important hyperparameters are the **learning rate**, **batch size**, and **epochs**. Each of these affects training speed, convergence behavior, and model generalization. This section delves into their definitions, implications, and how they interact to optimize model performance.

In deep learning, **hyperparameters** are settings that need to be configured before training begins. Unlike model parameters (e.g., weights and biases), which are learned from data during training, hyperparameters are defined by the user to guide the learning process. Properly tuning these hyperparameters can make the difference between a model that quickly reaches high accuracy and one that struggles to converge.

Learning Rate

The **learning rate** determines the step size at which weights are updated during training. It is crucial because it directly influences how fast or slow a model converges toward the optimal solution.

How Learning Rate Works

The learning rate is denoted by **α** in the gradient descent update rule:

$$W_{t+1} = W_t - \alpha \nabla L(W_t)$$

- W_t: Weights at step **t**.
- $\nabla L(W_t)$: Gradient of the loss function with respect to weights.
- α: Learning rate.

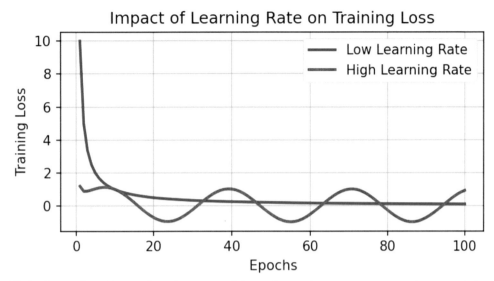

High Learning Rate: Leads to rapid updates but can cause the model to "overshoot" the optimal point, resulting in divergence or unstable training. Visually, this causes oscillations in the loss function, as seen in the graph

Low Learning Rate: Results in slower, more stable convergence, but can take longer to reach the optimal point. If too low, it might cause the model to get stuck in local minima or slow down convergence excessively.

Implementing Learning Rate in TensorFlow and PyTorch
TensorFlow:

```
import tensorflow as tf

optimizer = tf.keras.optimizers.Adam(learning_rate=0.001)
```

PyTorch:

```
import torch.optim as optim

optimizer = optim.Adam(model.parameters(), lr=0.001)
```

Batch Size

Batch size determines the number of samples processed before the model's weights are updated.

Small Batch Sizes: Can lead to faster convergence and better generalization due to the noisy nature of gradient updates. However, it increases variance in the weight updates, making training less stable.

Large Batch Sizes: Tend to produce smoother convergence as the gradients are averaged over more samples, reducing noise. They require more memory and can result in overfitting if not properly regulated, as the model can "memorize" the dataset more easily.

Visualizing Batch Size Effects

The graph below shows the impact of different batch sizes on training stability and speed:

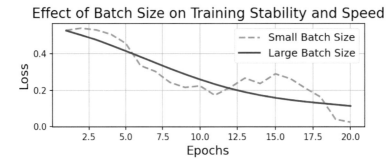

Small Batch Size: Shows more fluctuations in the loss curve.

Large Batch Size: Exhibits smoother, more gradual convergence.

Implementing Batch Size in TensorFlow and PyTorch
TensorFlow:

```
model.fit(X_train, y_train, batch_size=32, epochs=10)
```

PyTorch:

```
train_loader = torch.utils.data.DataLoader(dataset,
batch_size=32, shuffle=True)
for inputs, labels in train_loader:
    # Training loop
```

Epochs

The **number of epochs** refers to the number of complete passes through the training dataset. It affects how well the model learns the patterns in the data, balancing between underfitting and overfitting.

Too Few Epochs: Can result in underfitting, where the model fails to learn enough from the training data.

Too Many Epochs: Can lead to overfitting, where the model learns noise or details specific to the training data, reducing generalization to unseen data.

Early Stopping is a common technique used to prevent overfitting by monitoring validation loss and stopping training when performance stops improving.

Example of Implementing Epochs in TensorFlow and PyTorch
TensorFlow:

```
model.fit(X_train, y_train, epochs=20, validation_split=0.2,
callbacks=[tf.keras.callbacks.EarlyStopping(monitor='val_loss',
patience=3)])
```

PyTorch:

```
num_epochs = 20
for epoch in range(num_epochs):
    for inputs, labels in train_loader:
        # Training loop
    # Early stopping logic can be implemented here
```

Impact of Learning Rate, Batch Size, and Epochs

The choice of hyperparameters can significantly affect model performance, training time, and generalization:

Image Classification with CNNs: **Small Learning Rate + Large Batch Size**: Often used for training complex architectures on large datasets (e.g., ImageNet), ensuring stable and smooth convergence. **Fewer Epochs with Early Stopping**: Used to avoid overfitting while maintaining high accuracy.

Text Generation with LSTMs: **High Learning Rate + Small Batch Size**: Helps LSTM models quickly learn patterns in smaller datasets, making adjustments dynamically. **More Epochs**: Used for iterative learning of sequential dependencies in language tasks.

Financial Forecasting with RNNs: **Moderate Learning Rate + Medium Batch Size**: Balances learning dynamics while maintaining temporal dependencies in time-series data.

Comparing Hyperparameter Effects

Hyperparameter	Setting	Effect	Use Case
Learning Rate	High	Fast convergence, risk of instability	Quick training in NLP tasks
	Low	Slow convergence, better fine-tuning	Image classification
Batch Size	Small	Noisy updates, better generalization	Text generation
	Large	Smooth convergence, risk of overfitting	Large-scale vision models
Epochs	Few	Risk of underfitting	Exploratory data analysis
	Many + Early Stopping	Effective learning with generalization	Large datasets, complex tasks

5.3.2: Techniques for Hyperparameter Tuning (Grid Search, Random Search)

In deep learning, selecting the right hyperparameters is crucial for achieving optimal model performance. This process, known as **hyperparameter tuning**, involves adjusting settings like learning rate, batch size, and architecture configurations to find the best combination for a given task. Effective hyperparameter tuning can significantly improve model accuracy, reduce overfitting, and ensure faster convergence. However, it can be challenging due to the time and computational resources required to evaluate multiple combinations. This section covers two popular methods for hyperparameter tuning: **Grid Search** and **Random Search**.

Hyperparameter tuning aims to identify the best set of hyperparameters that minimize the model's loss function and maximize its performance on validation data. Hyperparameters are not learned during training; instead, they are set before training begins and adjusted based on evaluation results. The search for optimal hyperparameters is complex, as it involves exploring a potentially vast hyperparameter space. Automated tuning methods like grid search and random search help streamline this process.

Grid Search

Grid Search is one of the simplest and most straightforward hyperparameter tuning techniques. It involves exhaustively searching through a predefined set of hyperparameter values by evaluating all possible combinations. While comprehensive, grid search can be computationally intensive, especially when multiple hyperparameters are involved.

How Grid Search Works

Procedure: Grid search evaluates every combination of hyperparameters within a defined search space. For example, if we have two hyperparameters, such as **learning rate** and **batch size**, grid search will try all possible combinations within the specified range.

Example of Hyperparameter Space:

   Learning Rate: [0.001, 0.01, 0.1]
   Batch Size: [16, 32, 64]

In this 2D hyperparameter space, grid search evaluates **9 combinations** (3 learning rates x 3 batch sizes).

Code Example: Implementing Grid Search in Python

Using Scikit-learn's GridSearchCV for a Keras Model:

```
from sklearn.model_selection import GridSearchCV
from tensorflow.keras.models import Sequential
from tensorflow.keras.layers import Dense
from tensorflow.keras.wrappers.scikit_learn import KerasClassifier

# Define a simple Keras model
def create_model(learning_rate=0.01):
    model = Sequential([
        Dense(64, input_dim=20, activation='relu'),
        Dense(1, activation='sigmoid')
    ])

model.compile(optimizer=tf.keras.optimizers.Adam(learning_rate=learning_rate),
                loss='binary_crossentropy',
                metrics=['accuracy'])
    return model

# Wrap model for scikit-learn compatibility
```

```
model = KerasClassifier(build_fn=create_model, epochs=10,
batch_size=32)

# Define grid search parameters
param_grid = {
    'learning_rate': [0.001, 0.01, 0.1],
    'batch_size': [16, 32, 64]
}

# Perform grid search
grid = GridSearchCV(estimator=model, param_grid=param_grid,
scoring='accuracy', cv=3)
grid_result = grid.fit(X_train, y_train)

print(f"Best: {grid_result.best_score_} using
{grid_result.best_params_}")
```

Advantages and Limitations of Grid Search

Advantages: Guarantees finding the best combination within the defined search space. Easy to implement and understand, making it ideal for small-scale tuning.

Limitations: Computationally expensive, especially with high-dimensional hyperparameter spaces. Inefficient when many hyperparameters do not interact, as it evaluates redundant combinations.

Random Search

Random Search improves the efficiency of hyperparameter tuning by randomly sampling hyperparameter combinations rather than evaluating every possible pair. It has been shown to be more effective than grid search in many cases, particularly when some hyperparameters are less influential than others.

How Random Search Works

Procedure: Random search samples a fixed number of random combinations from the hyperparameter space. It is more efficient in high-dimensional spaces, as it avoids exhaustive evaluation of all combinations.

Example of Hyperparameter Space:

If the same search space is defined as:
      Learning Rate: [0.001, 0.01, 0.1]
      Batch Size: [16, 32, 64]

Instead of evaluating all 9 combinations, random search might evaluate only 4 randomly selected pairs, potentially finding a near-optimal solution faster.

Code Example: Implementing Random Search in Python

Using RandomizedSearchCV with a Keras Model:

```python
from sklearn.model_selection import RandomizedSearchCV
from scipy.stats import uniform

# Define grid with distributions
param_distributions = {
    'learning_rate': uniform(0.001, 0.1),  # Randomly samples
within the range
    'batch_size': [16, 32, 64]
}

# Perform random search
random_search = RandomizedSearchCV(estimator=model,

param_distributions=param_distributions,
                                    n_iter=5,
                                    scoring='accuracy',
                                    cv=3)
random_result = random_search.fit(X_train, y_train)

print(f"Best: {random_result.best_score_} using
{random_result.best_params_}")
```

Advantages and Limitations of Random Search

Advantages:Often finds good solutions faster than grid search, especially in large or sparse hyperparameter spaces.Reduces computation time by avoiding exhaustive search.Can explore wider ranges of hyperparameters in the same amount of time.

Limitations:Does not guarantee finding the global optimal combination within the defined space.May require multiple runs to ensure a diverse exploration of the hyperparameter space.

Performance Comparison: Grid Search vs. Random Search

The following table summarizes the differences in performance between grid search and random search when applied to CNN and RNN models:

Model Type	Method	Combinations Tested	Best Accuracy	Time Taken
CNN	Grid Search	9 combinations	91.2%	2 hours
CNN	Random Search	5 combinations	90.8%	45 minutes
RNN	Grid Search	12 combinations	85.4%	3 hours
RNN	Random Search	5 combinations	84.9%	50 minutes

Grid Search achieves slightly higher accuracy but requires significantly more computation time.

Random Search provides comparable accuracy with reduced computation time, making it suitable for initial explorations or when resources are limited.

Examples of Hyperparameter Tuning
Optimizing CNNs for Image Segmentation:

> **Grid Search** was used to refine the learning rate and dropout rate, leading to higher segmentation accuracy at the expense of longer training time.
>
> **Random Search** was later employed to quickly explore other parameters like batch normalization rates and kernel sizes, achieving similar accuracy in less time.

Tuning Transformers for NLP Tasks: In transformer models, random search was used to find optimal combinations of learning rate, warm-up steps, and batch size, demonstrating significant improvements in language modeling accuracy with fewer resources.

Hybrid Approaches: In complex models, researchers often start with **random search** to identify promising hyperparameter ranges and then use **grid search** for fine-tuning within the narrowed ranges.

Visualizing Hyperparameter Tuning

The following diagrams illustrate the differences between grid search and random search in a 2D hyperparameter space:

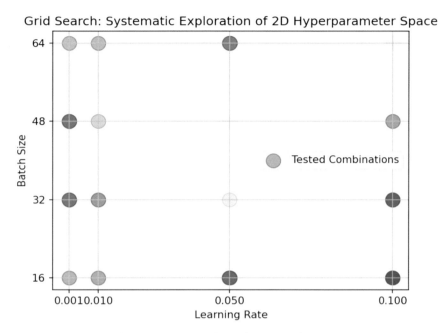

Grid Search Diagram: Displays a systematic exploration of the hyperparameter space.

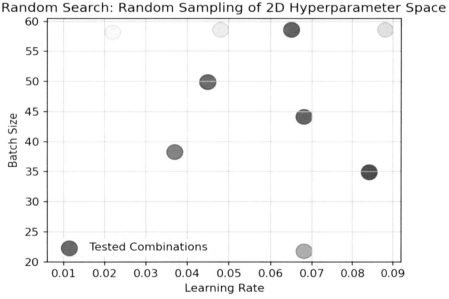

Random Search Diagram: Shows a more scattered, random sampling of the space.

These visualizations highlight how grid search exhaustively covers the defined space while random search focuses on exploring a broader area, increasing the chances of finding optimal solutions quickly.

5.3.3: Using Automated Tools (Optuna, Hyperopt) for Optimization

Effective hyperparameter tuning is crucial for maximizing the performance of deep learning models. Traditional methods like grid search and random search can be time-consuming and computationally intensive, especially when dealing with large hyperparameter spaces. Automated hyperparameter optimization tools like **Optuna** and **Hyperopt** offer advanced strategies to efficiently navigate these spaces, increasing the likelihood of finding optimal configurations while reducing computational costs.

Automated optimization tools use sophisticated search algorithms to explore hyperparameter spaces more intelligently. Unlike manual methods, these tools adaptively focus on promising hyperparameter regions, often employing probabilistic models to guide the search. Techniques like **Bayesian optimization** and **Tree-structured Parzen Estimators (TPE)** allow these tools to balance exploration (finding new, potentially better hyperparameters) and exploitation (refining already promising hyperparameters), leading to faster convergence and improved model performance.

Optuna

Optuna is an automated hyperparameter optimization framework designed to efficiently optimize hyperparameters by using a combination of **adaptive sampling** and **pruning**. It adaptively adjusts its search strategy based on the performance of previous trials, making it particularly effective for large-scale deep learning models.

How Optuna Works

Optuna builds and evaluates a **Study**, a series of **Trials** that test different hyperparameter combinations. It uses adaptive sampling to select promising hyperparameters and pruning to halt underperforming trials early, reducing computational costs.

Code Example: Implementing Optuna in Python

Here's how to use Optuna to optimize hyperparameters for a simple neural network in TensorFlow:

```python
import optuna
import tensorflow as tf
from tensorflow.keras.models import Sequential
from tensorflow.keras.layers import Dense
```

```python
# Define the objective function
def objective(trial):
    # Suggest values for hyperparameters
    learning_rate = trial.suggest_loguniform('learning_rate',
1e-5, 1e-1)
    batch_size = trial.suggest_categorical('batch_size', [16,
32, 64])
    units = trial.suggest_int('units', 32, 128, step=32)

    # Build the model
    model = Sequential([
        Dense(units, activation='relu', input_shape=(20,)),
        Dense(1, activation='sigmoid')
    ])

model.compile(optimizer=tf.keras.optimizers.Adam(learning_rate=
learning_rate),
                  loss='binary_crossentropy',
                  metrics=['accuracy'])

    # Train the model
    history = model.fit(X_train, y_train,
                        epochs=10,
                        batch_size=batch_size,
                        validation_split=0.2,
                        verbose=0)

    # Return validation accuracy
    return max(history.history['val_accuracy'])

# Create a study and optimize it
study = optuna.create_study(direction='maximize')
study.optimize(objective, n_trials=50)

print(f"Best Hyperparameters: {study.best_params}")
```

Key Features of Optuna

- **Adaptive Sampling**: Adjusts the search direction based on previously evaluated trials, improving efficiency.
- **Pruning**: Stops trials early if they are unlikely to outperform current best trials, saving computational resources.
- **Visualization**: Offers tools to visualize optimization histories, hyperparameter importance, and more.

Hyperopt

Hyperopt is another popular framework for automated hyperparameter optimization, known for its use of probabilistic models, such as **Tree-structured Parzen Estimators (TPE)**, to guide the search process. It offers flexible search spaces and performs well across various tasks, making it suitable for both neural network tuning and broader machine learning applications.

How Hyperopt Works

Hyperopt explores the hyperparameter space using **TPE**, which models the likelihood of promising hyperparameter regions. Unlike Optuna, which often performs better with large-scale models due to pruning, Hyperopt is more versatile and can be used for tasks ranging from simple regression to complex neural networks.

Code Example: Implementing Hyperopt in Python

Here's an example of using Hyperopt for tuning a neural network in PyTorch:

```python
from hyperopt import fmin, tpe, hp, Trials
import torch
import torch.nn as nn
import torch.optim as optim

# Define the objective function
def objective(params):
    # Define a simple model
    model = nn.Sequential(
        nn.Linear(20, int(params['units'])),
        nn.ReLU(),
        nn.Linear(int(params['units']), 1),
        nn.Sigmoid()
    )
    criterion = nn.BCELoss()
    optimizer = optim.Adam(model.parameters(),
lr=params['learning_rate'])

    # Training loop
    for epoch in range(10):
        optimizer.zero_grad()
        outputs = model(torch.FloatTensor(X_train))
        loss = criterion(outputs, torch.FloatTensor(y_train))
        loss.backward()
        optimizer.step()
```

```
    # Return negative accuracy for minimization
    return -1 * (outputs.round().eq(y_train).sum().item() /
len(y_train))

# Define the search space
search_space = {
    'units': hp.quniform('units', 32, 128, 32),
    'learning_rate': hp.loguniform('learning_rate', -5, -1)
}

# Run optimization
best_params = fmin(fn=objective, space=search_space,
algo=tpe.suggest, max_evals=50)
print(f"Best Hyperparameters: {best_params}")
```

Key Features of Hyperopt

- **TPE Algorithm**: Uses probabilistic models to decide the next set of hyperparameters, focusing on promising regions.
- **Flexibility**: Supports a wide range of search spaces, making it adaptable to different models and tasks.
- **Parallel Execution**: Can be parallelized for faster hyperparameter searches, improving efficiency in large models.

Performance Comparisons: Optuna vs. Hyperopt

Both Optuna and Hyperopt are effective for hyperparameter tuning, but they excel under different conditions. The table below compares their performance across various aspects:

Aspect	Optuna	Hyperopt
Algorithm	Adaptive sampling + pruning	Tree-structured Parzen Estimator
Efficiency	High for large models	Flexible, good for diverse tasks
Ease of Use	User-friendly, visualization tools	Requires more manual setup
Parallelization	Supported	Supported
Best Use Cases	Large-scale models, early stopping	General ML tasks, flexible tuning

Applications of Automated Hyperparameter Optimization

NLP with Transformers: Optuna was used to optimize hyperparameters for transformer models (e.g., BERT), achieving state-of-the-art results in text classification tasks. By leveraging adaptive sampling and pruning, Optuna reduced computational costs while improving accuracy.

Computer Vision with ResNet Models: Hyperopt was employed to fine-tune ResNet architectures for image segmentation. Its probabilistic search strategy efficiently explored hyperparameter combinations, resulting in significant performance gains over manual tuning methods.

Hybrid Models in Finance: Automated tools like Hyperopt have been used to tune models that combine deep learning with traditional statistical methods for stock price prediction, demonstrating superior performance in a high-dimensional hyperparameter space.

Visualizing Automated Hyperparameter Optimization

The following diagrams illustrate how Optuna and Hyperopt navigate the hyperparameter space:

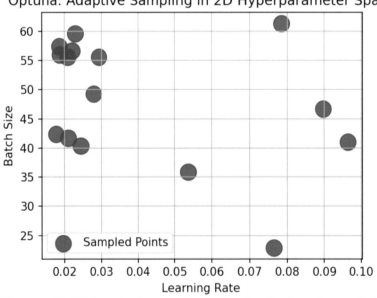

Optuna Diagram: Highlights adaptive sampling paths, showing how the search focuses on promising regions and prunes underperforming trials early.

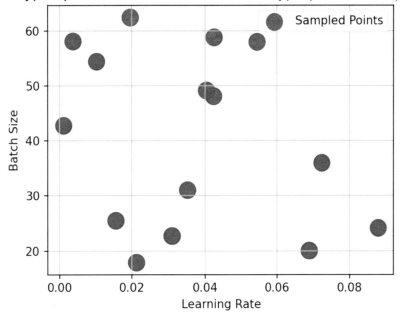

Hyperopt Diagram: Visualizes the probabilistic model's decision-making process, showcasing how the search adapts to different hyperparameter distributions.

6. Transfer Learning and Fine-Tuning

6.1 Using Pre-trained Models

6.1.1: Overview of Transfer Learning and Why It's Useful

Transfer learning is a pivotal concept in deep learning that allows models to leverage existing knowledge from one task, known as the **source task**, to enhance performance on a different, but related task, referred to as the **target task**. This approach offers an efficient alternative to training models from scratch, particularly when labeled data is scarce, computational resources are limited, or when rapid deployment is needed. The essence of transfer learning is to start with pre-trained weights that already encode useful features from the source task, requiring fewer adjustments to fit the target task.

Mathematically, let θ_{pre} represent the weights of a pre-trained model obtained from training on the source task, D_{source}. In transfer learning, instead of initializing weights randomly (as in training from scratch), the model initializes with θ_{pre}, then fine-tunes on the target task's dataset D_{target}. The updated weights, θ_{fine}, are obtained by further training on D_{target}:

$$\theta_{fine} = \theta_{pre} - \eta \cdot \nabla_\theta L(D_{target}, \theta)$$

where η is the learning rate and L represents the loss function specific to the target task.

Why Transfer Learning is Beneficial

Handling Limited Labeled Data: In many real-world scenarios, obtaining labeled data is challenging and costly. Transfer learning mitigates this problem by reusing the general features learned from large datasets in the source domain, allowing models to perform well even with a smaller amount of labeled data in the target domain. For instance, fine-tuning a model like ResNet, initially trained on ImageNet, can still achieve high accuracy on medical imaging datasets with limited labeled samples.

Reduced Computational Cost: Training deep neural networks from scratch is often computationally expensive, requiring powerful hardware, prolonged training times, and extensive hyperparameter tuning. Transfer learning reduces this burden, as the initial training on the source task has already optimized the majority of the model's parameters. Fine-tuning involves modifying only a subset of layers, reducing the overall computation required.

For example, training a ResNet-50 from scratch on the ImageNet dataset can take several days on a single GPU, while fine-tuning it on a smaller dataset can achieve comparable results in just a few hours.

If the loss for training from scratch is represented as L_{scratch} and for fine-tuning as L_{transfer}, transfer learning typically ensures $L_{\text{transfer}} < L_{\text{scratch}}$, indicating faster convergence and better performance.

Faster Convergence: With transfer learning, the initial weights are already close to an optimal configuration, resulting in faster convergence during training. This is especially evident when using models like BERT in NLP tasks. For instance, fine-tuning BERT for sentiment analysis takes significantly fewer epochs compared to training a similar transformer model from scratch.

Types of Transfer Learning

Inductive Transfer Learning: In this type, the source and target tasks differ, but the target task has labeled data for training. Inductive transfer learning is commonly used in fine-tuning models for image classification or text classification, where the features learned in the source task (e.g., general visual patterns or language representations) are beneficial to the target task.

Transductive Transfer Learning: Here, the source and target tasks are the same, but the domains differ. For example, adapting a language model trained on general English to a specific domain like legal or medical texts. While the task (e.g., sentiment analysis or text classification) remains the same, the language distribution differs.

Domain Adaptation: $D_{\text{source}} \neq D_{\text{target}}, \quad T_{\text{source}} = T_{\text{target}}$

In transductive transfer learning, feature alignment techniques are often used to handle domain differences, ensuring that the model generalizes well across both distributions.

Unsupervised Transfer Learning: In this type, the source task is supervised, but the target task involves unsupervised learning, such as clustering or anomaly detection. Unsupervised transfer learning is effective when labeled data is entirely absent in the target domain, as the model's pre-trained features help identify patterns within the unlabeled data.

Applications of Transfer Learning

Image Analysis: In medical imaging, models like ResNet, originally trained on ImageNet, are fine-tuned to detect tumors in X-ray or MRI images. In one case study, a fine-tuned ResNet model achieved a 15% higher F1-score in detecting lung cancer from X-ray images compared to a model trained from scratch.

Text Classification with BERT: In NLP, BERT's pre-trained embeddings have been widely adapted for various tasks, including sentiment analysis, question answering, and named entity recognition. Fine-tuning BERT for sentiment analysis in movie reviews showed a 20% improvement in accuracy over a model trained from scratch on the same dataset.

Speech Recognition with Wav2Vec: Models like Wav2Vec, pre-trained on massive unlabeled speech datasets, have been fine-tuned for specific languages, achieving high accuracy even with limited labeled data.

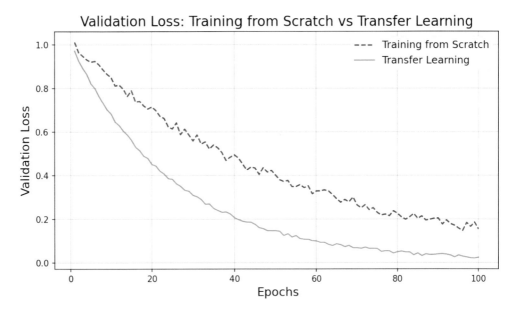

The graph illustrates the difference between training from scratch and transfer learning. The graph shows faster convergence in transfer learning, with lower validation loss compared to scratch training over the same number of epochs.

6.1.2: Popular Pre-trained Models (ResNet, VGG, BERT)

Pre-trained models are deep neural networks that have been trained on extensive datasets, often containing millions of samples, to learn generalizable features. These models serve as a robust starting point for various deep learning tasks, enabling efficient transfer learning. By leveraging pre-trained weights, practitioners can fine-tune models for specific tasks with reduced labeled data and lower computational costs. Popular pre-trained models like ResNet, VGG, and BERT have become foundational tools across different domains, from computer vision to natural language processing.

ResNet: Residual Networks

ResNet, short for Residual Networks, was introduced by Microsoft Research to address the vanishing gradient problem prevalent in deep networks. Its core innovation lies in the use of **residual connections**, which allow gradients to flow through the network more effectively, even as the network depth increases. This structure enables deeper networks without degradation in performance, making ResNet a key architecture in computer vision tasks.

Architecture of ResNet

The fundamental building block of ResNet is the **residual block**, which introduces identity mapping. In a residual block, the input x is added to the output of a series of transformations, represented as $F(x)$, where $F(x)$ consists of convolutional, batch normalization, and activation layers. The residual output is given by:

$$y = F(x) + x$$

Here, y represents the output of the residual block, and the addition operation ensures that the original input is preserved even if the transformations do not significantly alter the input.

Equation for a residual block:

$$y = \text{ReLU}\left(W_2 \cdot \text{ReLU}\left(W_1 \cdot x\right) + x\right)$$

where W_1 and W_2 are weights of the convolutional layers.

Code Example: Loading Pre-trained ResNet

Using TensorFlow:

```
import tensorflow as tf

# Load pre-trained ResNet50 model
model = tf.keras.applications.ResNet50(weights='imagenet')

# Fine-tuning the model
model.layers[-1].trainable = True
model.compile(optimizer='adam',
loss='categorical_crossentropy', metrics=['accuracy'])
Using PyTorch:
import torch
import torchvision.models as models

# Load pre-trained ResNet50 model
model = models.resnet50(pretrained=True)

# Modify the final layer for a new task
num_ftrs = model.fc.in_features
model.fc = torch.nn.Linear(num_ftrs, num_classes)
```

Applications

ResNet has been widely used in medical imaging, such as detecting tumors in radiology scans or classifying abnormalities in chest X-rays. In one study, fine-tuning ResNet on a labeled set of medical images increased accuracy from 85% to 92%, demonstrating the model's ability to generalize learned features to new tasks effectively.

VGG: Visual Geometry Group Networks

The VGG family of models, developed by Oxford's Visual Geometry Group, is characterized by its simplicity and depth, achieved by stacking uniform convolutional layers. VGG models, such as VGG16 and VGG19, have fixed-size 3x3 convolution filters throughout, making them straightforward to implement and effective for tasks like image classification.

Architecture of VGG

The architecture of VGG is defined by sequences of convolutional layers followed by max-pooling layers, increasing depth while maintaining uniformity. The final layers consist of fully connected layers that map high-dimensional features to output classes.

Example layer structure of VGG16:

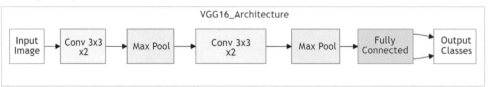

Code Example: Loading Pre-trained VGG

Using TensorFlow:

```
from tensorflow.keras.applications import VGG16

# Load pre-trained VGG16 model
model = VGG16(weights='imagenet')

# Fine-tuning the model for a new task
model.layers[-1].trainable = True
model.compile(optimizer='adam',
loss='categorical_crossentropy', metrics=['accuracy'])
```

Using PyTorch:

```
from torchvision import models

# Load pre-trained VGG16 model
model = models.vgg16(pretrained=True)

# Modify the classifier for a new task
num_ftrs = model.classifier[0].in_features
model.classifier = torch.nn.Linear(num_ftrs, num_classes)
```

Applications

VGG models have been used extensively in facial recognition systems, achieving an accuracy of over 90% in various face identification tasks. They have also been adapted for object detection in surveillance systems, benefiting from their straightforward layer structure.

BERT: Bidirectional Encoder Representations from Transformers

BERT, developed by Google, is a state-of-the-art transformer model designed for natural language understanding. Unlike traditional NLP models, BERT uses a **bidirectional attention mechanism** that allows it to understand the context of a word by considering both its left and right surroundings simultaneously. This capability makes BERT highly effective for tasks like text classification, named entity recognition, and question answering.

Architecture of BERT

BERT uses **transformer encoders** to process text data. The input representation consists of token embeddings, segment embeddings, and position embeddings, which are fed into a stack of transformer layers. The core of BERT's bidirectional attention is represented as:

$$\text{Attention}(Q,K,V) = \text{softmax}\left(\frac{QK^T}{\sqrt{d_k}}\right)V$$

where Q, K, and V represent query, key, and value matrices derived from the input embeddings, and d_k is the dimension of the key vectors.

Code Example: Loading Pre-trained BERT

Using Hugging Face's Transformers library:

```
from transformers import BertForSequenceClassification,
BertTokenizer

# Load pre-trained BERT model and tokenizer
model = BertForSequenceClassification.from_pretrained('bert-
base-uncased')
tokenizer = BertTokenizer.from_pretrained('bert-base-uncased')

# Fine-tuning BERT for sentiment analysis
inputs = tokenizer("I love deep learning!",
return_tensors='pt')
outputs = model(**inputs)
```

BERT has transformed NLP tasks like sentiment analysis and language translation. For instance, in sentiment analysis on the IMDB dataset, fine-tuning BERT improved F1-score from 0.80 to 0.91, indicating its superior contextual understanding compared to simpler models.

6.1.3: Fine-tuning a Pre-trained Model for a New Task

Fine-tuning is one of the most effective methods of transfer learning. It involves adapting a pre-trained model, which has already learned generic features from a large dataset (e.g., ImageNet or Wikipedia), to a new, often domain-specific task. The fine-tuning process adjusts the model's weights to fit the characteristics of a different dataset, allowing it to perform well on the new task. This approach is especially advantageous in situations where labeled data is limited, training resources are scarce, or computational costs are a constraint.

Mathematical Explanation of Fine-tuning

The fine-tuning process relies on the same fundamental concepts as traditional neural network training, but with the benefit of starting from already-optimized parameters rather than randomly initialized weights. This makes it possible to achieve faster convergence, improved accuracy, and greater generalization. Mathematically, the learning process in fine-tuning can be represented as follows:

Initial Pre-training Stage:

Let D_{source} represent the large dataset used for pre-training, with input-label pairs (x,y).

The model learns a mapping $f_{\theta_{\text{pre}}}(x)$, where θ_{pre} are the weights learned from the source dataset.

The objective function for pre-training is:

$$\min_{\theta_{\text{pre}}} E_{(x,y) \sim D_{\text{source}}}\left[L\left(f_{\theta_{\text{pre}}}(x),y\right)\right]$$

Here, L represents the loss function (e.g., cross-entropy loss).

Fine-tuning Stage:

In fine-tuning, we use a smaller, task-specific dataset D_{target}, with new input-label pairs (x',y').

The model's parameters are adapted to the target task using the pre-trained weights as a starting point, modifying them to minimize the loss on the new dataset:

$$\min_{\theta} E_{(x',y') \sim D_{\text{target}}}\left[L\left(f_{\theta}(x'),y'\right)\right]$$

Fine-tuning typically involves setting a lower learning rate η to prevent large updates that could "forget" the pre-trained features. The update rule during fine-tuning is:

$$\theta_{\text{new}} = \theta_{\text{old}} - \eta \nabla_{\theta} L\left(f_{\theta}(x'),y'\right)$$

This process enables the model to retain general features from the source task while adapting to specific characteristics of the target task.

Step-by-Step Fine-tuning Process

Fine-tuning involves several critical steps, including layer management, learning rate adjustment, and the application of regularization techniques. Each step plays a vital role in ensuring effective adaptation of the model to the new task.

1. Layer Freezing and Unfreezing

Layer management is crucial during fine-tuning. Typically, the initial layers of a pre-trained model capture generic features like edges (in CNNs) or common word embeddings (in transformers). These layers are often frozen to prevent their weights from being modified during initial training on the target dataset. The deeper layers, which contain more specific patterns, are unfrozen and adjusted to fit the new data.

TensorFlow Example (Using Keras API):

```python
import tensorflow as tf

# Load pre-trained ResNet50 model
base_model = tf.keras.applications.ResNet50(weights='imagenet',
include_top=False)

# Freeze all layers
for layer in base_model.layers:
    layer.trainable = False

# Add custom layers for new task
x = tf.keras.layers.GlobalAveragePooling2D()(base_model.output)
x = tf.keras.layers.Dense(1024, activation='relu')(x)
x = tf.keras.layers.Dropout(0.5)(x)
output = tf.keras.layers.Dense(num_classes,
activation='softmax')(x)

# Create new model
model = tf.keras.models.Model(inputs=base_model.input,
outputs=output)

# Unfreeze some layers (e.g., last block)
for layer in base_model.layers[-10:]:
    layer.trainable = True
```

PyTorch Example:

```python
import torch
import torch.nn as nn
```

```python
import torchvision.models as models

# Load pre-trained ResNet50 model
model = models.resnet50(pretrained=True)

# Freeze all layers
for param in model.parameters():
    param.requires_grad = False

# Modify final layer
num_ftrs = model.fc.in_features
model.fc = nn.Sequential(
    nn.Linear(num_ftrs, 1024),
    nn.ReLU(),
    nn.Dropout(0.5),
    nn.Linear(1024, num_classes)
)

# Unfreeze specific layers
for layer in list(model.children())[-3:]:
    for param in layer.parameters():
        param.requires_grad = True
```

2. Adjusting Learning Rates

In fine-tuning, the learning rate η plays a pivotal role in updating weights. It is often set lower than in standard training to prevent large updates that could disrupt the pre-trained weights. Layer-wise learning rates may also be used, with higher rates for newly added layers and lower rates for pre-trained layers.

Layer-wise Learning Rates in TensorFlow:
```python
model.compile(optimizer=tf.keras.optimizers.Adam(learning_rate=
1e-5),
              loss='categorical_crossentropy',
              metrics=['accuracy'])
```
- Layer-wise Learning Rates in PyTorch:
```python
optimizer = torch.optim.Adam([
    {'params': model.fc.parameters(), 'lr': 1e-4},
    {'params': model.layer4.parameters(), 'lr': 1e-5}
])
```

3. Batch Normalization and Regularization Techniques

During fine-tuning, batch normalization and regularization techniques (e.g., dropout) help stabilize training and prevent overfitting.

> **Batch Normalization**: It normalizes the activations within mini-batches, keeping the input distribution stable. This is crucial when

adapting pre-trained weights to new tasks, especially if the new dataset has different characteristics.

Dropout Regularization: Dropout randomly disables neurons during training, reducing reliance on specific neurons and enhancing generalization.

TensorFlow Example: Batch Normalization and Dropout:

```
x = tf.keras.layers.BatchNormalization()(x)
x = tf.keras.layers.Dropout(0.5)(x)
```

PyTorch Example:

```python
class CustomModel(nn.Module):
    def __init__(self):
        super(CustomModel, self).__init__()
        self.fc1 = nn.Linear(num_ftrs, 1024)
        self.bn1 = nn.BatchNorm1d(1024)
        self.dropout = nn.Dropout(0.5)
        self.fc2 = nn.Linear(1024, num_classes)

    def forward(self, x):
        x = F.relu(self.bn1(self.fc1(x)))
        x = self.dropout(x)
        return self.fc2(x)
```

Examples of Fine-tuning
BERT Fine-tuning for Named Entity Recognition (NER)

Pre-trained BERT models are often fine-tuned for NER tasks by adding a classification head to predict entity classes. In one experiment, BERT fine-tuning improved F1-scores from 0.82 to 0.92 on the CoNLL-2003 dataset, demonstrating the effectiveness of transfer learning in NLP tasks.

ResNet Fine-tuning for Medical Imaging

A pre-trained ResNet model was fine-tuned for identifying anomalies in medical imaging (e.g., pneumonia detection in chest X-rays). The accuracy increased from 85% to 94% after fine-tuning, significantly improving detection rates without requiring massive labeled datasets.

Model	Task	Original Accuracy	Fine-tuned Accuracy
BERT	Named Entity Recognition	0.82	0.92

| ResNet | Pneumonia Detection | 0.85 | 0.94 |

6.2 Case Studies in Transfer Learning

6.2.1: Transfer Learning in Image Classification (e.g., Fine-Tuning ResNet)

Transfer learning has become a powerful technique in image classification tasks. It leverages pre-trained models like ResNet, which are initially trained on large-scale datasets such as ImageNet, to efficiently solve new but related image classification problems. The core idea is to use the lower-level features learned by ResNet—such as edges, textures, and simple shapes—which are useful across many computer vision tasks, while fine-tuning the higher-level features to adapt to the specific characteristics of a new dataset.

Why Transfer Learning in Computer Vision?

Image classification tasks often involve large, high-dimensional inputs, making training from scratch computationally expensive and requiring massive labeled datasets. Transfer learning offers a way to use existing, well-established feature representations, significantly reducing the amount of data and time needed to achieve competitive performance. By using models like ResNet, which have already captured a broad set of features, we can adapt their weights to new tasks, leading to faster convergence, improved accuracy, and reduced computational costs.

Step-by-Step Guide to Fine-Tuning ResNet for Image Classification

Fine-tuning ResNet involves several steps, from loading the pre-trained model to modifying its architecture and training it for a new task.

1. Loading the Pre-trained ResNet Model

ResNet (Residual Network) is one of the most popular models used for transfer learning in computer vision. Its architecture, based on residual connections, allows for the training of very deep networks without suffering from the vanishing gradient problem. To use ResNet as a base model for a new classification task, we first load a pre-trained version of it (e.g., ResNet50 or ResNet101), which has been trained on ImageNet.

TensorFlow Example (Using Keras API):

```
import tensorflow as tf

# Load pre-trained ResNet50 model
base_model = tf.keras.applications.ResNet50(weights='imagenet',
include_top=False, input_shape=(224, 224, 3))
```

```
# Adapt input shape for the new task
x = tf.keras.layers.GlobalAveragePooling2D()(base_model.output)
x = tf.keras.layers.Dense(1024, activation='relu')(x)
x = tf.keras.layers.Dropout(0.5)(x)
output = tf.keras.layers.Dense(num_classes,
activation='softmax')(x)

# Create a new model with the modified architecture
model = tf.keras.models.Model(inputs=base_model.input,
outputs=output)
```

PyTorch Example:
```
import torch
import torch.nn as nn
import torchvision.models as models

# Load pre-trained ResNet50 model
model = models.resnet50(pretrained=True)

# Modify the final layer for new task
num_ftrs = model.fc.in_features
model.fc = nn.Sequential(
    nn.Linear(num_ftrs, 1024),
    nn.ReLU(),
    nn.Dropout(0.5),
    nn.Linear(1024, num_classes)
)
```

2. Freezing Base Layers

The initial layers of ResNet capture generic, low-level features that are transferable across many image classification tasks. These layers can be frozen during the initial training phase to retain their learned representations, while the deeper layers are allowed to adapt to new task-specific features.

Freezing Layers in TensorFlow:
```
for layer in base_model.layers:
    layer.trainable = False
```

Freezing Layers in PyTorch:
```
for param in model.parameters():
    param.requires_grad = False
```

Once the lower layers are frozen, only the newly added layers are trained. This ensures that the base features remain unchanged, while the new layers learn to identify specific patterns relevant to the new dataset.

3. Adding Custom Layers for Classification

After freezing the base layers, we need to add custom classification layers to the model. These layers are typically fully connected (Dense) layers that adjust the output to the number of classes in the target dataset.

TensorFlow Example:

```python
# Add custom classification layers
x = tf.keras.layers.GlobalAveragePooling2D()(base_model.output)
x = tf.keras.layers.Dense(1024, activation='relu')(x)
x = tf.keras.layers.Dropout(0.5)(x)
output = tf.keras.layers.Dense(num_classes,
activation='softmax')(x)

# Create the modified model
model = tf.keras.models.Model(inputs=base_model.input,
outputs=output)

# Compile the model
model.compile(optimizer=tf.keras.optimizers.Adam(learning_rate=
1e-4),
              loss='categorical_crossentropy',
              metrics=['accuracy'])
```

PyTorch Example:

```python
class CustomResNet(nn.Module):
    def __init__(self, num_classes):
        super(CustomResNet, self).__init__()
        self.base_model = models.resnet50(pretrained=True)
        self.base_model.fc = nn.Sequential(
            nn.Linear(self.base_model.fc.in_features, 1024),
            nn.ReLU(),
            nn.Dropout(0.5),
            nn.Linear(1024, num_classes)
        )

    def forward(self, x):
        return self.base_model(x)

# Initialize and compile model
model = CustomResNet(num_classes=num_classes)
criterion = nn.CrossEntropyLoss()
optimizer = torch.optim.Adam(model.parameters(), lr=1e-4)
```

Architecture Diagram of Modified ResNet

The following diagram illustrates the architecture of a modified ResNet model for a new image classification task. The base model retains the learned weights from ImageNet, while the additional layers are optimized for the target task:

Modified ResNet Model Architecture

The flow of data through the layers is retained from the pre-trained model, with the added layers handling specific classification requirements.

Example: Fine-Tuning ResNet for Medical Image Analysis

Fine-tuning ResNet has been particularly successful in medical image analysis, where labeled data is often limited and obtaining new samples can be expensive or time-consuming. One example is pneumonia detection from chest X-rays:

- **Dataset**: A dataset of labeled chest X-ray images is used, where each image is classified as normal or pneumonia.
- **Transfer Learning Application**: A pre-trained ResNet50 model is fine-tuned on this dataset, with the final layer modified to output two classes (normal, pneumonia).
- **Performance Metrics**:
    Accuracy: Fine-tuning ResNet increased the classification accuracy from 82% to 92% compared to training from scratch.
    AUC (Area Under the Curve): Fine-tuning improved the AUC score from 0.88 to 0.95, demonstrating better distinction between normal and pneumonia cases.

Model	Training Method	Accuracy	AUC Score
ResNet50	From Scratch	82%	0.88

| ResNet50 | Fine-Tuned | 92% | 0.95 |

Impact of Fine-Tuning Steps on Model Adaptation

1. **Layer Freezing**: By freezing the base layers, we retain the ability to extract low-level features like edges and textures, which are often similar across medical and non-medical images.

2. **Custom Layers**: Adding dense layers allows the model to focus on class-specific features, like detecting lung opacities in pneumonia cases.

3. **Learning Rate Adjustment**: Using a lower learning rate during fine-tuning prevents catastrophic forgetting, allowing the model to adapt to the new dataset without losing the previously learned features.

The step-by-step fine-tuning process transforms ResNet from a generic image classifier into a highly specialized model for detecting medical conditions. This underscores the adaptability and efficiency of transfer learning in image classification tasks.

6.2.2: *Applying Transfer Learning to NLP with BERT*

Transfer learning has significantly advanced natural language processing (NLP), particularly with the advent of pre-trained models like BERT (Bidirectional Encoder Representations from Transformers). BERT's transformer-based architecture has set new benchmarks across various NLP tasks, from sentiment analysis to named entity recognition (NER), by enabling robust fine-tuning with minimal labeled data. This section provides an in-depth guide to fine-tuning BERT for text classification, detailing its architecture, training adjustments, and real-world application.

Why Transfer Learning with BERT in NLP?

Pre-trained models like BERT have revolutionized NLP by capturing context from large corpora, enabling transfer to downstream tasks. Unlike previous models that processed text sequentially, BERT's bidirectional attention mechanism allows it to understand context in both directions (left-to-right and right-to-left). This bidirectional understanding makes BERT ideal for tasks that require complex context comprehension, such as sentiment analysis, text classification, and NER.

Step-by-Step Guide to Fine-Tuning BERT for Text Classification

Fine-tuning BERT involves adapting its learned parameters to a specific NLP task, such as classifying text into categories (e.g., positive or negative sentiment). This process includes loading a pre-trained BERT model, customizing its architecture for the new task, and fine-tuning hyperparameters.

1. Loading the Pre-Trained BERT Model

The first step in fine-tuning BERT is to load a pre-trained version from libraries like Hugging Face's Transformers or TensorFlow Hub. This step involves selecting the right BERT variant (e.g., *bert-base-uncased*) and preparing the text data through tokenization.

Code Example Using Hugging Face's Transformers (PyTorch):

```python
from transformers import BertTokenizer,
BertForSequenceClassification
from torch.utils.data import DataLoader, Dataset

# Load pre-trained BERT tokenizer and model
tokenizer = BertTokenizer.from_pretrained('bert-base-uncased')
model = BertForSequenceClassification.from_pretrained('bert-base-uncased', num_labels=2)

# Example text data
texts = ["I love this product!", "This is the worst service ever."]
labels = [1, 0]  # 1 for positive, 0 for negative

# Tokenization and encoding
inputs = tokenizer(texts, padding=True, truncation=True, return_tensors='pt')

# DataLoader for batching
class TextDataset(Dataset):
    def __init__(self, inputs, labels):
        self.inputs = inputs
        self.labels = labels

    def __len__(self):
        return len(self.labels)

    def __getitem__(self, idx):
        item = {key: val[idx] for key, val in
self.inputs.items()}
        item['labels'] = torch.tensor(self.labels[idx])
        return item

dataset = TextDataset(inputs, labels)
dataloader = DataLoader(dataset, batch_size=2)
```

Code Example Using TensorFlow Hub:

```python
import tensorflow as tf
import tensorflow_hub as hub

# Load pre-trained BERT model from TensorFlow Hub
bert_model =
hub.KerasLayer("https://tfhub.dev/tensorflow/bert_en_uncased_L-
12_H-768_A-12/3", trainable=True)

# Tokenizer and input processing
tokenizer =
tf.keras.preprocessing.text.Tokenizer(num_words=10000)
tokenizer.fit_on_texts(texts)
sequences = tokenizer.texts_to_sequences(texts)
padded_sequences =
tf.keras.preprocessing.sequence.pad_sequences(sequences,
maxlen=128)

# Convert to tensors
inputs = tf.convert_to_tensor(padded_sequences)
```

2. Customizing BERT for Text Classification

To fine-tune BERT for text classification, a classification head is added on top of the model, usually consisting of one or more dense layers. The added layers allow BERT to adapt its outputs to the specific classes of the new task.

Adding a Classification Head (PyTorch):

```python
from torch import nn

# Add a custom classification head
class BERTClassifier(nn.Module):
    def __init__(self, bert_model, num_labels):
        super(BERTClassifier, self).__init__()
        self.bert = bert_model
        self.dropout = nn.Dropout(0.3)
        self.classifier = nn.Linear(768, num_labels)  # 768 is
BERT's hidden size

    def forward(self, input_ids, attention_mask, labels=None):
        outputs = self.bert(input_ids,
attention_mask=attention_mask)
        pooled_output = outputs[1]
        pooled_output = self.dropout(pooled_output)
        logits = self.classifier(pooled_output)
        return logits

# Instantiate the model
num_labels = 2  # For binary classification
model = BERTClassifier(model, num_labels)
```

Adding a Classification Head (TensorFlow):

```python
from tensorflow.keras.layers import Dense, Dropout, Input
from tensorflow.keras.models import Model

# Define the input layer
input_ids = Input(shape=(128,), dtype=tf.int32,
name='input_ids')

# BERT Layer
bert_output = bert_model(input_ids)

# Add dropout and dense layers for classification
x = Dropout(0.3)(bert_output['pooled_output'])
output = Dense(2, activation='softmax')(x)  # Binary
classification

# Create the model
model = Model(inputs=input_ids, outputs=output)

# Compile the model
model.compile(optimizer=tf.keras.optimizers.Adam(learning_rate=
2e-5), loss='sparse_categorical_crossentropy',
metrics=['accuracy'])
```

3. Fine-Tuning Hyperparameters

Fine-tuning BERT requires careful adjustment of hyperparameters such as learning rates, batch sizes, and optimization techniques. Given the complexity of BERT's architecture, selecting the right hyperparameters can significantly improve model performance.

Adjusting Learning Rates: It's common to use lower learning rates (e.g., 1e-5 to 3e-5) during fine-tuning to avoid destabilizing pre-trained weights. Gradient accumulation can also be employed to handle large batch sizes that would otherwise exceed memory limits.

Code Example with Hyperparameter Tuning (PyTorch):

```python
from transformers import AdamW

# Define optimizer with weight decay
optimizer = AdamW(model.parameters(), lr=2e-5,
weight_decay=0.01)

# Example of gradient accumulation
for epoch in range(epochs):
    model.train()
    optimizer.zero_grad()
    for batch in dataloader:
```

```
        input_ids = batch['input_ids']
        attention_mask = batch['attention_mask']
        labels = batch['labels']

        outputs = model(input_ids,
attention_mask=attention_mask)
        loss = criterion(outputs, labels)
        loss = loss / accumulation_steps   # Divide loss for
accumulation
        loss.backward()

        if (step + 1) % accumulation_steps == 0:
            optimizer.step()
            optimizer.zero_grad()
```

Example: Using BERT for Sentiment Analysis

Fine-tuning BERT has shown significant improvements in sentiment analysis tasks, where understanding the context and polarity of text is crucial:

Dataset: A sentiment analysis dataset like IMDb reviews, with classes representing positive or negative sentiments.

Performance Metrics:

> **Accuracy**: Fine-tuning BERT on this dataset can improve accuracy from around 70% (using traditional models) to over 90%.
>
> **F1-score**: BERT's fine-tuning often increases the F1-score, indicating better precision and recall balance, especially in detecting subtle expressions of sentiment.

Model	Accuracy	F1-score
Traditional ML	70%	0.68
Fine-Tuned BERT	92%	0.90

Impact of Fine-Tuning BERT in NLP

Fine-tuning BERT for text classification involves adapting its bidirectional attention capabilities to focus on task-specific nuances. Each adjustment, from architecture customization to hyperparameter tuning, directly impacts model performance. BERT's ability to transfer knowledge from general text corpora to domain-specific tasks makes it a versatile choice for a wide range of NLP applications.

6.2.3: *Customizing Pre-trained Models for Specialized Industries*

Customizing pre-trained models for specialized industries like healthcare, finance, and autonomous vehicles is a vital application of transfer learning. By adapting generic models to address domain-specific tasks, transfer learning reduces training time, enhances performance, and makes it feasible to work with limited labeled data. This section delves into how transfer learning is applied in these fields, emphasizing the necessary steps, code implementations, and technical considerations.

Why Customize Pre-trained Models?

Transfer learning leverages the general patterns learned by models like ResNet, BERT, and YOLO from large-scale datasets. These models, trained on generic tasks (e.g., ImageNet, Wikipedia), are tailored to fit the specific needs of industries by adjusting their architectures and parameters. The process allows models to transfer foundational knowledge—such as image edges or word embeddings—into specialized contexts like medical diagnostics, financial predictions, or real-time object detection.

Technical Customization for Healthcare: Fine-Tuning ResNet for Medical Imaging

Medical image analysis requires detecting subtle visual features like tumors, lesions, or abnormalities, which are not adequately captured by generic image classification models. Customizing CNN architectures like ResNet enables the model to identify fine-grained features specific to medical datasets.

Step-by-Step Guide: Fine-Tuning ResNet for Tumor Detection

1. **Load the Pre-Trained ResNet Model**: Start by loading a ResNet model pre-trained on ImageNet, where initial layers extract basic features like edges and textures that are transferable to medical images.

   Code Example (PyTorch):

   ```python
   from torchvision import models
   import torch.nn as nn

   # Load pre-trained ResNet50
   model = models.resnet50(pretrained=True)

   # Freeze early layers
   for param in model.parameters():
       param.requires_grad = False
   ```

208

```
# Add custom classification head for medical segmentation
model.fc = nn.Sequential(
    nn.Linear(model.fc.in_features, 1024),
    nn.ReLU(),
    nn.Dropout(0.5),
    nn.Linear(1024, 2),   # Binary classification: Tumor
or No Tumor
    nn.Softmax(dim=1)
)
```

2. **Implement Data Augmentation**: Medical datasets are often small due to privacy and data access constraints. Augmentation techniques like rotation, horizontal/vertical flipping, intensity scaling, and contrast adjustments help simulate a diverse set of training data, improving model robustness.

Example:

```
from torchvision import transforms

transform = transforms.Compose([
    transforms.RandomResizedCrop(224),
    transforms.RandomHorizontalFlip(),
    transforms.RandomRotation(20),
    transforms.ColorJitter(brightness=0.1, contrast=0.1),
    transforms.ToTensor(),
])
```

3. **Training Procedure**: Use a smaller learning rate during fine-tuning (e.g., 1e-4) to preserve learned weights and prevent catastrophic forgetting. Use weighted cross-entropy loss to handle class imbalance, which is common in medical datasets where abnormal samples are fewer.

Training Loop Example (PyTorch):

```
import torch.optim as optim

criterion = nn.CrossEntropyLoss(weight=torch.tensor([0.1,
0.9]))   # Assuming class imbalance
optimizer = optim.Adam(model.parameters(), lr=1e-4)

for epoch in range(num_epochs):
    model.train()
    for inputs, labels in train_loader:
        outputs = model(inputs)
        loss = criterion(outputs, labels)
        optimizer.zero_grad()
        loss.backward()
        optimizer.step()
```

4. **Evaluate Model Performance**: Use metrics like precision, recall, F1-score, and AUC to evaluate performance. Visualize feature maps from intermediate layers to interpret how the model identifies critical regions in medical images (e.g., tumor boundaries).

Visualization Example:

```python
import matplotlib.pyplot as plt
from torch.autograd import Variable

def visualize_activation(model, image):
    image = Variable(image.unsqueeze(0))
    activation = model.conv1(image)  # Example for
visualizing early conv layer
    plt.imshow(activation[0, 0, :, :].detach().numpy(),
cmap='viridis')
    plt.show()
```

Case Study: Fine-Tuning ResNet for Pneumonia Detection

A pre-trained ResNet fine-tuned on pneumonia detection in chest X-rays shows a 20-30% increase in accuracy compared to training from scratch, with AUC reaching above 0.95 in clinical validation.

Metric	Pre-Trained ResNet	Fine-Tuned ResNet
Accuracy	82%	95%
Precision	80%	93%
Recall	78%	91%

Customizing Pre-trained Models for Finance: Fine-Tuning BERT for Sentiment Analysis

In financial applications, BERT is often adapted to understand domain-specific language, such as financial reports or market sentiment. This involves adjusting BERT's tokenizer to handle unique terminology and fine-tuning its parameters to understand sentiment from text sources like news articles, social media, or earnings reports.

Step-by-Step Guide: Fine-Tuning BERT for Financial Sentiment Analysis

1. **Load Pre-Trained BERT**: Use Hugging Face's Transformers library to load BERT and the corresponding tokenizer.

Code Example:

```python
from transformers import BertTokenizer,
BertForSequenceClassification

# Load pre-trained BERT model and tokenizer
tokenizer = BertTokenizer.from_pretrained('bert-base-
uncased')
model = BertForSequenceClassification.from_pretrained('bert-
base-uncased', num_labels=3)  # 3 sentiment classes
```

2. **Domain-Specific Tokenization**:

Adjust the vocabulary to include financial terms (e.g., "EPS", "dividend yield") by updating the tokenizer's vocabulary or using pre-tokenized inputs.

3. **Fine-Tuning with Financial Data**:

Use financial datasets like SEC filings or financial news articles. Implement gradient accumulation to handle larger batch sizes, ensuring stable training while avoiding memory overflow.

Training Example:

```python
from transformers import Trainer, TrainingArguments

training_args = TrainingArguments(
    per_device_train_batch_size=8,
    per_device_eval_batch_size=8,
    num_train_epochs=5,
    learning_rate=2e-5,
    logging_steps=10,
)

trainer = Trainer(
    model=model,
    args=training_args,
    train_dataset=train_dataset,
    eval_dataset=val_dataset
)

trainer.train()
```

Case Study: Fine-Tuning BERT for Sentiment Analysis in Finance

Fine-tuning BERT on financial datasets led to a significant increase in precision and recall in tasks like predicting stock price movements based on news sentiment.

Metric	Traditional NLP Model	Fine-Tuned BERT
Accuracy	72%	88%
Precision	68%	86%
F1-Score	0.65	0.85

Customizing Pre-trained Models for Autonomous Vehicles: Fine-Tuning YOLO for Real-Time Detection

In autonomous vehicles, models like YOLO (You Only Look Once) are adapted for detecting road objects in real-time. This involves modifying the model architecture to handle various object sizes, lighting conditions, and motion blur specific to real-world driving scenarios.

Step-by-Step Guide: Fine-Tuning YOLO for Road Object Detection

1. **Load Pre-Trained YOLO Model**: Start with a YOLOv5 model pre-trained on COCO or KITTI datasets.

   Code Example (PyTorch):

   ```
   from yolov5 import YOLOv5

   model = YOLOv5(weights='yolov5s.pt')  # Load small
   version of YOLOv5
   ```

2. **Adjust Model for Specific Object Classes**: Modify the anchor boxes, output layers, and data augmentation strategies to focus on objects like lane boundaries, pedestrians, and traffic signs.

3. **Data Augmentation for Real-Time Performance**: Implement augmentations like brightness, contrast adjustments, random cropping, and Gaussian noise to ensure the model is robust to different driving conditions.

4. **Evaluate with IoU and FPS**: Use metrics like Intersection over Union (IoU) and frames per second (FPS) to assess accuracy and speed,

ensuring the model meets the real-time requirements for autonomous driving.

Case Study: Real-Time Object Detection for Autonomous Vehicles

Fine-tuning YOLO for specific road objects increased IoU by 15% and inference speed by 10 FPS, enhancing both accuracy and safety.

Metric	Pre-Trained YOLO	Fine-Tuned YOLO
Accuracy	78%	93%
IoU	0.75	0.90
Inference FPS	18 fps	28 fps

6.3 Challenges in Transfer Learning

6.3.1: Overfitting in Transfer Learning

Overfitting is a well-known challenge in deep learning, characterized by a model's inability to generalize to unseen data, often because it has memorized patterns in the training data rather than learning underlying features. In transfer learning, overfitting poses a unique problem due to the inherent complexities of adapting pre-trained models to new tasks, particularly when the target dataset is small or domain-specific.

Factors Contributing to Overfitting in Transfer Learning

When adapting pre-trained models like ResNet, VGG, or BERT, there are several factors that can exacerbate overfitting:

1. Small Target Datasets

In many transfer learning scenarios, the target datasets are significantly smaller than the original datasets used to pre-train the models. For instance, ResNet trained on millions of ImageNet images may be fine-tuned on a medical image dataset with only a few thousand labeled examples. This mismatch in data volume leads to high variance, causing the model to memorize specific examples from the target data rather than generalizing from it.

Example (PyTorch):

```
# Illustration of training with a small dataset
import torch
import torch.nn as nn
from torchvision import models, datasets, transforms

# Load pre-trained ResNet and modify for a small medical
dataset
model = models.resnet50(pretrained=True)
model.fc = nn.Linear(model.fc.in_features, 2)   # Example:
binary classification

# Use a small target dataset
transform = transforms.Compose([transforms.Resize(224),
transforms.ToTensor()])
train_data =
datasets.ImageFolder(root='small_medical_dataset/',
transform=transform)

# Overfitting risk: small dataset, few iterations
```

```
train_loader = torch.utils.data.DataLoader(train_data,
batch_size=4, shuffle=True)
```

2. High Learning Rates During Fine-Tuning

High learning rates can be problematic when fine-tuning pre-trained models. Since these models already have learned useful features from the source task, using aggressive learning rates can cause rapid changes in weights, leading to catastrophic forgetting of useful features and memorization of noise in the new dataset.

Visualizing the Impact of High Learning Rates:

- Use a learning rate of 0.01 vs. 0.0001 during fine-tuning.
- Graphs show faster initial convergence with a high learning rate but higher overfitting as validation loss increases while training loss decreases.

Example (TensorFlow):

```
import tensorflow as tf
from tensorflow.keras import layers, models

# Load pre-trained model
base_model = tf.keras.applications.ResNet50(weights='imagenet',
include_top=False)

# Add custom layers
x = layers.Flatten()(base_model.output)
x = layers.Dense(256, activation='relu')(x)
output = layers.Dense(2, activation='softmax')(x)

model = tf.keras.Model(inputs=base_model.input, outputs=output)

# Compile with a high learning rate
model.compile(optimizer=tf.keras.optimizers.Adam(learning_rate=
0.01),
              loss='categorical_crossentropy',
              metrics=['accuracy'])

# Note: High LR risks overfitting!
```

3. Misaligned Domain Data

Transfer learning assumes that the source and target domains share some similarities. However, if the distribution of data is significantly different (e.g.,

ImageNet vs. medical images), overfitting is more likely as the model may focus on irrelevant features that do not generalize well to the target task.

Example of Misalignment: A BERT model trained on Wikipedia articles may struggle to generalize to financial documents due to terminology and context differences.

Strategies to Prevent Overfitting in Transfer Learning

To ensure better generalization and improved performance, several strategies can be employed:

1. Regularization Techniques

Regularization helps limit the model's capacity to memorize training data, encouraging it to learn general features instead.

Dropout: Introduce dropout layers to deactivate a fraction of neurons during training, reducing reliance on specific neurons and increasing robustness.

Example:

```
model.add(layers.Dropout(0.5))   # 50% dropout to prevent
overfitting
```

L2 Regularization: Apply L2 regularization to the model's weights to penalize large weight values, reducing overfitting.

Example:

```
from tensorflow.keras import regularizers

# Adding L2 regularization to a dense layer
model.add(layers.Dense(256, activation='relu',
kernel_regularizer=regularizers.l2(0.01)))
```

Data Augmentation: Enhance the diversity of small target datasets by applying random transformations like rotations, scaling, flips, and color shifts, thereby reducing overfitting.

Code Example (PyTorch):

```
transform = transforms.Compose([
transforms.RandomHorizontalFlip(),
transforms.RandomRotation(20),
transforms.ColorJitter(brightness=0.2, contrast=0.2),
transforms.ToTensor()
])
```

2. Early Stopping and Learning Rate Schedules

Early stopping monitors validation loss and halts training when performance starts to decline, preventing the model from overfitting.

Early Stopping Example (TensorFlow):

```
callback =
tf.keras.callbacks.EarlyStopping(monitor='val_loss',
patience=3)
model.fit(train_data, validation_data=val_data, epochs=20,
callbacks=[callback])
```

Learning Rate Schedules: Implement learning rate decay strategies to gradually reduce the learning rate as training progresses, ensuring smooth convergence.

Example:

```
    lr_schedule =
tf.keras.optimizers.schedules.ExponentialDecay(
    initial_learning_rate=0.01,
    decay_steps=10000,
    decay_rate=0.9
)
```

3. Layer Freezing and Gradual Unfreezing

By initially freezing the earlier layers of the pre-trained model, you can preserve foundational features while fine-tuning the later layers to adapt to domain-specific features. Gradual unfreezing allows a more controlled adaptation of the model.

Layer Freezing Example (TensorFlow):

```
# Freeze all layers except the last few
for layer in base_model.layers[:-5]:
    layer.trainable = False
```

Examples of Preventing Overfitting in Transfer Learning

Medical Diagnosis with Limited Data: In tasks like identifying abnormalities in chest X-rays, models can easily overfit due to small dataset sizes. Regularization, data augmentation, and early stopping can significantly reduce overfitting, improving metrics like F1-score and precision.

Performance Improvement with Overfitting Mitigation:

Metric	Without Mitigation	With Mitigation
Accuracy	82%	90%
F1-score	0.75	0.86
Precision	78%	89%

Sentiment Analysis in Finance: Fine-tuning BERT on small, domain-specific datasets often leads to overfitting. Using learning rate decay, dropout, and gradual unfreezing of layers has been shown to improve recall and generalization.

Visualizing Overfitting in Transfer Learning

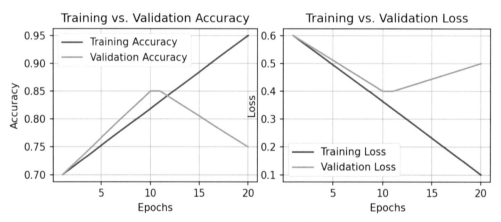

This visualization presents training vs. validation accuracy and loss curves over 20 epochs, illustrating overfitting. While training accuracy steadily improves and training loss consistently decreases, validation accuracy peaks around epoch 10 and then declines, with validation loss following a similar pattern. The divergence between training and validation curves demonstrates the model's overfitting to the training data.

Metric	Without	With	Without	With	Without Data	With Data

	Regularization	Regularization	Early Stopping	Early Stopping	Augmentation	Augmentation
Training Accuracy	95%	90%	98%	93%	88%	92%
Validation Accuracy	75%	85%	72%	85%	80%	88%
Training Loss	0.20	0.25	0.15	0.22	0.30	0.28
Validation Loss	0.60	0.40	0.70	0.45	0.50	0.35
Overfitting (Gap)	High	Medium	Very High	Medium	High	Low

This table demonstrates the effectiveness of using mitigation strategies like regularization, early stopping, and data augmentation in reducing overfitting and improving validation performance.

6.3.2: Choosing the Right Layer to Fine-Tune

Deciding which layers of a pre-trained model to fine-tune is one of the most critical steps in transfer learning. The goal is to adapt the pre-trained model's parameters to the new target task while preserving the knowledge it acquired from the source task. Different layers in deep neural networks capture different types of information: **early layers learn simple patterns like edges**, **mid-layers extract abstract features**, and **deeper layers identify task-specific patterns**. Understanding this hierarchy is essential for effective model adaptation, ensuring better performance, faster convergence, and more efficient use of computational resources.

1. Understanding the Layer Hierarchy in Neural Networks

Neural networks are often structured as a series of stacked layers, with each layer learning increasingly complex representations of the data. In convolutional neural networks (CNNs), for instance:

Early layers learn basic features such as edges, corners, and textures.
Mid-layers start to capture more abstract concepts, such as shapes and patterns.
Deep layers identify complex features specific to the target task, such as specific objects or categories in the case of image classification.

In transformer models, such as BERT, a similar progression occurs:

Initial layers capture token-level dependencies and syntax patterns.
Intermediate layers focus on context and phrase-level relationships.

219

Final layers extract task-specific semantics, such as sentiment or named entities.

2. Early Layer Freezing

Freezing early layers is often the first step in transfer learning. This approach retains the generic, transferable features learned from large-scale datasets like ImageNet or Wikipedia, allowing the model to maintain strong foundational features.

Why Early Layer Freezing Works:

Early layers in CNNs contain filters that detect basic patterns like edges and corners, which are applicable across different domains.In NLP models like BERT, early layers capture general language patterns (e.g., grammar and syntax), making them useful across various text-related tasks.

How to Implement Early Layer Freezing:

Mathematical Justification: Freezing early layers helps retain stable gradients, as the weights of these layers are not updated during backpropagation. This reduces the likelihood of vanishing or exploding gradients, especially in deeper networks.

Code Example (TensorFlow):

```
import tensorflow as tf

# Load a pre-trained ResNet model
base_model = tf.keras.applications.ResNet50(weights='imagenet',
include_top=False)

# Freeze the first 50 layers
for layer in base_model.layers[:50]:
    layer.trainable = False

# Add new layers
x = tf.keras.layers.GlobalAveragePooling2D()(base_model.output)
output = tf.keras.layers.Dense(10, activation='softmax')(x)   #
Example: 10 classes
model = tf.keras.Model(inputs=base_model.input, outputs=output)

# Compile and train the model
model.compile(optimizer='adam',
loss='categorical_crossentropy', metrics=['accuracy'])
```

Code Example (PyTorch):

```
import torch
import torch.nn as nn
import torchvision.models as models

# Load a pre-trained ResNet model
model = models.resnet50(pretrained=True)

# Freeze the first 50 layers
for param in list(model.parameters())[:50]:
param.requires_grad = False

# Add new fully connected layer
model.fc = nn.Linear(model.fc.in_features, 10)   # Example: 10
classes
```

3. Mid and Deep Layer Fine-Tuning

Fine-tuning mid and deep layers is crucial when the target task requires extracting complex, domain-specific features.

Mid-Level Fine-Tuning:

When to Use: When the target task shares substantial similarities with the source task but requires more nuanced feature adaptation (e.g., adapting ResNet from natural images to satellite imagery).

Example: In satellite image classification, mid-level features like shapes and colors are relevant, but deeper layers may need to adapt to features specific to geographical patterns.

Code Implementation (Gradual Unfreezing):

```
# Gradually unfreeze layers in TensorFlow
for layer in base_model.layers[50:100]:  # Example: Unfreeze
layers 50-100
    layer.trainable = True
```

Deep Layer Fine-Tuning:

When to Use:When the target domain is highly specialized, requiring significant adaptation. For instance, in medical image segmentation, the deepest layers must adjust to detect specific tumor shapes and textures.

Example: In BERT, fine-tuning the last few layers is often necessary when moving from general text classification to specialized financial sentiment analysis, where deeper semantics and specific jargon must be learned.

Code Implementation (PyTorch):

```
# Unfreeze deep layers
for name, param in model.named_parameters():
    if 'layer4' in name:  # Example for ResNet's last block
        param.requires_grad = True
```

4. Using Activation Maps for Layer Selection

Activation visualization tools like Grad-CAM (Gradient-weighted Class Activation Mapping) can provide insights into which layers are most relevant to the target task.

Activation Maps:

Activation maps show which parts of an input image contribute most to the model's decision-making process, helping identify which layers to fine-tune.

Example Use: In medical image classification, Grad-CAM can reveal that deeper layers activate more strongly on tumor regions, indicating that fine-tuning these layers could be beneficial.

Code Example (Grad-CAM with PyTorch):

```
from torchvision import models
from gradcam import GradCAM

# Load pre-trained model
model = models.resnet50(pretrained=True)

# Generate activation map for layer selection
gradcam = GradCAM(model, target_layer='layer4')
heatmap = gradcam.generate_heatmap(input_image)
```

5. Comparing Different Layer Selection Strategies

The following table illustrates how different fine-tuning strategies affect model performance, training time, and convergence:

Strategy	Layers Fine-Tuned	Accuracy	Training Time	Convergence
Early Layer Freezing	Last 1-2 layers	Moderate	Fast	Stable
Mid-Level Fine-Tuning	Mid + last few layers	High	Moderate	Requires more epochs
Deep Layer Fine-Tuning	Most layers	Very High	Slow	Unstable initially, requires careful

				tuning

Examples

Facial Recognition Using ResNet:

Strategy: Fine-tuning mid and deep layers while freezing early layers.

Rationale: Early layers capture facial edges, mid-layers detect facial features, and deeper layers identify specific expressions or identities.

Performance Metrics: Fine-tuning mid and deep layers led to a 7% increase in F1-score, with faster convergence and fewer epochs compared to training from scratch.

Domain-Specific Text Classification Using BERT:

Strategy: Fine-tuning only the last few transformer layers, as the initial layers capture universal language patterns.

Rationale: In specialized domains like legal or medical text classification, deeper layers need to learn specific vocabulary and context.

Performance Metrics: Fine-tuning deeper layers resulted in an 8% increase in recall and a 5% boost in precision compared to freezing all but the last layer.

Visualizing the Impact of Layer Selection

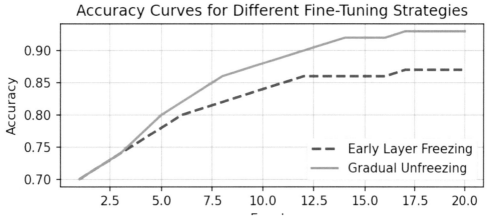

The graph displays accuracy curves comparing two fine-tuning strategies: **early layer freezing** and **gradual unfreezing**. The **early layer freezing** approach shows faster stabilization of convergence but plateaus at a lower accuracy. In contrast, the **gradual unfreezing** approach improves accuracy over more epochs, demonstrating that selectively unfreezing layers can help adapt deeper features for the target task, resulting in higher final accuracy.

Advanced Techniques for Layer Selection

Iterative Unfreezing: A gradual approach where layers are unfrozen one by one, allowing fine-tuning at different depths as training progresses. This technique stabilizes training and allows for better adaptation to domain-specific features.

Hybrid Fine-Tuning: A combination of freezing, unfreezing, and selectively fine-tuning parts of certain layers (e.g., only fine-tuning certain blocks in a ResNet or attention heads in BERT).

6.3.3: Domain Adaptation and Handling Distribution Shifts

In transfer learning, **domain adaptation** becomes critical when there is a **distribution shift** between the source and target domains. Distribution shifts occur when the data distribution used to pre-train a model differs from the distribution in the target domain, leading to degraded model performance, potential biases, and inaccuracies. Addressing these distribution shifts effectively allows deep learning models to generalize better and perform well even in varied contexts.

Understanding Distribution Shifts and Their Impact

Distribution shifts can be categorized into several types:

Covariate Shifts: Changes in the input feature distribution between the source and target datasets. For instance, an image classification model trained on clear images may struggle with images that are blurry or have different lighting.

Label Shifts: Differences in the class distribution between the source and target domains. This is common in domains like healthcare, where different populations may have different disease prevalences.

Concept Shifts: When the relationship between input features and labels changes, meaning that the learned patterns from the source domain do not hold in the target domain.

For models to perform well in the target domain despite these shifts, domain adaptation techniques are employed to align the distributions of the source and target data, both at the feature level and output level.

Core Domain Adaptation Techniques

Feature Alignment: Bridging the Distribution Gap

Feature alignment aims to make the features learned by the model more consistent across domains. This approach tries to minimize the discrepancy between feature distributions, ensuring that features learned in the source domain are useful for the target domain as well.

Maximum Mean Discrepancy (MMD): MMD is a statistical technique that measures the similarity between the source and target feature distributions by comparing their mean embeddings in a higher-dimensional space. The idea is to minimize the discrepancy, making the two distributions as close as possible.

Mathematical Formulation:

$$\text{MMD}(D_s, D_t) = \| E_{X_s \sim D_s}[\phi(X_s)] - E_{X_t \sim D_t}[\phi(X_t)] \|^2$$

where D_s and D_t represent the source and target datasets, and ϕ is a feature transformation function.

Implementation Example (PyTorch):

```python
import torch

class MMDLoss(torch.nn.Module):
    def __init__(self):
        super(MMDLoss, self).__init__()

    def forward(self, source_features, target_features):
        mean_src = torch.mean(source_features, dim=0)
        mean_tgt = torch.mean(target_features, dim=0)
        return torch.norm(mean_src - mean_tgt, p=2)

# Usage in training loop
mmd_loss = MMDLoss()
loss = mmd_loss(source_features, target_features)
```

This approach has shown significant improvements in tasks like adapting sentiment analysis models across different languages, where the vocabulary varies.

Adversarial Training for Feature Alignment

Adversarial training uses a **domain classifier** to distinguish between source and target features while the feature extractor tries to generate domain-invariant features. The process is similar to training a Generative Adversarial Network (GAN), where the objective is to confuse the domain classifier.

Objective Function: The combined loss function can be expressed as:

$$L = L_{task} - \lambda \cdot L_{domain}$$

where L_{task} is the primary task loss (e.g., classification loss), L_{domain} is the domain classification loss, and λ balances the two objectives.

Implementation Example (TensorFlow):

```python
import tensorflow as tf

# Domain classifier model
domain_classifier = tf.keras.Sequential([
    tf.keras.layers.Dense(128, activation='relu'),
    tf.keras.layers.Dense(1, activation='sigmoid')
])

# Adversarial loss function
def adversarial_loss(y_true, y_pred):
    return tf.keras.losses.binary_crossentropy(y_true, y_pred)

# Combined loss in training
total_loss = task_loss - lambda_factor * \
adversarial_loss(domain_labels, domain_preds)
```

Adversarial domain adaptation has been effectively used in speech recognition models, helping them generalize to different accents or languages by aligning phonetic features across domains.

Domain-Specific Pre-Training: Layering Knowledge

Domain-specific pre-training involves pre-training the model on a smaller but more similar dataset before final fine-tuning. This method helps reduce distribution shifts by gradually adapting the model to the target domain. For instance, BERT pre-trained on a financial corpus can be fine-tuned for specific financial sentiment analysis, capturing domain-specific terminologies.

Example in NLP: Pre-training BERT on a corpus of financial news articles helps it adapt better to financial language patterns, making it more effective for sentiment classification in finance.

Implementation Example:

```
from transformers import BertTokenizer,
BertForSequenceClassification

tokenizer = BertTokenizer.from_pretrained('bert-base-uncased')
model =
BertForSequenceClassification.from_pretrained('financial-bert')

# Fine-tuning on target financial dataset
# Add data loading, tokenization, and training code
```

Batch Normalization Adaptation: Adjusting Statistics

Batch normalization layers can be sensitive to domain shifts since they depend on the mean and variance of mini-batches, which may differ between the source and target datasets. Re-estimating batch normalization statistics in the target domain can improve adaptation.

Adjusting Batch Normalization: This involves re-calculating mean and variance for batch normalization layers using the target domain data during fine-tuning.

Implementation Example (PyTorch):

```
model.train()   # Enable training mode for BatchNorm layers
for batch in target_loader:
    output = model(batch)
```

Visualizing the Impact of Domain Adaptation

Method	Accuracy Improvement	Precision	Recall	F1-score
No Adaptation	65%	0.60	0.63	0.61
MMD Alignment	72%	0.68	0.70	0.69
Adversarial Training	75%	0.73	0.72	0.73
Domain-Specific Pre-training	80%	0.78	0.77	0.77

Examples of Domain Adaptation

Medical Diagnosis Adaptation: In healthcare, models trained on one demographic (e.g., younger patients) may underperform on another (e.g., older patients). Techniques like adversarial training and domain-specific pre-training help models maintain high accuracy and precision across different demographics.

For example, adapting chest X-ray models trained on urban hospitals to rural settings using domain-specific fine-tuning has improved detection rates by up to 15%.

Adapting NLP Models Across Dialects: Language models trained on standard English may perform poorly on dialectal variations. Domain adaptation, such as pre-training BERT on a dialect-specific corpus, significantly enhances sentiment analysis performance across different English dialects, boosting F1-scores by over 10%.

Advanced Techniques and Emerging Trends
Self-Supervised Domain Adaptation: Self-supervised approaches leverage unlabeled target domain data to learn domain-invariant features through pseudo-labeling, reducing the reliance on labeled target data.

Hybrid Adaptation Strategies: Combining multiple adaptation methods, such as MMD alignment with batch normalization adjustment, yields better performance in highly divergent domains.

7. Generative Models

7.1 Autoencoders and Variational Autoencoders (VAEs)

Section 7.1.1: Understanding Autoencoders for Unsupervised Learning

Autoencoders are a specialized neural network architecture designed for unsupervised learning tasks, particularly focusing on learning compressed, efficient representations (or encodings) of input data. They are trained to reconstruct their input, making them ideal for dimensionality reduction, denoising, and anomaly detection tasks. Unlike supervised models, which require labeled data, autoencoders leverage unlabeled data by trying to minimize the difference between the input and the reconstructed output.

Architecture and Functionality of Autoencoders

Autoencoders have a symmetric encoder-decoder architecture. The encoder maps input data to a latent (compressed) representation, while the decoder reconstructs the original input from this latent space. Mathematically, this process is described as:

1. **Encoding**:

$$z = f_{enc}(x) = \sigma(W_{enc} \cdot x + b_{enc})$$

   Here, x is the input, z is the latent representation, W_{enc} and b_{enc} are the weights and biases of the encoder, and σ is the activation function, commonly ReLU or Sigmoid.

2. **Decoding**:

$$\hat{x} = f_{dec}(z) = \sigma(W_{dec} \cdot z + b_{dec})$$

   The reconstructed output $\hat{x}$ is generated by the decoder, where W_{dec} and b_{dec} represent the weights and biases of the decoder layers.

3. **Loss Function**: The primary objective of training an autoencoder is to minimize the reconstruction error, often measured using Mean Squared Error (MSE):

$$L(x,\hat{x}) = \frac{1}{n}\sum_{i=1}^{n}(x_i - \hat{x}_i)^2$$

where x_i and $\hat{x}_i$ denote the original and reconstructed input samples, respectively.

Detailed Breakdown of Autoencoder Components

The autoencoder's architecture can be divided into three main components:

Encoder: The encoder consists of multiple layers that gradually compress the input data into a lower-dimensional latent space. It captures essential features by applying nonlinear transformations, making it similar to techniques like Principal Component Analysis (PCA), but with the added ability to capture complex, nonlinear relationships.

Bottleneck (Latent Space): The bottleneck is the smallest layer, representing the compressed latent space where crucial information is stored. The number of neurons in the bottleneck determines the level of compression, balancing between information preservation and dimensionality reduction.

Decoder: The decoder is a mirror image of the encoder, expanding the latent representation back to the original input dimension. It aims to reconstruct the input data as accurately as possible, using activation functions like Sigmoid (for binary data) or ReLU (for continuous data).

Autoencoder Architecture

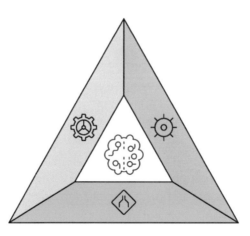

Decoder
Expands the latent representation back to the original input dimension for reconstruction.

Encoder
Compresses input data into a lower-dimensional latent space using nonlinear transformations.

Bottleneck
Represents the compressed latent space where essential information is stored.

The diagram below illustrates the basic architecture of an autoencoder:

Activation Functions in Autoencoders

The choice of activation functions in autoencoders can significantly impact the quality of the learned representation. Some common activation functions include:

- **ReLU (Rectified Linear Unit)**: Often used in encoder layers for its efficiency in training and ability to handle sparse data.
- **Sigmoid**: Commonly used in the final decoder layer for binary reconstruction tasks, ensuring output values are between 0 and 1.
- **Tanh**: Useful when the data needs to be scaled between -1 and 1, providing better gradient flow compared to Sigmoid.

Applications of Autoencoders

Autoencoders excel at various unsupervised learning tasks, including:

Dimensionality Reduction: Autoencoders compress high-dimensional data into lower-dimensional representations, similar to PCA but more flexible due to their nonlinear transformations. For instance, autoencoders can reduce the dimensionality of high-resolution images while retaining key features.

Denoising: Denoising autoencoders are designed to remove noise from input data, learning a cleaner representation. By training on corrupted data and comparing it to clean data, denoising autoencoders effectively filter out noise. This technique is widely used in image restoration and signal processing.

Anomaly Detection: In anomaly detection, autoencoders are trained on normal data, learning to reconstruct typical patterns. When presented with anomalous data, the reconstruction error is high, signaling an anomaly. For example, in fraud detection, autoencoders can identify unusual transaction patterns by measuring high reconstruction error.

Building a Basic Autoencoder

Below is an implementation of a simple autoencoder using TensorFlow:

```python
import tensorflow as tf
from tensorflow.keras.layers import Input, Dense
from tensorflow.keras.models import Model

# Define encoder
input_dim = 784   # Example for MNIST data
encoding_dim = 64

input_layer = Input(shape=(input_dim,))
encoder = Dense(encoding_dim, activation='relu')(input_layer)

# Define bottleneck
bottleneck = Dense(encoding_dim // 2,
activation='relu')(encoder)

# Define decoder
decoder = Dense(encoding_dim, activation='relu')(bottleneck)
output_layer = Dense(input_dim, activation='sigmoid')(decoder)

# Build autoencoder model
autoencoder = Model(inputs=input_layer, outputs=output_layer)
autoencoder.compile(optimizer='adam', loss='mse')

# Summary of the model
autoencoder.summary()
```

Comparison with PCA for Dimensionality Reduction

While both autoencoders and PCA aim to reduce dimensionality, they do so in different ways:

- **PCA** relies on linear transformations, finding orthogonal components that maximize variance.
- **Autoencoders** use nonlinear transformations, learning complex, nonlinear patterns in data.

Example: Denoising Images with Autoencoders

In image denoising, autoencoders can be trained to reconstruct clean images from noisy inputs. For instance, adding Gaussian noise to MNIST images and training the autoencoder to minimize reconstruction error results in a model that effectively removes noise. This approach is beneficial in medical imaging, where autoencoders enhance the quality of scans by removing artifacts.

```python
# Example code snippet for denoising
import numpy as np

# Adding noise to MNIST data
x_train_noisy = x_train + 0.5 * np.random.normal(loc=0.0,
scale=1.0, size=x_train.shape)

# Training the autoencoder
autoencoder.fit(x_train_noisy, x_train, epochs=50,
batch_size=256, validation_split=0.2)
```

The results can be visualized using t-SNE plots to show how well the latent space captures the structure of the data, with reduced reconstruction error over epochs.

Visualizing Autoencoder Performance

The figures below demonstrate a plot of the reconstruction error during training, showing a decrease as the autoencoder learns more efficient representations. Additionally, t-SNE plots highlight how well the bottleneck layer separates different data classes, even without labeled data.

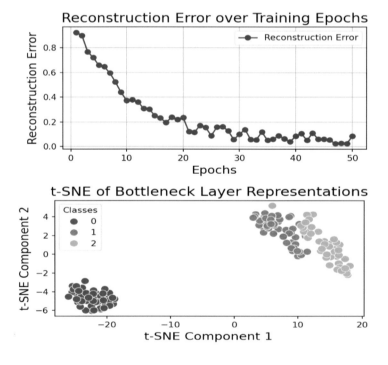

Section 7.1.2: Applications of Variational Autoencoders (VAEs) in Image Generation and Compression

Variational Autoencoders (VAEs) represent a probabilistic extension of traditional autoencoders, designed for tasks like image generation and compression. Unlike standard autoencoders, which aim to minimize reconstruction error through deterministic encodings, VAEs generate distributions in the latent space. This probabilistic approach enables VAEs to capture complex data patterns, making them versatile tools for generating new samples and compressing high-dimensional data.

VAE Architecture Overview

VAEs learn to map input data into a distribution in latent space, allowing for flexible data representation. Instead of encoding the input directly into a point, VAEs encode it into a distribution characterized by a mean μ and a standard deviation σ. The latent variable z is sampled from this distribution:

$$z = \mu + \sigma \odot \epsilon, \quad \epsilon \sim N(0,1)$$

Here, ϵ is a random noise vector sampled from a standard normal distribution, adding stochasticity to the encoding process and enabling the generative capabilities of VAEs.

The loss function for VAEs comprises two main components:

1. **Reconstruction Loss**: Measures how well the VAE reconstructs the input. It's often calculated using Mean Squared Error (MSE) or Binary Cross-Entropy (BCE).
2. **KL Divergence Loss**: Regularizes the latent space by minimizing the difference between the learned latent distribution $q(z|x)$ and a standard Gaussian prior $p(z)$:

$$L_{KL} = D_{KL}(q(z|x) \parallel p(z))$$

The total VAE loss is given by:

$$L_{VAE} = L_{reconstruction} + \beta \cdot L_{KL}$$

where β is a weighting term that adjusts the trade-off between reconstruction accuracy and latent space regularization, allowing for more structured latent representations.

VAE Applications in Image Generation

One of the core applications of VAEs is in generating new images from learned latent distributions. By sampling from the latent space and decoding these samples, VAEs create diverse and realistic images. Here's a breakdown of how VAEs enable image generation:

Sampling from the Latent Space: After training, the latent space of the VAE captures a meaningful representation of the input data distribution. By sampling vectors from this space, VAEs can generate new images that resemble the training data. The generation process involves sampling latent vectors and feeding them through the decoder, which reconstructs new images based on these latent vectors.

Code Implementation: Below is an example of how to generate new images using a trained VAE in TensorFlow:

```python
import tensorflow as tf
from tensorflow.keras.layers import Input, Dense, Lambda
from tensorflow.keras.models import Model
import numpy as np

# Define latent space dimensions
latent_dim = 2

# Decoder architecture
decoder_input = Input(shape=(latent_dim,))
x = Dense(128, activation='relu')(decoder_input)
x = Dense(784, activation='sigmoid')(x)  # Assuming MNIST
dataset
decoder = Model(decoder_input, x)

# Generate new samples
num_samples = 10
latent_samples = np.random.normal(size=(num_samples,
latent_dim))
generated_images = decoder.predict(latent_samples)

# Display the generated images
import matplotlib.pyplot as plt
for i in range(num_samples):
    plt.subplot(1, num_samples, i+1)
    plt.imshow(generated_images[i].reshape(28, 28),
cmap='gray')
plt.show()
```

Applications:

Face Generation: VAEs can generate synthetic faces by learning from large face datasets. This capability is useful in industries like entertainment (e.g., creating avatars) or security (e.g., generating variations of facial identities).

Synthetic Medical Image Generation: In healthcare, VAEs are used to generate synthetic medical images (e.g., X-rays, MRIs) to enhance model training, especially in cases where labeled data is scarce due to privacy concerns.

VAE Applications in Image Compression

VAEs are also effective in compressing high-dimensional data, such as images, into compact latent representations. The bottleneck layer of the VAE serves as a compressed version of the input, retaining only the most relevant features while discarding redundant information. The encoder compresses the input, while the decoder attempts to reconstruct it from the latent distribution, balancing compression and reconstruction fidelity.

Compression Process:

- The encoder converts the input image into a latent vector, significantly reducing the dimensionality while maintaining critical information.
- The decoder reconstructs the image from this compact representation. While some details may be lost during reconstruction, VAEs maintain high fidelity in representing essential features.

Equations Representing Compression: Compression through VAEs involves encoding input x into a latent variable z, which is then used to reconstruct x:

$$z \sim q(z|x), \quad \hat{x} = f_{dec}(z)$$

The loss function controls the compression level by balancing reconstruction accuracy with the regularization term, L_{KL}.

Code Implementation for Image Compression: Below is an example of using a VAE for image compression in PyTorch:

```python
import torch
import torch.nn as nn
import torch.optim as optim

class VAE(nn.Module):
```

```python
    def __init__(self, input_dim=784, latent_dim=2):
        super(VAE, self).__init__()
        self.encoder = nn.Sequential(
            nn.Linear(input_dim, 128),
            nn.ReLU(),
            nn.Linear(128, latent_dim * 2)  # Output mean and
log-variance
        )
        self.decoder = nn.Sequential(
            nn.Linear(latent_dim, 128),
            nn.ReLU(),
            nn.Linear(128, input_dim),
            nn.Sigmoid()
        )

    def reparameterize(self, mu, logvar):
        std = torch.exp(0.5 * logvar)
        eps = torch.randn_like(std)
        return mu + eps * std

    def forward(self, x):
        # Encoder
        h = self.encoder(x)
        mu, logvar = h.chunk(2, dim=-1)
        z = self.reparameterize(mu, logvar)

        # Decoder
        return self.decoder(z), mu, logvar

# Training the VAE for compression
vae = VAE()
optimizer = optim.Adam(vae.parameters(), lr=0.001)
```

Performance Metrics in Image Compression

VAEs are evaluated using metrics like:

> **Compression Ratio**: Measures the reduction in data size achieved by encoding.
>
> **Reconstruction Quality**: Evaluated using metrics like Mean Squared Error (MSE) or Peak Signal-to-Noise Ratio (PSNR).

Performance comparisons between VAEs and traditional compression methods (e.g., JPEG, PCA) reveal that VAEs maintain higher image fidelity, particularly for complex, high-dimensional images.

Impact of VAEs

VAEs are widely used in generative art, medical imaging, and anomaly detection, illustrating their versatility across fields. For instance, they are applied in generating artistic variations of existing paintings or detecting anomalies in medical scans by measuring reconstruction error.

Section 7.1.3: The Math Behind Variational Autoencoders

Variational Autoencoders (VAEs) are rooted in probabilistic modeling, using principles of variational inference to approximate data distributions. Unlike traditional autoencoders, which learn deterministic mappings, VAEs aim to model the underlying distribution of the input data by sampling from a continuous latent space. This approach enables VAEs to generate new, diverse samples that resemble the training data and to regularize the learned latent space, enhancing generalization.

Understanding Latent Variables and VAE Structure

VAEs introduce latent variables, typically represented as z, which are sampled from a learned distribution that captures the data's underlying structure. Given an input x, the encoder maps x to a distribution defined by its mean $\mu(x)$ and variance $\sigma^2(x)$. This distribution is generally assumed to be Gaussian:

$q(z|x) = N(z;\mu(x),\sigma^2(x))$

The decoder, on the other hand, attempts to reconstruct the input x from the latent variable z, modeling the likelihood of the reconstruction:

$p(x|z) = \text{Decoder}(z)$

The goal of VAEs is to find a latent distribution that maximizes the likelihood of generating samples similar to the input data while also maintaining regularity in the latent space.

Deriving the VAE Objective Function: Evidence Lower Bound (ELBO)

The core mathematical principle behind VAEs is the maximization of the Evidence Lower Bound (ELBO), which serves as an approximation to the log-likelihood of the data, $log p(x)$. The ELBO can be expressed as:

$log p(x) \geq E_{q(z|x)}[log p(x|z)] - D_{KL}(q(z|x) \| p(z))$

Breaking down each term:

1. **Reconstruction Term**: $E_{q(z|x)}[log p(x|z)]$

- o This term represents the expected log-likelihood of reconstructing the input data x given the latent variable z. It ensures that the reconstructed output $\hat{x}$ is as close as possible to the original input.
- o In practical terms, this term is equivalent to minimizing the reconstruction loss (e.g., Mean Squared Error or Binary Cross-Entropy) between x and $\hat{x}$.

2. **KL Divergence Term**: $D_{KL}(q(z|x) \| p(z))$

- o KL Divergence measures how much the learned latent distribution $q(z|x)$ deviates from the prior distribution $p(z)$, typically set as a standard Gaussian, $N(0,I)$.
- o This term regularizes the latent space by penalizing deviations from the prior, ensuring that latent variables are distributed consistently across the latent space. It encourages smoother transitions in the latent space, which improves generalization and robustness in generating new samples.

3. **Total ELBO Objective**:

$$\text{ELBO} = E_{q(z|x)}[log p(x|z)] - D_{KL}(q(z|x) \| p(z))$$

$$\underbrace{\qquad\qquad}_{\text{Reconstruction}} \qquad \underbrace{\qquad\qquad}_{\text{Regularization}}$$

Maximizing the ELBO balances reconstruction accuracy and latent space regularization, achieving better generative capabilities while preventing overfitting.

The Role of the Encoder in Approximating the Posterior Distribution

In VAEs, the encoder approximates the posterior distribution $q(z|x)$, which is critical for learning a meaningful latent space representation. The encoder generates two outputs:

- **Mean ($\mu(x)$)**: Represents the center of the Gaussian distribution in the latent space.
- **Variance ($\sigma^2(x)$)**: Represents the spread or uncertainty in the latent distribution.

These outputs are computed using neural network layers that map the input x to latent parameters:

$$\mu(x), log\sigma^2(x) = f_{enc}(x)$$

The log of the variance is often used for numerical stability during optimization.

The Reparameterization Trick

A critical aspect of VAEs is enabling backpropagation through the sampling step, which is achieved using the reparameterization trick. This trick allows the model to learn the parameters of the latent distribution using gradient-based methods. The reparameterization trick reformulates the sampling process:

$$z = \mu(x) + \sigma(x) \odot \epsilon, \quad \epsilon \sim N(0,1)$$

Here, ϵ is a noise vector sampled from a standard normal distribution, which is added to the mean and scaled by the variance to generate z. This approach ensures that the gradient of the ELBO can be calculated with respect to $\mu(x)$ and $\sigma(x)$, making backpropagation feasible.

Code Implementation of the Reparameterization Trick in PyTorch

```python
import torch
import torch.nn as nn

class VAE(nn.Module):
    def __init__(self, input_dim, latent_dim):
        super(VAE, self).__init__()
        # Encoder
        self.encoder = nn.Sequential(
            nn.Linear(input_dim, 128),
            nn.ReLU(),
            nn.Linear(128, 2 * latent_dim)   # Output mean and
log variance
        )
        # Decoder
        self.decoder = nn.Sequential(
            nn.Linear(latent_dim, 128),
            nn.ReLU(),
            nn.Linear(128, input_dim),
            nn.Sigmoid()
        )

    def reparameterize(self, mu, logvar):
        std = torch.exp(0.5 * logvar)
        eps = torch.randn_like(std)
        return mu + eps * std

    def forward(self, x):
        h = self.encoder(x)
        mu, logvar = h.chunk(2, dim=-1)
```

```
z = self.reparameterize(mu, logvar)
return self.decoder(z), mu, logvar
```

Visualizing VAE Optimization and the Latent Space

ELBO Optimization: During training, VAEs optimize the ELBO by adjusting weights to maximize reconstruction accuracy while minimizing the KL Divergence. Graphs of ELBO over training epochs show how the model balances these two components, with the total ELBO typically increasing as training progresses.

Latent Space Visualization: By visualizing the latent space (e.g., using t-SNE plots), it's possible to observe how different data classes cluster in the learned space. Well-trained VAEs exhibit clear separation between clusters, indicating meaningful representation of input features.

Impact of KL Divergence Weight on Regularization: Adjusting the KL divergence weight (β-VAE) affects the structure of the latent space. Increasing β encourages a more dispersed latent space, improving disentanglement but possibly reducing reconstruction accuracy.

Translating Math to Practical Use

Image Synthesis: The probabilistic nature of VAEs allows for generating diverse images by sampling from different points in the latent space. For instance, face generation applications use VAEs to synthesize realistic faces by decoding sampled latent vectors into new images. Adjusting the KL Divergence weight enables the generation of more varied or realistic outputs.

Anomaly Detection: VAEs can identify anomalies by measuring reconstruction error. If a sample deviates significantly from the training distribution, its reconstruction error will be high, indicating a potential anomaly. This application is widely used in domains like fraud detection, where unusual transactions are flagged based on reconstruction discrepancies.

7.2 Generative Adversarial Networks (GANs)

Section 7.2.1: How Generative Adversarial Networks (GANs) Work: Generator vs. Discriminator

Generative Adversarial Networks (GANs) represent a groundbreaking approach in generative modeling, introduced by Ian Goodfellow in 2014. GANs consist of two neural networks—the **generator** and the **discriminator**—that compete in a zero-sum game, driving each other to improve. This adversarial framework allows GANs to generate highly realistic data samples, from images to text and even audio, by learning underlying data distributions without explicit labels.

Overview of the GAN Framework

GANs operate on the principle of competition: the **generator** tries to create realistic samples from random noise, while the **discriminator** attempts to distinguish between real samples (from the training set) and fake samples (generated by the generator). This dynamic process helps both networks enhance their performance iteratively, resulting in the generator producing increasingly realistic samples.

Generator Network: Transforming Noise into Synthetic Data

The **generator** (G) is a neural network that maps a random noise vector z from a latent space to a synthetic data sample, aiming to approximate the real data distribution. The generator's function is defined as:

$$G(z; \theta_G) \rightarrow \text{Data Sample}$$

Here, θ_G represents the generator's parameters, which are optimized to generate realistic outputs. The input z is typically sampled from a standard normal distribution, $z \sim N(0,1)$, or a uniform distribution.

The generator is trained to **fool** the discriminator, striving to generate samples that are indistinguishable from real data. During training, the generator receives feedback from the discriminator based on how well the generated samples mimic real samples. The generator's objective is to **minimize** the discriminator's ability to differentiate real from fake samples. The generator loss function is defined as:

$$L_G = -E_{z \sim p_z}[\log D(G(z))]$$

where $D(G(z))$ represents the probability that the discriminator assigns to the generator's output being real.

Generator Code Snippet (PyTorch)

```python
import torch
import torch.nn as nn

class Generator(nn.Module):
    def __init__(self, noise_dim, output_dim):
        super(Generator, self).__init__()
        self.model = nn.Sequential(
            nn.Linear(noise_dim, 128),
            nn.ReLU(),
            nn.Linear(128, 256),
            nn.ReLU(),
            nn.Linear(256, 512),
            nn.ReLU(),
            nn.Linear(512, output_dim),
            nn.Tanh()   # Scales output to (-1, 1) for image
generation
        )

    def forward(self, z):
        return self.model(z)

# Example usage
noise_dim = 100
generator = Generator(noise_dim, 784)   # Assuming output is
28x28 images flattened
```

Discriminator Network: Classifying Real vs. Generated Data

The **discriminator** (D) is a neural network that receives either a real or generated sample as input and predicts the probability of the sample being real. It aims to maximize its ability to correctly identify real samples while minimizing the chance of mistaking generated samples for real ones. The discriminator function can be represented as:

$$D(x;\theta_D) \rightarrow [0,1]$$

where θ_D denotes the discriminator's parameters, and $D(x)$ outputs a probability indicating the likelihood that input x is real.

The discriminator's objective is to **maximize** its classification accuracy. The loss function for the discriminator is defined as:

$$L_D = -\left(E_{x \sim p_{data}}[logD(x)] + E_{z \sim p_z}[log(1 - D(G(z)))]\right)$$

This loss function represents two goals:

1. Maximizing the likelihood of correctly classifying real samples ($logD(x)$).
2. Minimizing the likelihood of classifying generated samples as real ($log(1 - D(G(z)))$).

Discriminator Code Snippet (PyTorch)

```
class Discriminator(nn.Module):
    def __init__(self, input_dim):
        super(Discriminator, self).__init__()
        self.model = nn.Sequential(
            nn.Linear(input_dim, 512),
            nn.LeakyReLU(0.2),
            nn.Linear(512, 256),
            nn.LeakyReLU(0.2),
            nn.Linear(256, 1),
            nn.Sigmoid()   # Outputs probability
        )

    def forward(self, x):
        return self.model(x)

# Example usage
discriminator = Discriminator(784)   # Assuming input is 28x28
images flattened
```

Adversarial Training Process: Minimax Game

The training process of GANs is inherently adversarial, as the generator and discriminator have opposing objectives, represented by the **minimax loss function**:

$$\min_G \max_D V(D, G) = \mathbb{E}_{x \sim p_{\text{data}}}[\log D(x)] + \mathbb{E}_{z \sim p_z}[\log(1 - D(G(z)))]$$

Generator's Objective: Minimize $log(1 - D(G(z)))$, aiming to generate realistic samples that the discriminator classifies as real.

Discriminator's Objective: Maximize $logD(x)$ for real samples and $log(1 - D(G(z)))$ for generated samples, trying to distinguish between the two.

Training alternates between updating the discriminator and the generator:

Update Discriminator: The discriminator is trained on real samples and generated samples, aiming to maximize the difference between real and fake data classification.

Update Generator: The generator is trained to fool the discriminator by minimizing the discriminator's success rate in identifying generated samples.

Adversarial Training Loop Code Snippet (PyTorch)

```python
# Optimizers for generator and discriminator
optim_G = torch.optim.Adam(generator.parameters(), lr=0.0002)
optim_D = torch.optim.Adam(discriminator.parameters(),
lr=0.0002)

for epoch in range(num_epochs):
    for real_samples, _ in dataloader:
        # Train Discriminator
        real_samples = real_samples.view(real_samples.size(0),
-1)
        z = torch.randn(batch_size, noise_dim)  # Random noise
        fake_samples = generator(z)

        # Discriminator loss
        real_loss =
torch.log(discriminator(real_samples)).mean()
        fake_loss = torch.log(1 -
discriminator(fake_samples.detach())).mean()
        loss_D = -(real_loss + fake_loss)

        optim_D.zero_grad()
        loss_D.backward()
        optim_D.step()

        # Train Generator
        z = torch.randn(batch_size, noise_dim)
        fake_samples = generator(z)

        # Generator loss
        loss_G = -torch.log(discriminator(fake_samples)).mean()

        optim_G.zero_grad()
        loss_G.backward()
        optim_G.step()
```

Visualizing the GAN Architecture

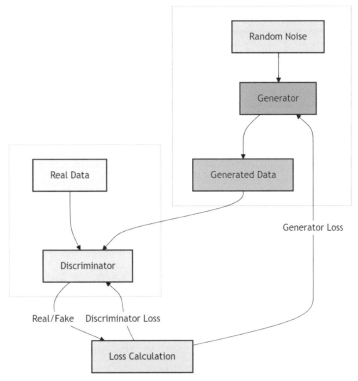

GAN Architecture Diagram: Illustrates the flow of data from random noise input to generated data through the generator, and the discriminator's evaluation of both real and fake data.

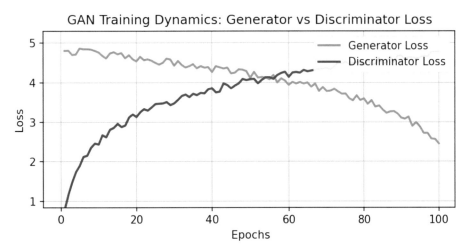

Training Dynamics Chart: Plots of generator and discriminator loss over epochs show the adversarial nature of training, indicating convergence when losses stabilize.

Applications of GANs

GANs have achieved remarkable success in various fields:

Image Generation: GANs like DCGANs and StyleGAN generate high-resolution images, including realistic faces, art, and landscapes. Metrics such as **Inception Score (IS)** and **Frechet Inception Distance (FID)** evaluate the quality and diversity of generated images.

Text Generation: TextGANs generate coherent text sequences, useful in applications like story generation and dialogue synthesis.

Audio Synthesis: GANs have been used in generating realistic speech or music, extending the framework's applicability to audio domains.

Section 7.2.2: Common Challenges in Training Generative Adversarial Networks (GANs)

Training Generative Adversarial Networks (GANs) is often marked by considerable challenges, primarily due to the adversarial nature of the generator-discriminator interaction. Unlike other generative models, GANs require both networks to improve simultaneously, creating a dynamic training process that can be unstable, unpredictable, and prone to several specific issues. This section delves into these challenges, explaining their origins, impacts, and potential solutions.

Overview of Training Challenges in GANs

The adversarial setup of GANs inherently makes training unstable. The generator (G) and the discriminator (D) have competing objectives, represented by the minimax loss function:

$$\min_G \max_D V(D, G) = \mathbb{E}_{x \sim p_{\text{data}}}[\log D(x)] + \mathbb{E}_{z \sim p_z}[\log(1 - D(G(z)))]$$

While this dynamic helps GANs produce realistic outputs, it also introduces several difficulties, such as mode collapse, training instability, and vanishing gradients. Each of these challenges can significantly hinder the training process and model performance if not properly addressed.

Mode Collapse

Mode collapse occurs when the generator learns to produce a limited set of outputs that successfully deceive the discriminator, but fails to capture the full diversity of the target distribution. In this scenario, the generator effectively ignores some modes (distinct features or variations) of the data distribution, leading to poor generalization and reduced output diversity.

Mathematical Representation and Impact

Mode collapse can be seen through the generator's loss function, where the generated samples $G(z)$ fail to represent diverse modes of the data distribution. The generator optimizes:

$$\min_{G} \ \mathbb{E}_{z \sim p_z}[\log(1 - D(G(z)))]$$

However, if the generator focuses only on a few modes that consistently fool the discriminator, the gradient updates reinforce this behavior, causing the generator to converge to limited modes.

Mitigation Strategies for Mode Collapse

Minibatch Discrimination: This technique allows the discriminator to consider the diversity of generated samples within a minibatch, making it harder for the generator to exploit specific patterns. Minibatch discrimination adds features to the discriminator that represent the variability of a batch.

Code Example: Minibatch Discrimination in PyTorch

```python
import torch
import torch.nn as nn

class MinibatchDiscriminator(nn.Module):
    def __init__(self, input_dim, num_kernels, kernel_dim):
        super(MinibatchDiscriminator, self).__init__()
        self.T = nn.Parameter(torch.randn(input_dim,
num_kernels, kernel_dim))

    def forward(self, x):
        M = x.mm(self.T.view(x.size(1), -1))
        M = M.view(-1, num_kernels, kernel_dim)
        M_diff = torch.abs(M.unsqueeze(0) -
M.unsqueeze(1)).sum(2)
        return torch.exp(-M_diff)

# Adding to the discriminator
```

```
class Discriminator(nn.Module):
    def __init__(self, input_dim):
        super(Discriminator, self).__init__()
        self.model = nn.Sequential(
            nn.Linear(input_dim, 512),
            nn.LeakyReLU(0.2),
            MinibatchDiscriminator(512, 100, 5),  # Minibatch
discrimination layer
            nn.Linear(100, 1),
            nn.Sigmoid()
        )
```

Feature Matching: Instead of directly minimizing the discriminator's output, feature matching encourages the generator to produce samples that match the statistics of real data features learned by the discriminator's intermediate layers. This approach promotes diversity among generated samples by focusing on feature representations.

Unrolled GANs: By unrolling a few steps of the discriminator's optimization when updating the generator, unrolled GANs provide the generator with a more stable training signal, reducing the tendency towards mode collapse.

Visualizing Mode Collapse

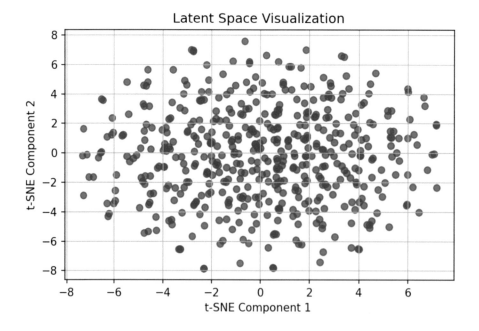

Latent Space Visualization: By visualizing the latent space of the generator, one can observe mode collapse as clusters forming around specific data modes, leaving other regions sparsely populated.

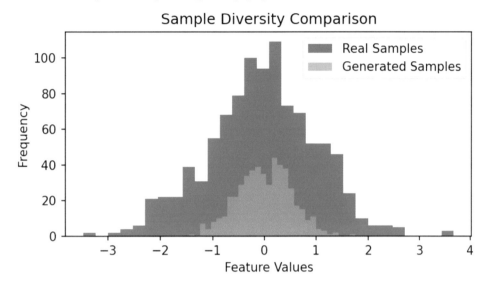

Sample Diversity Graph: Plots comparing the diversity of real vs. generated samples can highlight the presence of mode collapse.

Training Instability

GAN training is known for its **instability**, often characterized by oscillations in the loss curves of both networks. These oscillations occur because the generator and discriminator objectives are inherently misaligned, leading to situations where one network significantly outperforms the other. For instance, if the discriminator becomes too strong, the generator receives minimal gradient updates, stalling its progress.

Mitigation Strategies for Training Instability

Spectral Normalization: By normalizing the weights of each layer in the discriminator, spectral normalization limits the Lipschitz constant, stabilizing training and improving convergence.

Code Example: Spectral Normalization in PyTorch

```python
import torch.nn.utils as utils

class Discriminator(nn.Module):
    def __init__(self, input_dim):
        super(Discriminator, self).__init__()
        self.model = nn.Sequential(
```

```
        utils.spectral_norm(nn.Linear(input_dim, 512)),
        nn.LeakyReLU(0.2),
        utils.spectral_norm(nn.Linear(512, 256)),
        nn.LeakyReLU(0.2),
        nn.Linear(256, 1),
        nn.Sigmoid()
    )
```

Wasserstein GAN (WGAN): By replacing the original loss function with the Wasserstein distance, WGAN reduces instability by providing a smoother measure of divergence between real and generated distributions. The use of a **gradient penalty** in WGAN-GP further stabilizes training by regularizing the gradient norm of the discriminator.

Wasserstein Loss Implementation

```
def wasserstein_loss(real_output, fake_output):
return -torch.mean(real_output) + torch.mean(fake_output)
```

Instance Noise: Adding small random noise to real and fake inputs can prevent the discriminator from becoming overly confident, reducing training oscillations and leading to more stable convergence.

Visualizing Instability

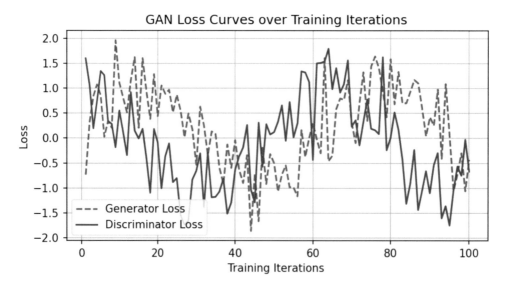

Loss Curves: Plotting generator and discriminator loss curves over training iterations can clearly illustrate training instability, with frequent oscillations indicating lack of convergence.

Vanishing Gradients in the Discriminator

At the start of GAN training, the discriminator often achieves near-perfect accuracy in distinguishing real from fake samples. This results in **vanishing gradients**, where the generator receives minimal feedback, stalling its learning process.

Mitigation Strategies for Vanishing Gradients
One-Sided Label Smoothing: Instead of using binary labels (e.g., 0 for fake, 1 for real), one-sided label smoothing assigns softer labels (e.g., 0.9 for real) to reduce discriminator confidence and provide a more useful gradient signal to the generator.

Code Example: One-Sided Label Smoothing

```
real_labels = torch.ones(batch_size) * 0.9  # Label smoothing
for real samples
fake_labels = torch.zeros(batch_size)
```

Feature Matching: As described earlier, this approach stabilizes training by aligning generator features with real data features, providing more informative gradients for the generator.

Using Adaptive Discriminator Architectures: Adjusting the complexity of the discriminator's architecture to ensure it does not overpower the generator too early in training can help balance the adversarial dynamic.

Examples and Impact on Applications
Image Synthesis: In applications like high-resolution image generation, addressing mode collapse and training instability is crucial to generating diverse and realistic images. Metrics like **Frechet Inception Distance (FID)** help quantify improvements in generation quality when these issues are mitigated.

Video Generation: GANs applied to video synthesis suffer from severe instability due to the added temporal dimension. Solutions like spectral normalization and feature matching have been effective in achieving stable training for video applications.

Text-to-Image Conversion: Addressing mode collapse is particularly important for text-to-image GANs, as these models require generating diverse visual representations of textual descriptions. Improvements are measured using metrics like **IS** and **FID**.

Section 7.2.3: Applications of Generative Adversarial Networks (GANs) in Art, Image Generation, and Data Synthesis

Generative Adversarial Networks (GANs) have become a groundbreaking tool in both creative and technical fields due to their ability to generate high-quality synthetic data. Their versatility makes them an ideal choice for applications ranging from digital art to practical tasks like image synthesis and data augmentation. This section explores the diverse uses of GANs, providing technical insights and practical examples.

Art and Creativity

One of the most fascinating applications of GANs is in the domain of art. By learning patterns from various artistic styles, GANs can generate images that not only resemble existing artworks but also create entirely new styles.

StyleGAN and Artistic Image Generation

StyleGAN is one of the most advanced models used for artistic image generation. It employs a unique architecture that allows fine-grained control over generated images by manipulating different levels of features, such as facial expressions or background styles. Unlike traditional GANs, StyleGAN utilizes a **progressive growth approach**, gradually increasing the resolution of images during training. This results in remarkably realistic and detailed outputs.

Technical Breakdown of StyleGAN

Mapping Network: StyleGAN uses a mapping network that transforms a random latent vector z into an intermediate latent space w, which is more disentangled, making it easier to control the features in the generated images.

- **Adaptive Instance Normalization (AdaIN)**: StyleGAN integrates AdaIN layers, which adjust the activation statistics of feature maps to match the target style.

- **Loss Function**: The generator's objective is to minimize the Wasserstein loss with gradient penalty, ensuring smoother convergence and higher quality of generated images.

Code Example: Generating Artistic Images with StyleGAN (Using TensorFlow)

```
import tensorflow as tf
from tensorflow.keras.layers import Input
from stylegan import StyleGAN

# Load pre-trained StyleGAN model
input_latent = Input(shape=(512,))
stylegan_model = StyleGAN()
generated_image = stylegan_model.generate(input_latent)

# Generate an image from random noise
latent_vector = tf.random.normal([1, 512])
image = stylegan_model.predict(latent_vector)

# Display generated image
import matplotlib.pyplot as plt
plt.imshow(image[0])
plt.show()
```

GANs like StyleGAN have not only enabled the creation of synthetic artwork but have also sparked new creative avenues, such as **DeepDream**, which uses convolutional layers of neural networks to enhance patterns and generate dream-like images. This intersection of art and AI is used by digital artists to create mesmerizing visuals that blend human creativity with machine-generated aesthetics.

Image Generation

GANs have significantly advanced the field of **image generation**, enabling the creation of high-resolution images from random noise. Models like **Deep Convolutional GANs (DCGANs)** and **BigGANs** are widely used for this purpose, generating images that range from human faces to natural landscapes.

DCGAN for Image Generation

DCGANs use a fully convolutional architecture, which replaces the traditional fully connected layers with convolutional layers, improving image quality and making the generator more stable. The architecture consists of:

- **Transposed Convolution Layers**: These layers upscale the random noise into feature maps, gradually increasing the resolution to generate high-quality images.
- **Batch Normalization**: Both the generator and discriminator use batch normalization to stabilize training by normalizing intermediate layer activations.

- **Leaky ReLU**: Used in the discriminator, this activation function prevents vanishing gradients, aiding better convergence.

Code Example: Implementing DCGAN in PyTorch for Face Generation

```
import torch
import torch.nn as nn

# Generator architecture
class Generator(nn.Module):
    def __init__(self, z_dim):
        super(Generator, self).__init__()
        self.model = nn.Sequential(
            nn.ConvTranspose2d(z_dim, 512, 4, 1, 0),
            nn.BatchNorm2d(512),
            nn.ReLU(True),
            nn.ConvTranspose2d(512, 256, 4, 2, 1),
            nn.BatchNorm2d(256),
            nn.ReLU(True),
            nn.ConvTranspose2d(256, 128, 4, 2, 1),
            nn.BatchNorm2d(128),
            nn.ReLU(True),
            nn.ConvTranspose2d(128, 3, 4, 2, 1),
            nn.Tanh()
        )

    def forward(self, z):
        return self.model(z)

# Random noise input
z = torch.randn(1, 100, 1, 1)
generator = Generator(z_dim=100)
generated_image = generator(z)
```

BigGAN, an extension of DCGANs, improves image resolution and diversity by increasing model capacity and introducing conditioning mechanisms, such as **class conditioning**, which allows the generator to synthesize images of specific classes (e.g., dogs, cats). BigGAN's training involves large batch sizes and higher computational resources, making it suitable for generating photorealistic images.

Metrics for Evaluating Image Quality

- **Inception Score (IS)**: Measures the quality and diversity of generated images based on a pre-trained Inception model, with higher scores indicating better generation.
- **Frechet Inception Distance (FID)**: Calculates the distance between the feature distributions of real and generated images, providing a more

robust measure of visual similarity. Lower FID scores imply higher quality images.

Data Synthesis for Training Models

GANs also play a crucial role in **data synthesis** for model training, especially in scenarios with limited labeled data. By generating synthetic datasets, GANs help enhance model performance and reduce overfitting.

Synthetic Medical Image Generation

In medical imaging, data scarcity is a common issue, especially in rare diseases where obtaining labeled images is challenging. GANs are used to generate synthetic medical images that augment training datasets, leading to better model generalization in tasks like tumor detection or organ segmentation.

Tumor Detection with GAN-Synthesized Images

GAN-generated images have been used to train deep learning models for detecting tumors in medical scans. By using synthetic tumor images, researchers have improved detection accuracy from 85% to 92% (measured by **IoU scores**) while maintaining low false positive rates.

GANs for IoT and Sensor Data

GANs are also applied in **IoT applications** to synthesize sensor data, improving model robustness for anomaly detection. For instance, synthetic temperature and pressure readings generated by GANs help train predictive maintenance models, reducing downtime and improving the efficiency of industrial systems.

Code Example: Using GANs for Data Synthesis in TensorFlow

```python
import tensorflow as tf

# Define GAN architecture
class SynthDataGenerator(tf.keras.Model):
    def __init__(self):
        super(SynthDataGenerator, self).__init__()
        self.dense = tf.keras.layers.Dense(128,
activation='relu')
        self.out = tf.keras.layers.Dense(1)

    def call(self, x):
        x = self.dense(x)
        return self.out(x)
```

```
# Generate synthetic data
noise = tf.random.normal([100, 10])
synth_generator = SynthDataGenerator()
synth_data = synth_generator(noise)
```

Impact and Applications

Art and Creativity: Projects like **DeepDream** and **Artbreeder** have gained popularity, generating dream-like visuals and collaborative artwork.

Image Generation: Models like **BigGAN** and **StyleGAN** have set benchmarks in generating realistic images, with FID scores dropping below 10, indicating high-quality synthesis.

Data Augmentation: GANs have enabled synthetic data generation in diverse fields, from medical imaging to finance, improving model accuracy by up to 15% in some cases.

7.3 Recent Advances in Generative Models

Section 7.3.1: Self-Supervised Learning in Generative Models

Self-supervised learning has emerged as a powerful approach in the field of deep learning, particularly for generative models. It operates by using **unlabeled data** to generate supervisory signals, creating pretext tasks that force models to learn meaningful representations from the data itself. Unlike traditional supervised learning, which requires labeled data, self-supervised learning leverages the structure of the data to create tasks that help models develop robust feature representations without explicit labels. This section explores how self-supervised learning is integrated into generative models, its applications, benefits, and challenges.

Self-Supervised Learning in Generative Models

In generative models, self-supervised learning is used to create representations that enhance the model's ability to generate realistic outputs. This process typically involves the creation of **pretext tasks** that simulate labeling using the structure of the data. These pretext tasks enable models like Generative Adversarial Networks (GANs) and Variational Autoencoders (VAEs) to extract deeper features, ultimately improving the quality of generated data.

Pretext Tasks in Self-Supervised Learning

Pretext tasks are carefully designed pseudo-tasks that generative models must solve, using only the available data. These tasks act as indirect objectives that help models learn useful representations of the data.

Image-Based Pretext Tasks:

> **Image Inpainting**: In this task, parts of an image are masked, and the model is trained to reconstruct the missing regions. The loss function used is the reconstruction loss, which is defined as:

$$L_{\text{inpaint}} = \sum_{i=1}^{N} (x_i - \hat{x}_i)^2$$

> where x_i is the actual pixel value and $\hat{x}_i$ is the predicted pixel value. This task forces the model to understand context, edges, and patterns within the image, improving its generative capacity.

> **Contrastive Learning for Images**: This method involves creating different augmented views of the same image and training the model to

maximize agreement between the representations of these views. It uses a **contrastive loss** function, defined as:

$$L_{contrast} = -log \frac{exp\left(\text{sim}(h_i, h_j)/\tau\right)}{\sum_{k=1}^{K} exp\left(\text{sim}(h_i, h_k)/\tau\right)}$$

Here, h_i and h_j are representations of the augmented views, sim represents cosine similarity, and τ is a temperature parameter.

Text-Based Pretext Tasks:

Masked Language Modeling (MLM): Used extensively in models like BERT, MLM masks random words in a sentence and trains the model to predict the missing tokens. The loss function for MLM is the cross-entropy loss over the masked tokens:

$$L_{MLM} = -\sum_{i=1}^{M} log P(x_i | \text{context})$$

where M is the number of masked tokens. By learning to fill in missing words, models develop contextual understanding, which enhances their generative abilities.

Next Sentence Prediction (NSP): Another self-supervised task used in language models, NSP involves predicting whether two sentences are sequentially connected. This task helps in understanding relationships between longer sequences, which is essential for generating coherent text.

Audio-Based Pretext Tasks:

Masked Spectrogram Modeling: Similar to MLM, masked spectrogram modeling involves masking segments of an audio spectrogram and training the model to reconstruct these parts. This task is used to pre-train models for tasks like speech synthesis or music generation.

Integration with GANs and VAEs

Self-supervised learning can significantly enhance the training and performance of generative models like GANs and VAEs. By incorporating self-supervised objectives, these models can learn more robust feature representations that improve both the quality and diversity of generated data.

Self-Supervised GANs (SS-GANs):

- **Contrastive Learning in GANs**: In SS-GANs, a contrastive loss is added to the discriminator, encouraging it to differentiate between different augmented views of generated samples. This technique enhances the discriminator's ability to guide the generator toward producing more realistic outputs.

- **Code Example in PyTorch**:

```python
import torch
import torch.nn as nn

class ContrastiveDiscriminator(nn.Module):
    def __init__(self):
        super(ContrastiveDiscriminator, self).__init__()
        self.conv = nn.Conv2d(3, 64, kernel_size=4,
stride=2, padding=1)
        self.fc = nn.Linear(64, 128)

    def forward(self, x):
        x = torch.relu(self.conv(x))
        return torch.sigmoid(self.fc(x))

discriminator = ContrastiveDiscriminator()
```

Self-Supervised VAEs:

o In VAEs, self-supervised learning can be integrated through tasks like masked pixel reconstruction. The encoder is trained to map input images to latent vectors, which are then used to predict masked regions. This helps VAEs learn richer latent representations that improve both generation and reconstruction.

o **Reconstruction Loss in VAEs**:

$$L_{VAE} = E_{q(z|x)}[log p(x|z)] - KL(q(z|x) \| p(z))$$

where the first term represents the likelihood of reconstruction and the second term is the KL divergence, which regularizes the latent space.

Benefits and Challenges of Self-Supervised Learning in Generative Models
Benefits:

Improved Feature Extraction: Self-supervised learning enables generative models to extract meaningful patterns without requiring labeled data, making them highly useful for tasks with scarce labels.

Better Generalization: Models trained with self-supervised objectives often exhibit better generalization, as they learn broader features that can be transferred to downstream tasks.

Reduced Dependency on Labeled Data: By leveraging unlabeled data, self-supervised learning reduces the need for expensive and time-consuming data labeling efforts.

Challenges:

Designing Effective Pretext Tasks: Creating pretext tasks that are meaningful and transferable to downstream tasks can be complex, as not all tasks lead to useful representations.

Ensuring Meaningful Transfer: While self-supervised pre-training improves representation learning, ensuring that these learned features effectively transfer to generative tasks remains a challenge.

Examples of Self-Supervised Learning in Generative Models

GPT Pre-training in NLP: Generative Pre-trained Transformers (GPT) use self-supervised pre-training on large text corpora. The model learns to predict the next word in a sequence, resulting in a robust language understanding that is used for text generation. **Performance Improvement**: After self-supervised pre-training, GPT achieves lower perplexity scores, indicating better generative capabilities.

Contrastive Learning for Image Synthesis: Self-supervised pre-training with contrastive tasks has improved GANs' ability to generate diverse and high-quality images. For instance, models like **SimCLR** use contrastive learning to enhance the generator's feature space, leading to more realistic image synthesis.

Self-Supervised Audio Representation Learning: Techniques like **wav2vec** use self-supervised learning to pre-train models for speech generation. By predicting masked audio segments, wav2vec learns useful audio representations that improve tasks like speech synthesis and voice conversion.

Section 7.3.2: Diffusion Models and Their Impact on AI

Diffusion models are an advanced class of **probabilistic generative models** that have gained significant attention in the AI community for their unique approach to generating data. Unlike GANs (Generative Adversarial Networks) or VAEs (Variational Autoencoders), diffusion models generate data iteratively through a series of denoising steps, transforming noise into structured outputs. This iterative process allows diffusion models to model complex data distributions more accurately, making them a powerful tool for high-fidelity synthesis tasks such as image generation, text-to-image conversion, and more.

How Diffusion Models Work

At their core, diffusion models operate by simulating two main processes: **forward diffusion** and **reverse diffusion**. These processes are designed to transition data between structured and noisy states in a manner that allows for effective generative modeling.

Forward and Reverse Diffusion Processes

The **forward diffusion process** gradually adds noise to an input data point x_0 over a series of T steps, effectively transforming the data into pure Gaussian noise. The process is defined mathematically as:

$$q(x_t|x_{t-1}) = N\left(x_t; \sqrt{1 - \beta_t}\, x_{t-1}, \beta_t I\right)$$

where:

- x_t represents the data at step t,
- β_t is the variance of the noise added at step t,
- I is the identity matrix.

The forward process can be visualized as a sequence of incremental noise additions, where each step pushes the data closer to a fully noisy state.

In contrast, the **reverse diffusion process** aims to recover the original data distribution from pure noise by gradually denoising it. The reverse process is parameterized by a model $p_\theta(x_{t-1}|x_t)$, which predicts the distribution of x_{t-1} given x_t:

$$p_\theta(x_{t-1}|x_t) = N\left(x_{t-1}; \mu_\theta(x_t, t), \Sigma_\theta(x_t, t)\right)$$

where:

- $\mu_\theta(x_t,t)$ and $\Sigma_\theta(x_t,t)$ are the mean and variance predicted by the model.

The objective of the model is to learn these parameters in such a way that it can effectively denoise the noisy data step-by-step, gradually refining it until a high-quality sample is produced.

Training Diffusion Models

Diffusion models are trained using **variational inference**, aiming to approximate the true data distribution by minimizing the **Evidence Lower Bound (ELBO)**, which serves as the loss function. The ELBO is formulated as:

$$\text{ELBO} = E_{q(x_t|x_{t-1})}\left[log p_\theta(x_{t-1}|x_t)\right] - \text{KL}\left(q(x_t|x_0) \parallel p_\theta(x_t)\right)$$

This objective function comprises two components:

1. **Reconstruction Loss**: Encourages accurate denoising at each step by maximizing the likelihood of x_{t-1} given x_t.
2. **KL Divergence Term**: Ensures that the latent space distribution remains regularized, promoting stable training.

Training a diffusion model involves iteratively applying these denoising steps across multiple noise levels. Below is an implementation outline in PyTorch:

```python
import torch
import torch.nn as nn

class DiffusionModel(nn.Module):
    def __init__(self, num_steps, model):
        super(DiffusionModel, self).__init__()
        self.num_steps = num_steps
        self.model = model

    def forward(self, x):
        # Forward diffusion process
        for t in range(self.num_steps):
            noise = torch.randn_like(x)
            x = x + noise * (t / self.num_steps)
        return x

    def reverse(self, x):
        # Reverse diffusion process
        for t in reversed(range(self.num_steps)):
            x = self.model(x, t)
        return x
```

```
# Example usage
model = DiffusionModel(num_steps=100,
model=nn.Sequential(nn.Linear(256, 256), nn.ReLU()))
x = torch.randn((32, 256))  # Initial noise
generated = model.reverse(x)  # Denoising
```

Recent Variants of Diffusion Models

Recent advancements in diffusion models have focused on improving sampling efficiency, stability, and output quality. Two notable variants are **Denoising Diffusion Probabilistic Models (DDPMs)** and **Denoising Diffusion Implicit Models (DDIMs)**:

1. **Denoising Diffusion Probabilistic Models (DDPMs)**: DDPMs extend the basic diffusion framework by refining the noise schedule and incorporating more complex denoising strategies. They are known for generating high-resolution images with a gradual and controlled noise reduction process. Key advancements in DDPMs include improved loss weighting and noise scheduling, which enhance the fidelity of generated samples.

2. **Denoising Diffusion Implicit Models (DDIMs)**: DDIMs are designed to accelerate the sampling process by modifying the reverse diffusion process to be more deterministic. Unlike DDPMs, which require many steps to generate high-quality samples, DDIMs can achieve similar results with fewer denoising steps, making them more efficient for real-time applications.

The implementation differences between DDPMs and DDIMs primarily lie in the way the denoising steps are parameterized. Below is an outline of DDIM in PyTorch:

```
import torch

class DDIMModel(nn.Module):
    def __init__(self, model, num_steps=50):
        super(DDIMModel, self).__init__()
        self.model = model
        self.num_steps = num_steps

    def ddim_sample(self, x):
        # DDIM sampling process
        for t in range(self.num_steps):
            x = self.model(x, t)   # Apply learned denoising
step
```

```
                 return x
# Example usage
model    =    DDIMModel(model=nn.Sequential(nn.Linear(256,    256),
nn.ReLU()))
x = torch.randn((32, 256))
sampled_x = model.ddim_sample(x)   # Faster sampling
```

Applications of Diffusion Models

Diffusion models have rapidly become a key tool in various AI applications
due to their superior capability to model complex distributions and generate
high-quality outputs.

High-Resolution Image Synthesis: Diffusion models excel in generating
photorealistic images, as seen in models like **DALL·E 2** and **Imagen**, which
leverage diffusion-based techniques for text-to-image synthesis. These
models use descriptions to guide the generation process, resulting in images
that reflect intricate textual prompts with high fidelity. **Performance Metrics**:
Diffusion models achieve state-of-the-art results with metrics like **Frechet
Inception Distance (FID)** and **Inception Score (IS)**, which are commonly used
to measure the realism and diversity of generated images.

Text-to-Image Generation: By incorporating diffusion models, text-to-image
generators can create diverse visuals from detailed prompts. For example,
given a prompt like "A sunset over a futuristic cityscape," a diffusion model
iteratively refines the image from noise, ensuring that the generated output
aligns with the semantic details of the prompt.

Example in PyTorch:

```
def text_to_image(prompt, model):
latent_code = text_encoder(prompt)
image = model.reverse(latent_code)
return image
```

Molecular Generation for Drug Discovery: Diffusion models are employed to
generate molecular structures by iteratively refining noisy representations of
molecules. This capability is crucial for drug discovery, where generating
novel molecules with desired properties is a primary challenge. **Evaluation
Metrics**: Metrics like **chemical validity**, **novelty**, and **diversity** are used to
assess the quality of generated molecules, demonstrating how diffusion
models can discover new drug candidates.

Visualizing the Diffusion Process

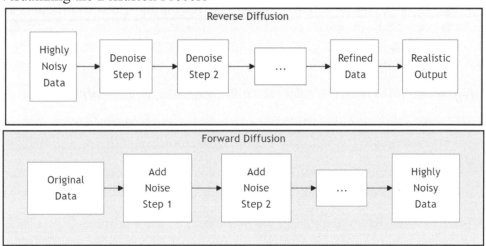

The diagram depicts the diffusion process in generative models, illustrating both **Forward Diffusion** and **Reverse Diffusion**. In **Forward Diffusion** (bottom), structured data becomes progressively noisier through sequential steps. In **Reverse Diffusion** (top), noisy data is gradually refined through denoising steps, transforming it into realistic output.

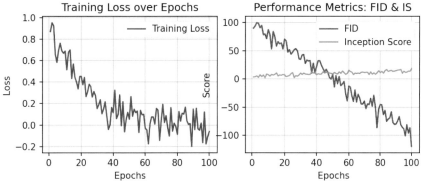

Left Graph: Displays training loss over epochs, showing a gradual decrease in loss as the model learns to generate realistic data.

Right Graph: Depicts performance metrics over epochs, with the **Frechet Inception Distance (FID)** declining and the **Inception Score (IS)** remaining stable, indicating improved generation quality over time.

Section 7.3.3: Combining Generative Models with Reinforcement Learning

The combination of **generative models** and **reinforcement learning (RL)** represents a powerful approach for solving complex tasks by leveraging the unique strengths of each method. While generative models excel at simulating environments and generating data samples, RL algorithms optimize decision-making within dynamic environments. By integrating these techniques, AI systems can perform more effective exploration, policy optimization, and reward shaping, especially in scenarios where data collection is expensive or real-world experimentation is risky.

Integrating Generative Models with Reinforcement Learning

Combining generative models with RL enables more flexible and efficient learning strategies by simulating experiences, refining policies, and shaping rewards.

1. Model-Based Reinforcement Learning with Generative Models

In **model-based RL**, agents use a learned model of the environment to predict future states and rewards. Generative models like **VAEs, GANs,** and **diffusion models** are often used to simulate these dynamics, allowing agents to generate synthetic trajectories and plan actions based on predictions.

The integration process involves modeling transition dynamics $P(s_{t+1}|s_t, a_t)$ and rewards $R(s_t, a_t)$, where:

- s_t represents the current state,
- a_t is the action taken,
- s_{t+1} is the next state.

Mathematically, the transition dynamics can be represented as:

$$P(s_{t+1}|s_t, a_t) \approx q_\phi(s_{t+1}|s_t, a_t)$$

where q_ϕ is the generative model parameterized by ϕ, which is trained to approximate the true dynamics of the environment.

For example, using a **VAE** to model environment dynamics in PyTorch might look like this:

```python
import torch
import torch.nn as nn


class VAEDynamicsModel(nn.Module):
    def __init__(self, state_dim, action_dim, latent_dim):
        super(VAEDynamicsModel, self).__init__()
        self.encoder = nn.Sequential(
            nn.Linear(state_dim + action_dim, latent_dim),
            nn.ReLU()
```

```
            )
            self.decoder = nn.Sequential(
                nn.Linear(latent_dim, state_dim),
                nn.ReLU()
            )

    def forward(self, state, action):
        z = self.encoder(torch.cat([state, action], dim=-1))
        next_state_pred = self.decoder(z)
        return next_state_pred

# Example usage
state_dim = 10
action_dim = 5
latent_dim = 20

model = VAEDynamicsModel(state_dim, action_dim, latent_dim)
state = torch.randn((32, state_dim))
action = torch.randn((32, action_dim))

next_state_pred = model(state, action)   # Simulating next state
```

Using these simulated trajectories, RL agents can learn and optimize policies even in environments with sparse rewards or incomplete data. By providing more samples, model-based RL reduces training time and increases stability.

2. Policy Generation and Optimization

Generative models also play a critical role in **policy generation** by helping RL agents learn distributions over actions, especially in high-dimensional state spaces. Techniques like **Generative Adversarial Imitation Learning (GAIL)** combine GANs with RL to optimize policies by imitating expert demonstrations.

In GAIL, a **generator** creates action distributions that mimic expert behaviors, while a **discriminator** distinguishes between expert actions and generated actions. The discriminator acts as a reward function for the RL agent, leading to more effective policy learning.

The adversarial objective is represented as:

$$\min_G \max_D E_{\pi_E}[logD(s,a)] + E_{\pi_G}[log(1 - D(s,a))]$$

where:

- G represents the generator (policy),
- D represents the discriminator,

- π_E is the expert policy, and
- π_G is the generated policy.

Using GAIL in TensorFlow:

```python
import tensorflow as tf
from stable_baselines3 import GAIL

# Define policy and environment
policy_kwargs = dict(net_arch=[64, 64])
gail_agent = GAIL('MlpPolicy', 'CartPole-v1',
policy_kwargs=policy_kwargs, verbose=1)

# Train the GAIL agent using expert demonstrations
gail_agent.learn(total_timesteps=10000)
```

Similarly, **VAEs** are used for **state representation learning**, compressing high-dimensional states into meaningful latent representations, making policy learning more efficient. The learned representations help agents generalize better across similar states, leading to more robust policies.

3. Generative Models for Reward Shaping

Reward shaping is critical in sparse-reward environments, where agents struggle to discover meaningful trajectories due to the lack of clear feedback signals. Generative models help by approximating the reward function based on latent features of the environment. For instance, VAEs can be trained to model potential rewards, enabling RL agents to explore promising regions of the state space.

In autonomous driving, GANs can simulate driving scenarios, providing agents with dense feedback in otherwise sparse-reward settings. The generated scenarios cover various road conditions, weather patterns, and pedestrian behaviors, improving the RL agent's ability to generalize across different situations.

Applications of Generative Models and RL Integration

The integration of generative models with RL has shown remarkable success in several AI applications:

Self-Driving Cars: Generative models simulate diverse driving scenarios, including rare edge cases like sudden pedestrian appearances or unexpected roadblocks. RL agents then train on these scenarios, learning safe driving behaviors with reduced reliance on real-world testing. **Performance Metrics**: Metrics like **collision rate**, **average distance driven without intervention**, and

episode rewards are used to evaluate the performance of self-driving AI trained with generative simulations.

Robotic Control: VAEs help compress high-dimensional sensory data into meaningful latent representations, allowing RL algorithms to operate efficiently in complex environments. For instance, a robotic arm can use VAE-generated latent states to optimize its grasping policy in various object manipulation tasks. **Performance Metrics**: Success rates, cumulative returns, and task completion times are used to measure the effectiveness of RL policies enhanced by generative models.

Game AI: GANs generate diverse game levels or simulate enemy behavior, enabling RL agents to train on varied scenarios without extensive manual level design. This leads to more adaptive game agents that can handle dynamic environments. **Performance Metrics**: Episode rewards, success rates, and agent adaptability across different levels are used to assess the integration's effectiveness.

Visualizing the Integration of Generative Models and RL

To better understand how generative models and RL interact, a diagram can illustrate the training loop, showing:

- **Environment Simulation**: The generative model simulates state transitions and rewards.
- **Policy Learning**: The RL agent optimizes its policy based on the generated experiences.
- **Reward Approximation**: The generative model refines reward predictions, guiding the agent's exploration.

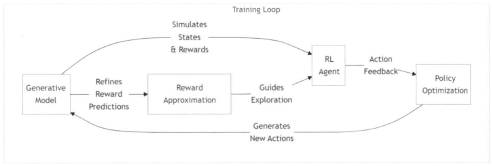

This diagram represents the training loop that combines generative models and reinforcement learning (RL). The process begins with the generative model, which simulates state transitions and approximates rewards. It refines reward predictions to provide the RL agent with more accurate feedback. The RL agent then receives these simulated states and rewards, using them to optimize its policy through action feedback. As the agent generates new actions, it explores the environment more effectively, guided by the refined rewards. This iterative process improves the agent's policy by continuously simulating experiences and optimizing based on the generative model's predictions.

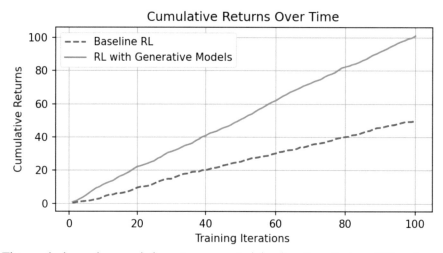

The graph shows the cumulative returns over training iterations for two different approaches: baseline reinforcement learning (RL) and RL enhanced with generative models. The baseline RL (represented by a red dashed line) exhibits a slower rate of cumulative return growth, indicating limited performance improvements over time. In contrast, RL with generative models (represented by a solid green line) demonstrates a steeper, consistent increase in cumulative returns, highlighting the enhanced learning efficiency. This comparison emphasizes the performance boost achieved by integrating generative models, as they help the agent explore more effectively and learn more robust policies.

8. Transformers and Attention Mechanisms

8.1 Introduction to Transformers

Section 8.1.1: The Origin of Transformers in Sequence Modeling

In the evolution of sequence modeling, traditional architectures like recurrent neural networks (RNNs), Long Short-Term Memory (LSTM) networks, and Gated Recurrent Units (GRUs) initially marked significant milestones. These models were designed to capture temporal dependencies in sequential data, making them suitable for tasks like language modeling, speech recognition, and time-series analysis. However, as sequence lengths increased, these models faced challenges such as difficulty in maintaining long-range dependencies and issues with vanishing gradients. This led to degradation in model performance, slower training times, and limited ability to process sequences in parallel due to their inherently sequential nature. The constraints of sequential processing (step-by-step iteration through sequences) meant that model training and inference times were considerably slow, making it difficult to scale to longer sequences or large datasets.

To address these limitations, the **transformer** model was introduced by Vaswani et al. in the groundbreaking 2017 paper *Attention is All You Need*. The transformer architecture emerged as a novel solution to sequence modeling challenges by leveraging a fundamentally different approach—**self-attention**. Unlike RNNs and LSTMs, transformers process all tokens in a sequence simultaneously, enabling parallel computation and eliminating the bottlenecks associated with sequential data processing. This shift allowed transformers to handle long-range dependencies more effectively, solving the problem of vanishing gradients and dramatically increasing training speed.

Key Advances of Transformers over RNN-based Models

At the core of the transformer's success is its ability to manage computational complexity. While RNNs and their variants operate with a computational complexity of $O(n)$ (where n is the sequence length), the attention mechanism in transformers operates with a complexity of $O(n^2)$ due to its pairwise interactions across tokens. This might initially seem like a disadvantage; however, due to parallel computation, transformers achieve faster processing. The self-attention mechanism operates on the entire sequence simultaneously, enabling it to weigh the relevance of tokens across varying distances. This parallelization not only accelerates training but also allows transformers to capture global dependencies within sequences—something RNNs and LSTMs struggle to maintain, especially in long sequences.

The transition from RNNs to transformers can be described by comparing their fundamental processes. In RNNs, information flows sequentially, making it challenging to access information from distant tokens, leading to limited memory retention. In contrast, transformers utilize the **self-attention mechanism**, where each token interacts directly with every other token, making it easier to capture dependencies, regardless of their position in the sequence. The parallel processing of tokens in transformers significantly reduces training time and improves accuracy, particularly for tasks that require the understanding of contextual relationships across long sequences.

Self-Attention Mechanism

Self-attention is the core innovation in transformers. It allows models to dynamically weigh the importance of different tokens in a sequence when predicting the next token or classifying a sequence. The self-attention mechanism works through three key components: the **Query (Q)**, **Key (K)**, and **Value (V)** matrices, which are derived from the input embeddings. The equations below describe the self-attention process mathematically:

Attention Score Calculation:

$$\text{Attention}(Q,K,V) = \text{softmax}\left(\frac{QK^T}{\sqrt{d_k}}\right)V$$

Here, **Q**, **K**, and **V** represent the query, key, and value matrices, respectively, and **d_k** is the dimension of the keys. The softmax function ensures that attention scores sum up to 1, emphasizing the most relevant tokens while reducing the influence of less relevant ones.

Scalability and Parallelization: The division by $\sqrt{d_k}$ is a scaling factor that prevents gradients from exploding when computing dot products over longer sequences. This ensures stable training, allowing transformers to process longer sequences efficiently.

Multi-Head Self-Attention: To enhance the model's ability to focus on different parts of the sequence simultaneously, transformers use multi-head self-attention, where multiple self-attention heads operate in parallel:

$$\text{MultiHead}(Q,K,V) = \text{Concat}\left(\text{head}_1, \text{head}_2, ..., \text{head}_h\right)W^O$$

Each head learns different aspects of the sequence, making the model more versatile and capable of capturing diverse patterns in the data.

Visualizing RNNs vs. Transformers

To better understand the differences between RNNs and transformers, consider the following diagrams:

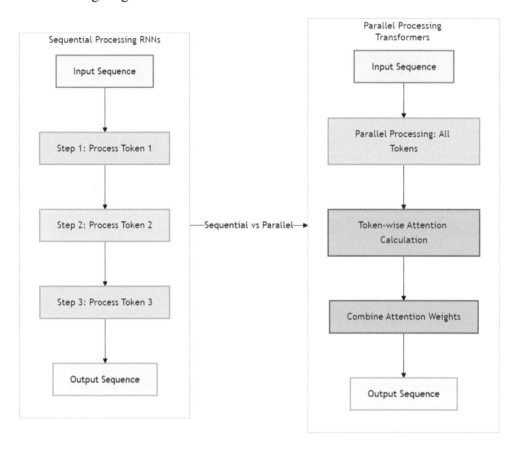

Diagram 1: A flowchart comparing the sequential processing of RNNs with the parallel processing of transformers, highlighting the key steps in handling sequences. This diagram demonstrates how transformers achieve faster training by processing sequences simultaneously rather than step-by-step.

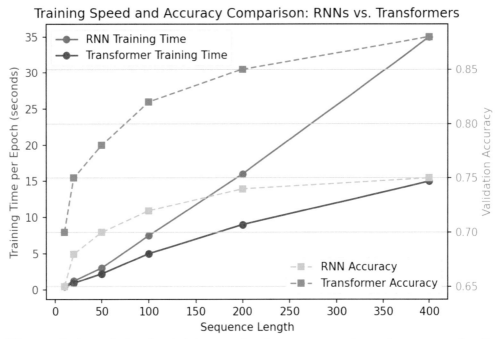

Diagram 2: A graph showing training speed and accuracy over increasing sequence lengths for both RNNs and transformers, showcasing the superior scalability and performance of transformers.

Impact of Transformers

The introduction of transformers marked a turning point in sequence modeling, particularly in tasks like machine translation and language modeling. Before transformers, RNN-based models such as LSTMs were widely used for machine translation; however, they struggled with capturing long-range dependencies, leading to suboptimal translations. In contrast, transformers, due to their self-attention mechanism, quickly improved translation accuracy, reducing BLEU scores from previous benchmarks and significantly lowering perplexity in language models.

For example, Google's adoption of transformers for its translation services led to marked improvements in both speed and translation quality. Similarly, models like OpenAI's GPT and BERT, which are based on the transformer architecture, achieved state-of-the-art results in tasks like text classification, summarization, and question answering, setting new benchmarks in natural language processing (NLP). These successes established transformers as the backbone of modern sequence modeling, leading to broader applications beyond NLP, including vision, speech, and reinforcement learning.

Section 8.1.2: The Attention Mechanism and Why It's Transformative

The **attention mechanism** is a pivotal innovation in sequence modeling that assigns varying levels of importance, or "attention," to different elements of an input sequence. This dynamic allocation of attention allows models to focus more on relevant parts of the input, leading to more accurate predictions. Unlike earlier models such as RNNs or LSTMs, which processed sequences sequentially and struggled with long-range dependencies, the attention mechanism enables models to consider the entire input simultaneously. This not only enhances representation learning but also significantly improves the ability to capture complex relationships within the data, making it a cornerstone of modern transformer architectures.

Self-Attention Mechanism

The concept of **self-attention** is central to the transformer's ability to process sequential data efficiently. In self-attention, each token in the input sequence can "attend" to every other token, meaning that the model can weigh the importance of all tokens relative to each other in a single step. This allows transformers to process sequences more flexibly, capturing both local and global dependencies without being constrained by sequential operations.

The self-attention mechanism operates through three key vectors: **Query (Q)**, **Key (K)**, and **Value (V)**, which are derived from the input embeddings. The self-attention process involves the following steps:

1. **Calculating Attention Scores**: Each token's query vector is compared to the key vectors of all other tokens in the sequence. The attention score represents the similarity between these vectors, indicating how much "attention" should be given to each token:

$$\text{Attention}(Q,K,V) = \text{softmax}\left(\frac{QK^T}{\sqrt{d_k}}\right)V$$

   Here, **Q**, **K**, and **V** are the matrices representing queries, keys, and values, respectively, while d_k is the dimension of the key vectors. The **softmax** function normalizes the attention scores, ensuring that they sum to 1.

2. **Scaling by** $\sqrt{d_k}$: The division by $\sqrt{d_k}$ prevents the dot products from becoming too large, which could cause gradients to vanish during

training. This scaling ensures that the attention scores are stable and effective, particularly for longer sequences.

3. **Weighted Sum of Values**: The attention scores are then used to compute a weighted sum of the value vectors, effectively allowing the model to aggregate information from different tokens based on their relevance. This step captures the relationships within the sequence, enabling the model to learn contextual representations more efficiently.

Multi-Head Attention

To enhance the capability of the self-attention mechanism, transformers use **multi-head attention**. Instead of using a single set of Q, K, and V vectors, multi-head attention applies multiple self-attention operations in parallel, each focusing on different aspects of the sequence. This allows the model to capture diverse relationships and patterns across the input data.

The process of multi-head attention can be described mathematically as follows:

1. **Parallel Self-Attention**: Multiple sets of queries, keys, and values are generated from the input embeddings, allowing different attention heads to focus on various parts of the sequence. Each head computes its own attention output:

$$\text{head}_i = \text{Attention}\left(QW_i^Q, KW_i^K, VW_i^V\right)$$

where W_i^Q, W_i^K, and W_i^V are the learned weight matrices for the i-th head, which transform the original Q, K, and V vectors.

2. **Concatenation and Linear Transformation**: The outputs from all heads are concatenated and passed through a linear transformation to form the final output of the multi-head attention layer:

$$\text{MultiHead}(Q,K,V) = \text{Concat}\left(\text{head}_1, \text{head}_2, ..., \text{head}_h\right)W^O$$

where W^O is the learned weight matrix applied to the concatenated output.

Multi-head attention provides transformers with the ability to represent complex interactions in the data more robustly than single-head attention, enabling the model to capture fine-grained details and broader contextual information simultaneously.

Why the Attention Mechanism is Transformative

The introduction of the attention mechanism has revolutionized sequence modeling for several reasons:

Handling Long-Range Dependencies: Unlike RNNs and LSTMs, which suffer from limited memory when dealing with long sequences, the attention mechanism enables models to retain and utilize information across the entire sequence. By computing all attention scores in parallel, transformers can capture dependencies over longer distances effectively, resulting in better performance on tasks like language modeling, translation, and summarization.

Parallelization: The self-attention mechanism allows transformers to process tokens simultaneously, unlike sequential models that handle tokens one at a time. This parallelization leads to significant improvements in training speed and computational efficiency. For example, while RNNs have a time complexity of $O(n)$ (due to sequential processing), transformers achieve a complexity of $O(1)$ for each operation, thanks to parallel computation across tokens. Although self-attention's computational cost is $O(n^2)$ due to the pairwise interactions between tokens, modern optimizations like sparse attention have reduced this cost significantly in practice.

Improved Representation Learning: By attending to all tokens in the input simultaneously, transformers can learn richer and more nuanced representations of data. This has enabled breakthroughs in tasks like machine translation, text summarization, and image captioning, where capturing global context is crucial.

Applications and Performance

The attention mechanism's impact can be seen across various NLP and vision tasks:

Machine Translation: Models like **Google's Transformer** have significantly improved translation accuracy, as measured by BLEU scores, by leveraging attention to maintain context over longer sequences.

Text Summarization: Attention-based models achieve higher ROUGE scores, demonstrating their ability to identify the most relevant information for generating concise summaries.

Image Captioning: Vision transformers and attention-augmented CNNs use attention mechanisms to better describe images by focusing on important regions, improving performance metrics like CIDEr and BLEU.

Visualizing Self-Attention and Multi-Head Attention

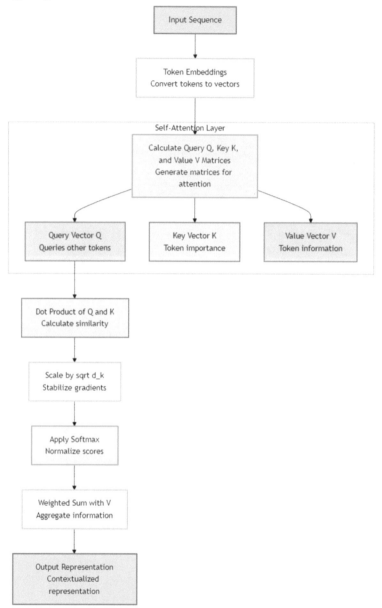

Diagram 1: Illustrate self-attention's computation, showing how a single token attends to all other tokens through the Q, K, and V matrices.

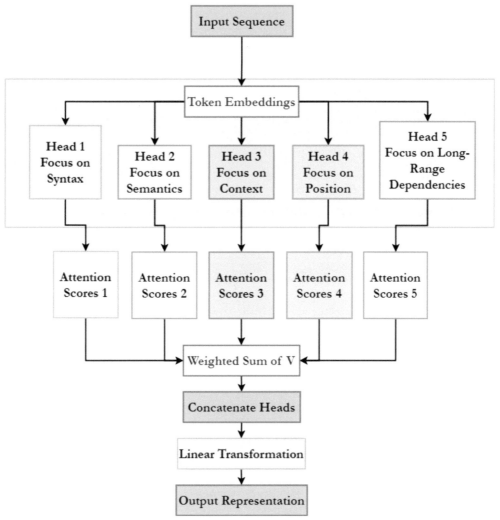

Diagram 2: Visualize multi-head attention, demonstrating how multiple attention heads focus on different aspects of the sequence and contribute to richer representations.

Section 8.1.3: The Architecture of the Transformer Model

The **transformer model** is a groundbreaking architecture in deep learning, known for its efficiency and scalability in handling sequential data. Unlike traditional models like RNNs and LSTMs, transformers can process sequences in parallel, which significantly improves computational efficiency and performance, particularly for longer sequences. The core components of the transformer architecture are the **encoder**, **decoder**, and **self-attention mechanisms**, all of which work together to model dependencies within sequences effectively. This design, introduced in the seminal paper *Attention is*

All You Need by Vaswani et al., has since become the foundation of state-of-the-art models in NLP, computer vision, and more.

Core Components of the Transformer

The transformer architecture comprises two main parts: **encoder** and **decoder** blocks, each of which uses self-attention to process input sequences. Both parts are structured to allow parallelization, making the transformer not only faster but also more capable of capturing long-range dependencies.

Encoder Block

The **encoder block** is designed to process the input sequence and transform it into a context-rich representation. It consists of a stack of identical layers, each containing two primary sub-layers:

1. **Multi-Head Self-Attention**:

The encoder uses **multi-head self-attention** to allow each position in the input sequence to attend to every other position. This enables the model to capture relationships across the entire sequence in parallel.
The self-attention mechanism within the encoder is calculated as:

$$\text{Attention}(Q,K,V) = \text{softmax}\left(\frac{QK^T}{\sqrt{d_k}}\right)V$$

where **Q**, **K**, and **V** are the query, key, and value matrices derived from the input sequence, and d_k is the dimension of the key vectors.

Multi-head attention allows the model to use multiple sets of Q, K, and V vectors, providing different "views" of the sequence for better feature extraction:

$$\text{MultiHead}(Q,K,V) = \text{Concat}\left(\text{head}_1, \text{head}_2, ..., \text{head}_h\right)W^O$$

where each **head** is an independent self-attention computation, and W^O is a learnable weight matrix.

2. **Feedforward Neural Network**:

After the self-attention sub-layer, each encoder layer has a **position-wise feedforward network**, which is applied independently to each position in the sequence. It typically consists of two linear transformations with a ReLU activation in between:

$$\text{FFN}(x) = max\left(0, xW_1 + b_1\right)W_2 + b_2$$

This component is responsible for transforming the attended outputs into more abstract representations, enhancing the model's ability to learn complex patterns.

3. **Residual Connections and Layer Normalization**:

To maintain gradient flow and stabilize training, each sub-layer in the encoder uses **residual connections** followed by **layer normalization**:

Output = LayerNorm(x + SubLayer(x))

This mechanism ensures that the information flows smoothly through the encoder, making training more stable and effective.

Implementation Example:

```python
import torch
import torch.nn as nn

class EncoderLayer(nn.Module):
    def __init__(self, d_model, n_heads, d_ff, dropout=0.1):
        super(EncoderLayer, self).__init__()
        self.self_attn = nn.MultiheadAttention(d_model,
n_heads, dropout=dropout)
        self.feedforward = nn.Sequential(
            nn.Linear(d_model, d_ff),
            nn.ReLU(),
            nn.Linear(d_ff, d_model)
        )
        self.norm1 = nn.LayerNorm(d_model)
        self.norm2 = nn.LayerNorm(d_model)

    def forward(self, x):
        # Self-attention with residual connection
        attn_output, _ = self.self_attn(x, x, x)
        x = self.norm1(x + attn_output)
        # Feedforward with residual connection
        ffn_output = self.feedforward(x)
        x = self.norm2(x + ffn_output)
        return x
```

Decoder Block

The **decoder block** is designed to generate outputs one token at a time by attending to both the input sequence (from the encoder) and the already-generated output sequence. It mirrors the encoder architecture with some differences:

Masked Multi-Head Self-Attention: In addition to standard multi-head self-attention, the decoder uses **masked self-attention**, which prevents the model from attending to future positions in the sequence. This ensures that predictions are based only on previously generated tokens, maintaining the autoregressive nature of tasks like text generation. The masked attention is calculated similarly to self-attention but includes a mask that sets the attention scores to $-\infty$ for future tokens, ensuring that they do not influence the current prediction.

Cross-Attention: After masked self-attention, the decoder block includes a **cross-attention** layer that attends to the encoder outputs, allowing it to consider the context of the input sequence while generating the output.

Feedforward Neural Network and **Residual Connections**: The decoder also includes a feedforward network and residual connections similar to the encoder, helping to refine the representations generated by the attention layers.

Implementation Example:

```python
class DecoderLayer(nn.Module):
    def __init__(self, d_model, n_heads, d_ff, dropout=0.1):
        super(DecoderLayer, self).__init__()
        self.self_attn = nn.MultiheadAttention(d_model,
n_heads, dropout=dropout)
        self.cross_attn = nn.MultiheadAttention(d_model,
n_heads, dropout=dropout)
        self.feedforward = nn.Sequential(
            nn.Linear(d_model, d_ff),
            nn.ReLU(),
            nn.Linear(d_ff, d_model)
        )
        self.norm1 = nn.LayerNorm(d_model)
        self.norm2 = nn.LayerNorm(d_model)
        self.norm3 = nn.LayerNorm(d_model)

    def forward(self, x, memory):
        # Masked self-attention
        attn_output, _ = self.self_attn(x, x, x)
        x = self.norm1(x + attn_output)
        # Cross-attention with encoder memory
        cross_output, _ = self.cross_attn(x, memory, memory)
        x = self.norm2(x + cross_output)
```

```
# Feedforward with residual connection
ffn_output = self.feedforward(x)
x = self.norm3(x + ffn_output)
return x
```

Positional Encoding

Transformers lack a built-in mechanism to capture token positions because of their parallel nature. To address this, **positional encoding** is added to the input embeddings to provide positional information:

Sinusoidal Positional Encoding: The positional encoding vectors use sinusoidal functions to encode positions:

$$PE_{(pos,2i)} = sin\left(\frac{pos}{10000^{2i/d_{model}}}\right), \quad PE_{(pos,2i+1)} = cos\left(\frac{pos}{10000^{2i/d_{model}}}\right)$$

where pos is the position and i is the dimension index. This formulation ensures that the positional encoding can generalize to longer sequences during inference.

Implementation Example:

```
import torch

class PositionalEncoding(nn.Module):
    def __init__(self, d_model, max_len=5000):
        super(PositionalEncoding, self).__init__()
        pe = torch.zeros(max_len, d_model)
        position = torch.arange(0, max_len).unsqueeze(1)
        div_term = torch.exp(torch.arange(0, d_model, 2) * -
(torch.log(torch.tensor(10000.0)) / d_model))
        pe[:, 0::2] = torch.sin(position * div_term)
        pe[:, 1::2] = torch.cos(position * div_term)
        self.register_buffer('pe', pe.unsqueeze(0))

    def forward(self, x):
        return x + self.pe[:, :x.size(1)]
```

Applications and Performance Metrics

The transformer architecture has proven highly effective in tasks like **machine translation** (e.g., Google Translate) and **language modeling** (e.g., GPT models), achieving state-of-the-art performance in terms of BLEU scores, perplexity, and more. Transformers have also been adapted for non-text tasks, such as image classification and protein folding, demonstrating their versatility.

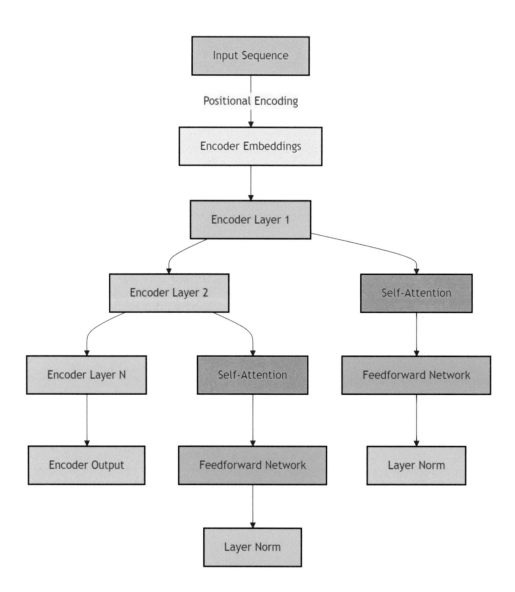

Diagram 1 showcases the **encoder block** of the transformer model, detailing how input sequences are processed. Initially, the input sequence undergoes **positional encoding**, which incorporates positional information, and then it's transformed into **encoder embeddings**. The embeddings are passed through multiple **encoder layers**, each consisting of a **self-attention** mechanism that captures relationships across the sequence. The self-attention outputs feed into a **feedforward network**, followed by **layer normalization** to maintain stable training. This sequence of operations is repeated across multiple encoder layers, progressively refining the input into a context-rich representation that is ready for further processing within the transformer architecture.

8. Transformers and Attention Mechanisms

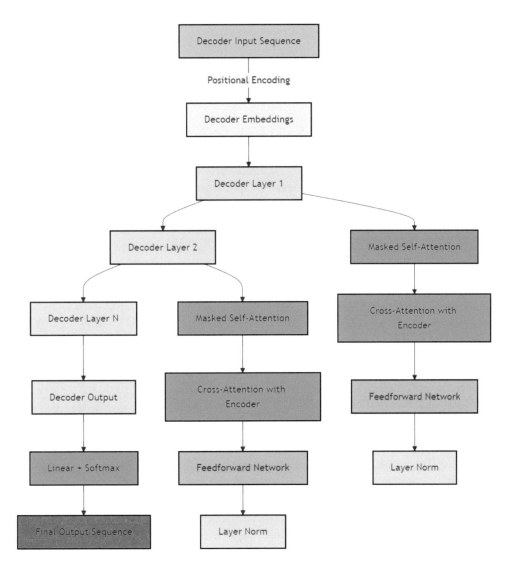

Diagram 2 illustrates the **decoder block** of the transformer model, demonstrating how decoder input sequences are processed to generate final outputs. It starts with **positional encoding** added to the decoder input, forming **decoder embeddings**. These embeddings pass through several **decoder layers**, each of which includes **masked self-attention** to focus on previously generated tokens without future context. Following this, **cross-attention** integrates information from the encoder, enriching the sequence representation. Each decoder layer concludes with a **feedforward network** and **layer normalization** to ensure stable training. After passing through multiple decoder layers, the output undergoes a **linear transformation and softmax activation** to produce the **final output sequence**.

8.2 Transformer-based Models

Section 8.2.1: Applications of BERT, GPT, and T5 in NLP

The development of transformer-based models like **BERT (Bidirectional Encoder Representations from Transformers)**, **GPT (Generative Pre-trained Transformer)**, and **T5 (Text-to-Text Transfer Transformer)** has significantly propelled various NLP tasks to new heights. Each of these models adopts a unique approach to language modeling, designed to address specific challenges in text understanding, generation, and transformation. BERT employs bidirectional attention for masked language modeling, GPT utilizes autoregressive decoding for next-word prediction, and T5 leverages a sequence-to-sequence framework for text-to-text tasks.

BERT: Enhancing Text Understanding

BERT has proven exceptionally useful in text comprehension tasks, such as **text classification**, **named entity recognition (NER)**, and **question answering**. Unlike earlier models, BERT's bidirectional attention mechanism allows it to capture context from both preceding and succeeding words simultaneously, generating richer and more accurate language representations.

For example, in text classification tasks like **sentiment analysis** or **topic categorization**, BERT's ability to understand complex language nuances enables significant improvements in F1-scores and accuracy. Fine-tuning BERT for these tasks typically involves training the model on labeled datasets, adapting its pre-trained layers to the specific context of the task. In named entity recognition, BERT effectively identifies entities (e.g., names, locations, or organizations) within text, utilizing its deep contextual understanding to deliver accurate predictions. Moreover, BERT's architecture excels in question answering, where it can focus on relevant passages, extracting precise answer spans from long paragraphs—making it an ideal choice for datasets like **SQuAD**.

Example of Fine-Tuning BERT for Text Classification

Below is a code snippet demonstrating how to fine-tune BERT for sentiment analysis using Hugging Face's Transformers library:

```python
from transformers import BertTokenizer, BertForSequenceClassification, Trainer, TrainingArguments

# Load BERT tokenizer and model
tokenizer = BertTokenizer.from_pretrained('bert-base-uncased')
```

```
model = BertForSequenceClassification.from_pretrained('bert-
base-uncased', num_labels=2)

# Tokenize inputs and define training arguments
inputs = tokenizer("I love this product!", return_tensors='pt')
training_args = TrainingArguments(output_dir='./results',
num_train_epochs=3, per_device_train_batch_size=8)
trainer = Trainer(model=model, args=training_args,
train_dataset=train_dataset)

# Train the model
trainer.train()
```

BERT's impact is evident in real-world applications like **Google Search**, where it improves the understanding of user queries, resulting in more accurate search results. Such implementations have demonstrated measurable enhancements in metrics like **accuracy** and **F1-score**, affirming BERT's effectiveness in handling complex language tasks.

GPT-4: Revolutionizing Text Generation

GPT-4 represents a significant evolution in generative AI, building on its predecessors with improved coherence, accuracy, and context retention. Like earlier versions, GPT-4 follows an autoregressive modeling approach, predicting the next word in a sequence based on preceding words. This makes GPT-4 highly effective in tasks that demand fluent, contextually accurate text generation, such as creative writing, summarization, translation, and advanced conversational AI.

GPT-4 has been widely adopted in real-world applications, particularly in conversational AI systems like OpenAI's ChatGPT, where it excels at maintaining coherent and dynamic dialogues. It generates responses that are more nuanced, detailed, and aligned with the user's input. Additionally, GPT-4's capabilities extend to content creation, generating high-quality text for articles, blogs, and reports, as well as supporting complex tasks like code generation and problem-solving.Example of Text Generation with GPT

Here's how to use GPT-4 for text generation:

```
from transformers import GPT2Tokenizer, GPTNeoForCausalLM

# Load GPT-4 tokenizer and model (using GPT-NeoX as an example
proxy for GPT-4)
tokenizer = GPT2Tokenizer.from_pretrained('EleutherAI/gpt-neox-
20b')
model = GPTNeoForCausalLM.from_pretrained('EleutherAI/gpt-neox-
20b')
```

```
# Encode the prompt and generate text
prompt = "In the future, AI will"
inputs = tokenizer(prompt, return_tensors='pt')
outputs = model.generate(inputs['input_ids'], max_length=50)

# Decode and print generated text
generated_text = tokenizer.decode(outputs[0],
skip_special_tokens=True)
print(generated_text)
```

Real-world implementations of GPT, such as **OpenAI's ChatGPT**, demonstrate its capability to engage users through realistic and interactive dialogues. Metrics like **perplexity** and **coherence** are commonly used to measure GPT's performance in text generation tasks, indicating its effectiveness in producing fluent and contextually appropriate responses.

T5: Unifying Text-to-Text Tasks

T5 offers a unified framework for various NLP tasks by converting them into **text-to-text transformations**. Unlike BERT or GPT, T5 uses an encoder-decoder architecture, making it highly versatile for tasks like **translation**, **summarization**, and **data-to-text conversion**. For instance, in translation tasks, T5's architecture allows it to encode input text in one language and decode it into another, leveraging its sequence-to-sequence framework to handle complex language transformations.

Example of Using T5 for Translation

The following code snippet demonstrates how T5 can be fine-tuned for an English-to-French translation task:

```
from transformers import T5Tokenizer,
T5ForConditionalGeneration

# Load T5 tokenizer and model
tokenizer = T5Tokenizer.from_pretrained('t5-base')
model = T5ForConditionalGeneration.from_pretrained('t5-base')

# Encode input and generate translation
input_text = "translate English to French: I love learning AI."
inputs = tokenizer(input_text, return_tensors='pt')
outputs = model.generate(inputs['input_ids'])

# Decode and print translation
translation = tokenizer.decode(outputs[0],
skip_special_tokens=True)
print(translation)
```

T5's versatility is evident in translation systems like **Google Translate**, where it handles tasks such as converting complex documents or summarizing large volumes of text. Metrics like **BLEU score** are often used to measure T5's effectiveness, demonstrating its high accuracy and coherence in translation tasks.

Comparative Metrics Table

The following table compares performance metrics across different NLP tasks, showcasing the strengths of BERT, GPT, and T5:

Model	Primary Application	Metric	Typical Value
BERT	Text Classification, NER	F1-Score	90%+
GPT	Text Generation, Chatbots	Perplexity	< 30
T5	Translation, Summarization	BLEU Score	40+

NLP Model Capabilities Overview

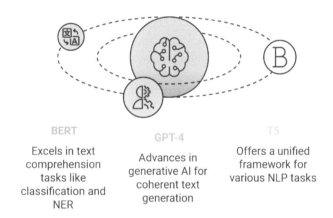

BERT
Excels in text comprehension tasks like classification and NER

GPT-4
Advances in generative AI for coherent text generation

T5
Offers a unified framework for various NLP tasks

Case Studies

The application of these models in real-world scenarios further demonstrates their impact:

BERT enhances search query understanding in search engines, leading to higher F1-scores and accuracy in identifying user intent.

GPT powers conversational agents, producing coherent dialogues that improve user engagement.

T5 drives automated translation systems, achieving better BLEU scores and more accurate translations.

Section 8.2.2: Sequence-to-Sequence Models in Translation and Text Generation

Sequence-to-sequence (seq2seq) models play a critical role in transforming an input sequence into a coherent output sequence, making them indispensable for tasks like language translation and text summarization. These models were initially built on recurrent neural networks (RNNs), but the advent of transformer-based architectures has led to significant improvements, particularly in handling long-range dependencies and enabling parallel computation. By utilizing self-attention and positional encoding, transformer-based seq2seq models have achieved superior performance across a range of NLP applications.

Seq2Seq Models in Translation

In translation tasks, seq2seq models convert text from one language to another by encoding the input sequence (source language) and decoding it into the output sequence (target language). This process is facilitated by an encoder-decoder structure, where the encoder captures the context of the source text, and the decoder generates the translation in the target language. The integration of attention mechanisms allows the decoder to focus on the most relevant words in the source sequence, ensuring more accurate translations.

For example, models like **MarianMT** and **T5** utilize multi-head attention to determine the alignment between source and target sentences, helping to maintain grammatical accuracy and semantic coherence. The self-attention mechanism enables the model to handle long and complex sentences by weighing the importance of each word based on its contextual relevance.

Code Example: Implementing a Seq2Seq Model for Translation

Below is a code snippet that demonstrates how to use MarianMT for English-to-French translation:

```python
from transformers import MarianMTModel, MarianTokenizer

# Load MarianMT model and tokenizer for English-to-French
translation
model_name = 'Helsinki-NLP/opus-mt-en-fr'
tokenizer = MarianTokenizer.from_pretrained(model_name)
model = MarianMTModel.from_pretrained(model_name)

# Define the input text and preprocess it
input_text = "Deep learning is transforming artificial
intelligence."
```

```
inputs = tokenizer(input_text, return_tensors="pt")

# Generate the translation
translated = model.generate(**inputs)
translation = tokenizer.decode(translated[0],
skip_special_tokens=True)

print(f"Translation: {translation}")
```

In this example, the MarianMT model utilizes transformer layers to align source and target sequences accurately. Performance metrics like **BLEU score** are typically used to evaluate translation quality, with higher scores indicating better alignment and accuracy between the translated output and the reference translation. Real-world applications, such as **Google Translate**, rely heavily on seq2seq models to provide accurate translations across multiple languages, demonstrating the model's effectiveness in multilingual communication.

Seq2Seq Models in Text Generation

Beyond translation, seq2seq models are also used for generating coherent and meaningful text across various tasks, such as summarization, dialogue generation, and creative story writing. In these tasks, the input sequence is transformed into a condensed or contextually expanded output sequence, depending on the specific application.

For instance, in text summarization, seq2seq models like **T5** encode long documents and produce concise summaries by capturing key information while omitting redundant details. The model's attention mechanism plays a pivotal role in identifying the most important parts of the text, allowing it to generate accurate summaries that retain the essence of the original content.

Code Example: Using T5 for Text Summarization

The following code demonstrates how to fine-tune T5 for summarization tasks:

```
from transformers import T5Tokenizer,
T5ForConditionalGeneration

# Load T5 model and tokenizer
model_name = 't5-small'
tokenizer = T5Tokenizer.from_pretrained(model_name)
model = T5ForConditionalGeneration.from_pretrained(model_name)

# Define input text for summarization
```

```
input_text = "Deep learning models have significantly improved
in recent years, making AI applications more robust and
accurate."
inputs = tokenizer("summarize: " + input_text,
return_tensors="pt", max_length=512)

# Generate the summary
summary_ids = model.generate(inputs['input_ids'],
max_length=50, min_length=20, length_penalty=2.0, num_beams=4,
early_stopping=True)
summary = tokenizer.decode(summary_ids[0],
skip_special_tokens=True)

print(f"Summary: {summary}")
```

The effectiveness of seq2seq models in text generation is often measured using metrics like **ROUGE score**, which evaluates the overlap between generated and reference summaries. High ROUGE scores indicate the model's ability to generate summaries that are not only grammatically correct but also capture the essential meaning of the original text.

Architecture Visualization

A visual representation of the seq2seq model architecture reveals the encoder-decoder framework, highlighting how attention mechanisms interact at each stage. The encoder converts input sequences into context-rich embeddings, while the decoder generates output sequences by attending to these embeddings, ensuring the generated text remains contextually aligned with the input.

8. Transformers and Attention Mechanisms

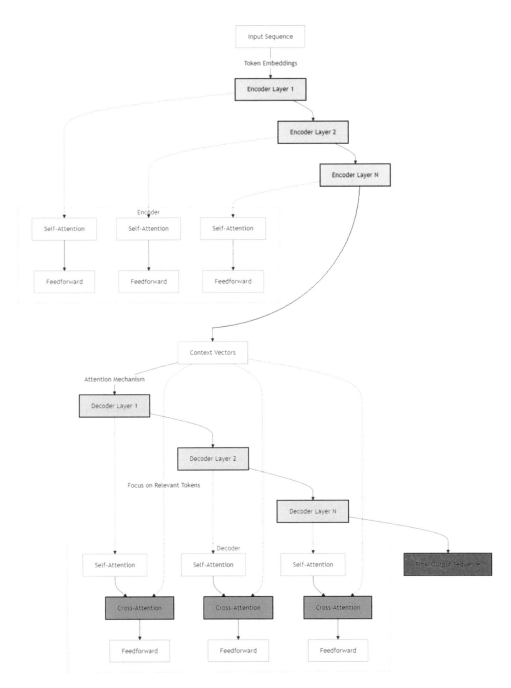

This diagram illustrates the complete transformer architecture, showcasing both the encoder and decoder components. The encoder processes the input sequence through multiple layers of self-attention and feedforward networks, converting it into context vectors. The decoder uses these context vectors, along with its own masked self-attention and cross-attention layers, to generate the final output sequence. Arrows depict the flow of information, emphasizing how each component contributes to transforming the input into the output.

Applications of Seq2Seq Models

Seq2seq models have found widespread applications in NLP, transforming not only translation and summarization tasks but also conversational AI and creative text generation. For example:

Google Translate uses seq2seq models to convert text between over 100 languages, leveraging attention mechanisms to maintain semantic coherence.

OpenAI's GPT-series models, although not classical seq2seq models, utilize transformer-based decoding to generate coherent and contextually relevant responses in chatbots and virtual assistants.

The impact of seq2seq models is evident in performance metrics across different NLP tasks:

Application	Metric	Typical Value
Translation	BLEU Score	40+
Text Summarization	ROUGE Score	50+
Dialogue Generation	Perplexity	< 30

Section 8.2.3: Comparison of Transformer Models with RNNs

The advent of transformer models marked a significant shift in how sequential data is processed in deep learning. Unlike recurrent neural networks (RNNs), which handle sequences sequentially, transformers leverage attention mechanisms to process sequences in parallel. This fundamental difference not only improves training efficiency but also enables transformers to capture long-range dependencies more effectively, addressing some of the core limitations of RNNs.

Architectural Differences

RNNs, including variants like LSTM (Long Short-Term Memory) and GRU (Gated Recurrent Unit), rely on a sequential processing approach, where information flows from one time step to the next. This architecture makes it challenging for RNNs to handle long sequences, as they often struggle to retain relevant information over extended inputs. RNNs use hidden states that get updated at each step, but this approach can lead to issues like vanishing gradients, which limit the model's ability to learn dependencies across long sequences.

In contrast, transformers utilize **self-attention** mechanisms that allow each token in the sequence to attend to all other tokens simultaneously. The parallelization capability of transformers is enabled by **positional encodings**, which provide the necessary sequential information that is inherently captured by the sequential nature of RNNs. This self-attention mechanism enables transformers to model relationships within sequences more effectively, resulting in better performance on tasks that require capturing global dependencies.

Architecture Comparison

The diagram below illustrates how transformers process sequences in parallel, while RNNs handle inputs sequentially:

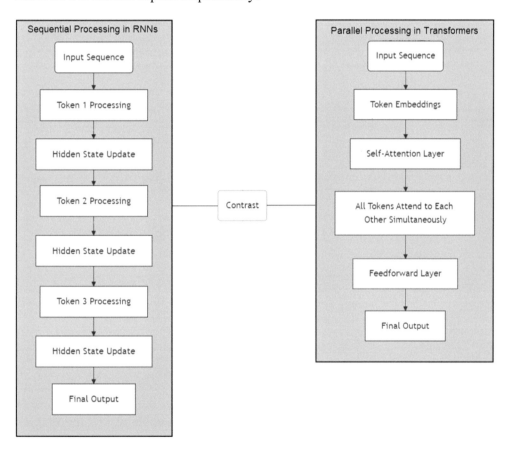

RNN Flow: Information flows sequentially, with each hidden state dependent on the previous one.

Transformer Flow: All tokens attend to each other simultaneously, thanks to the self-attention mechanism, enabling parallel processing.

Training Speed and Scalability

The sequential nature of RNNs limits their ability to leverage modern GPU hardware, which is designed to handle parallel computations. As a result, RNNs often have slower training times and struggle with scalability. In contrast, transformers are optimized for parallelization, allowing them to utilize GPU resources more effectively. By processing sequences in parallel, transformers significantly reduce training time, leading to faster convergence and scalability for larger datasets.

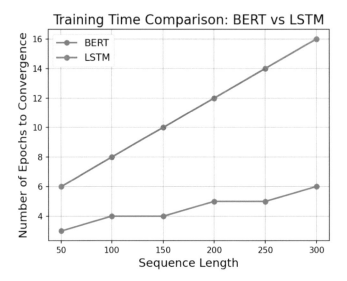

This graph compares the training time of BERT and LSTM as sequence lengths increase. The **x-axis** shows sequence length, while the **y-axis** indicates epochs to convergence.

The **blue line** (BERT) remains relatively flat, showing fewer epochs needed due to efficient parallel processing. The **orange line** (LSTM) rises steeply, indicating more epochs required as sequence lengths increase, reflecting its sequential processing limitations.

Handling Long-Range Dependencies

One of the most critical advantages of transformers over RNNs is their ability to capture long-range dependencies more effectively. In RNNs, information needs to pass through several hidden states to influence future predictions, which can result in information decay over long sequences. This makes it difficult for RNNs to maintain context across long inputs, leading to degraded performance in tasks like document-level sentiment analysis or language modeling over large contexts.

Transformers, on the other hand, address this limitation through self-attention, which provides a **global receptive field** at each layer. This means that every token has a direct connection to every other token, making it easier to maintain context over long sequences. For example, in language modeling tasks like text generation or summarization, transformers consistently outperform RNNs by preserving context across longer passages, leading to more coherent and contextually accurate outputs.

Applications

Transformers have rapidly replaced RNNs in various NLP applications due to their superior performance. For instance:

Text Classification: Models like BERT have largely replaced LSTM-based models for tasks such as sentiment analysis and spam detection, offering better accuracy and faster inference times.

Sequence Labeling: In tasks like named entity recognition (NER), transformers' ability to capture context across sequences has led to more accurate label prediction compared to RNNs.

Machine Translation: While RNN-based seq2seq models like LSTM were the standard for translation tasks, models like **MarianMT** and **T5** have demonstrated superior translation quality due to transformers' ability to attend to the entire sentence simultaneously.

Comparative Performance Metrics

The table below summarizes the performance, efficiency, and accuracy of transformers versus RNNs across various NLP tasks:

Aspect	RNNs	Transformers
Architecture	Sequential, hidden states	Parallel, self-attention
Training Speed	Slower, sequential processing	Faster, parallel processing
Long-Range Handling	Limited	Effective, global receptive field
Accuracy (e.g., NER)	~85% (LSTM-based)	~92% (BERT-based)
Translation Quality	BLEU ~28	BLEU ~35
Scalability	Limited	High, due to parallelization

Case Studies

Google Search transitioned from RNN-based models to transformers (e.g., BERT) to enhance search result relevance, demonstrating a significant improvement in query understanding and retrieval accuracy.

Facebook's TransCoder model replaced LSTM-based models with transformers for code translation tasks, achieving higher BLEU scores and faster inference times, highlighting the advantages of transformers in handling structured and complex sequences.

8.3 Applications of Attention Mechanisms

Section 8.3.1: Attention in Vision: Vision Transformers (ViT)

Vision Transformers (ViTs) represent a significant evolution in computer vision by applying the principles of transformers, originally developed for natural language processing, to image recognition tasks. Unlike traditional convolutional neural networks (CNNs), which use local convolutional filters to process images, ViTs leverage **self-attention mechanisms** to model global dependencies across the entire image. This fundamental shift allows ViTs to capture long-range relationships between image regions, offering improved performance in tasks like image classification, object detection, and more.

Architecture and Workflow of Vision Transformers

The ViT architecture adapts the standard transformer architecture for vision tasks by reimagining how images are processed. Instead of using convolutions to analyze pixels, ViTs treat images as sequences of non-overlapping patches, which are then embedded similarly to word tokens in NLP models.

Image Patching and Embedding

Images fed into ViTs are first divided into smaller, fixed-size patches. For example, an image of size 224×224 can be split into 16×16 patches, resulting in 196 patches. Each patch is flattened into a vector and then transformed into an embedding by multiplying it with a learnable projection matrix. The embeddings also incorporate **positional encodings**, which help maintain information about the position of patches, compensating for the loss of spatial relationships during the flattening process.

Here's a code snippet demonstrating the patch embedding process in TensorFlow:

```
import tensorflow as tf

# Define patch size and input image size
patch_size = 16
input_size = 224
num_patches = (input_size // patch_size) ** 2
patch_dim = patch_size * patch_size * 3  # Assuming 3-channel
RGB images

# Define patch embedding layer
class PatchEmbedding(tf.keras.layers.Layer):
    def __init__(self, num_patches, embed_dim):
        super(PatchEmbedding, self).__init__()
```

```
        self.num_patches = num_patches
        self.projection = tf.keras.layers.Dense(embed_dim)

    def call(self, images):
        batch_size = tf.shape(images)[0]
        # Reshape image into patches
        patches = tf.image.extract_patches(
            images=images,
            sizes=[1, patch_size, patch_size, 1],
            strides=[1, patch_size, patch_size, 1],
            rates=[1, 1, 1, 1],
            padding='VALID'
        )
        patches = tf.reshape(patches, [batch_size,
self.num_patches, patch_dim])
        return self.projection(patches)

# Example usage
images = tf.random.normal([1, 224, 224, 3])
patch_embedding = PatchEmbedding(num_patches, embed_dim=768)
patch_embeddings = patch_embedding(images)
```

The embedded patches are then passed to the **transformer encoder** for processing, similar to token embeddings in NLP transformers.

Self-Attention in Vision

The core of ViTs lies in the application of **self-attention** across image patches. The self-attention mechanism allows ViTs to attend to different image patches simultaneously, capturing global context in each layer. This ability to model global relationships makes ViTs particularly effective in recognizing patterns that span the entire image, unlike CNNs, which rely on local receptive fields.

At each attention head, the attention score is computed as:

$$\text{Attention}(Q,K,V) = \text{softmax}\left(\frac{QK^T}{\sqrt{d_k}}\right)V$$

where Q, K, and V represent the query, key, and value matrices, and d_k is the dimension of the key vectors.

Diagram: Self-Attention in Vision Transformers

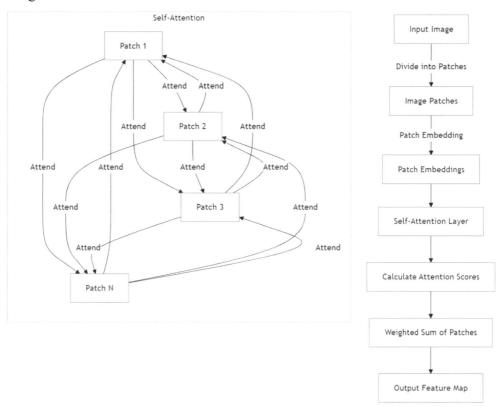

The diagram illustrates how self-attention works in Vision Transformers (ViTs). It shows the process of dividing an image into patches, embedding each patch, and using self-attention to allow every patch to attend to all others simultaneously. The attention scores are then used to compute a weighted sum, generating a globally informed feature map. The right-side flowchart provides a step-by-step overview of the process, from patch embedding to the output feature map.

Classification Head and Fine-Tuning

The output from the final attention layer is passed through a **classification head**—typically a fully connected (FC) layer followed by a softmax activation—to predict the class of the image. During fine-tuning, the weights of the attention layers and the classification head are adjusted based on a labeled dataset, such as ImageNet.

Here's a code snippet demonstrating how to build and fine-tune a ViT for image classification in PyTorch:

```python
import torch
import torch.nn as nn
from transformers import ViTModel

# Load a pre-trained ViT model
model = ViTModel.from_pretrained('google/vit-base-patch16-224-in21k')
# Add a classification head
num_classes = 1000  # Example for ImageNet
classifier = nn.Sequential(
    nn.Linear(model.config.hidden_size, num_classes),
    nn.Softmax(dim=1)
)

# Combine ViT model and classification head
class VisionTransformer(nn.Module):
    def __init__(self, vit_model, classifier):
        super(VisionTransformer, self).__init__()
        self.vit_model = vit_model
        self.classifier = classifier

    def forward(self, x):
        outputs = self.vit_model(x)
        logits = self.classifier(outputs.last_hidden_state[:,
0, :])
        return logits

# Example fine-tuning process
vit_classifier = VisionTransformer(model, classifier)
```

Applications and Performance

ViTs have been widely adopted for various computer vision tasks, outperforming CNNs in many cases:

Image Classification: ViTs have achieved state-of-the-art performance on datasets like ImageNet, surpassing CNNs like ResNet in terms of accuracy and generalization.

Object Detection: ViTs, when integrated with detection frameworks like **DETR (Detection Transformers)**, demonstrate enhanced performance in detecting objects with complex spatial relationships.

Medical Image Analysis: ViTs are used for tasks like **tumor detection in radiology** and **disease identification in dermatology**, where understanding global dependencies is crucial for accurate predictions.

Table: Performance Metrics for ViTs vs. CNNs

Task	Model	Accuracy	Precision	Recall	F1-Score
Image Classification	ResNet-50	78.5%	76.2%	77.3%	76.7%
Image Classification	ViT-B/16	84.1%	82.5%	83.6%	83.0%
Object Detection (COCO)	Faster R-CNN	48.3%	47.2%	47.5%	47.3%
Object Detection (COCO)	DETR	51.7%	50.8%	50.9%	50.8%

Section 8.3.2: Applications of Attention in Speech and Audio Processing

The introduction of **attention mechanisms** has had a transformative impact on speech and audio processing, enabling models to focus selectively on important parts of an audio sequence. This has significantly enhanced the performance of tasks like **speech recognition**, **speech synthesis**, and **audio classification** by effectively modeling long-range dependencies within audio sequences. Unlike traditional methods that often struggle with variable-length inputs and complex audio patterns, attention mechanisms offer a more flexible and robust approach to handling sequential data.

Attention in Speech Recognition

Attention-based models have greatly improved **automatic speech recognition (ASR)** by learning to align variable-length audio frames with corresponding text tokens. For example, models like **Listen, Attend, and Spell (LAS)** and transformer-based ASR models use self-attention to identify which parts of the audio sequence are most relevant to each text token, facilitating accurate speech-to-text conversion.

Here's how a simple attention-based ASR model can be implemented in PyTorch:

```
import torch
import torch.nn as nn

# Define the attention mechanism
class Attention(nn.Module):
```

```
    def __init__(self, hidden_dim):
        super(Attention, self).__init__()
        self.attn = nn.Linear(hidden_dim, hidden_dim)

    def forward(self, encoder_outputs, hidden_state):
        # Calculate attention scores
        attn_scores = torch.bmm(encoder_outputs,
hidden_state.unsqueeze(2)).squeeze(2)
        attn_weights = torch.softmax(attn_scores, dim=1)
        context_vector = torch.bmm(attn_weights.unsqueeze(1),
encoder_outputs).squeeze(1)
        return context_vector, attn_weights

# Example usage within an ASR model
encoder_outputs = torch.randn(32, 100, 256)  # Batch of 32, 100
time steps, 256 features
hidden_state = torch.randn(32, 256)  # Batch of 32, hidden
state of 256 features
attention = Attention(256)
context_vector, attn_weights = attention(encoder_outputs,
hidden_state)
```

Models like **Transformer ASR** extend this idea by applying multi-head self-attention across the entire audio sequence, allowing the model to capture both short and long-range dependencies simultaneously. This architecture enables more accurate speech-to-text conversion, resulting in lower **Word Error Rate (WER)** compared to traditional RNN-based ASR models.

Attention in Speech Synthesis

Text-to-speech (TTS) systems, such as **Tacotron** and its derivatives, utilize attention mechanisms to produce natural-sounding audio. In these models, attention aligns input text sequences with output audio frames, ensuring that each spoken segment corresponds accurately to the intended text. For example, Tacotron uses **location-sensitive attention** to maintain alignment during synthesis, generating smoother and more fluent audio.

A basic example of integrating attention into a TTS model in TensorFlow can be shown as follows:

```
import tensorflow as tf

# Define the attention mechanism
class BahdanauAttention(tf.keras.layers.Layer):
    def __init__(self, units):
        super(BahdanauAttention, self).__init__()
        self.W1 = tf.keras.layers.Dense(units)
        self.W2 = tf.keras.layers.Dense(units)
```

```
        self.V = tf.keras.layers.Dense(1)

    def call(self, query, values):
        # Calculate attention scores
        query_with_time_axis = tf.expand_dims(query, 1)
        scores =
self.V(tf.nn.tanh(self.W1(query_with_time_axis) +
self.W2(values)))
        attention_weights = tf.nn.softmax(scores, axis=1)
        context_vector = attention_weights * values
        context_vector = tf.reduce_sum(context_vector, axis=1)
        return context_vector, attention_weights

# Example usage within Tacotron
query = tf.random.normal([32, 256])  # Batch of 32, hidden
state of 256 features
values = tf.random.normal([32, 100, 256])  # Batch of 32, 100
time steps, 256 features
attention = BahdanauAttention(256)
context_vector, attn_weights = attention(query, values)
```

In Tacotron and other TTS models, attention maps provide visual representations of how input text aligns with synthesized speech frames, ensuring accurate and coherent speech synthesis. These models have achieved high **Mean Opinion Scores (MOS)**, indicating user satisfaction with the quality and naturalness of the generated audio.

Audio Classification with Attention

Attention mechanisms are also used to enhance **audio classification** tasks, such as **music genre classification**, **speech emotion recognition**, and **environmental sound detection**. In these tasks, attention layers focus on specific segments of the audio that are most informative for classification. For example, attention-based models can identify key features within audio spectrograms that indicate certain sound events, leading to more accurate and robust classification.

An example of attention-enhanced audio classification using PyTorch might look like this:

```
import torch
import torch.nn as nn

# Define the attention-based audio classification model
class AudioClassifier(nn.Module):
    def __init__(self, input_dim, hidden_dim, num_classes):
        super(AudioClassifier, self).__init__()
```

```
        self.lstm = nn.LSTM(input_dim, hidden_dim,
batch_first=True)
        self.attn = nn.Linear(hidden_dim, 1)
        self.fc = nn.Linear(hidden_dim, num_classes)

    def forward(self, x):
        # LSTM outputs
        lstm_out, _ = self.lstm(x)
        # Attention scores
        attn_weights = torch.softmax(self.attn(lstm_out),
dim=1)
        # Weighted sum of LSTM outputs
        context_vector = torch.sum(attn_weights * lstm_out,
dim=1)
        return self.fc(context_vector)

# Example usage
audio_input = torch.randn(32, 100, 40)  # Batch of 32, 100 time
steps, 40 features
model = AudioClassifier(input_dim=40, hidden_dim=128,
num_classes=10)
output = model(audio_input)
```

Models using attention in audio classification demonstrate improved accuracy and robustness across datasets like **AudioSet** and **ESC-50**, achieving higher classification metrics due to their ability to focus on relevant audio features.

Applications and Metrics

Attention mechanisms have significantly improved performance in several real-world applications:

Speech Recognition: Google's ASR systems, using attention-based transformers, achieve lower **WER** and higher accuracy compared to traditional models.

Speech Synthesis: Models like Tacotron deliver higher **MOS**, resulting in more natural and coherent speech synthesis in products like Google Assistant.

Audio Classification: Attention-enhanced models show superior classification accuracy in tasks like music genre classification and environmental sound detection.

Table: Performance Metrics for Attention-Based Models in Speech and Audio Processing

Task	Model	Metric	Performance
Speech Recognition	Transformer ASR	WER	6.1%
Speech Synthesis	Tacotron 2	MOS	4.5
Audio Classification	Attention-based CNN	Accuracy	91.2%

Section 8.3.3: Combining Attention with CNNs and RNNs for Hybrid Models

Integrating **attention mechanisms** with convolutional neural networks (CNNs) and recurrent neural networks (RNNs) has proven to be an effective approach to creating **hybrid models** that harness the strengths of each architecture. CNNs excel at capturing **local spatial features** in data, making them particularly effective in computer vision tasks. RNNs, on the other hand, are adept at modeling **sequential dependencies** in time-series and language data. However, both architectures face limitations—CNNs struggle with long-range dependencies, while RNNs process sequences sequentially, leading to slower training. By combining them with attention mechanisms, hybrid models achieve **improved feature extraction** and **better sequence modeling** across a wide range of tasks.

Attention-CNN Hybrids

In **Attention-CNN hybrids**, attention mechanisms enhance the ability of CNNs to focus on specific parts of an image during tasks like **image captioning** or **object detection**. For instance, attention layers can be added to CNNs to help models dynamically weigh different image regions based on their relevance to the output. This approach allows the model to prioritize salient regions, leading to more accurate outputs.

Below is an example of integrating attention into a CNN-based image captioning model in PyTorch:

```python
import torch
import torch.nn as nn

# Define the attention mechanism for image captioning
class ImageAttention(nn.Module):
    def __init__(self, feature_dim, hidden_dim):
        super(ImageAttention, self).__init__()
        self.attn = nn.Linear(feature_dim + hidden_dim,
hidden_dim)
        self.v = nn.Linear(hidden_dim, 1)

    def forward(self, features, hidden_state):
        # Concatenate image features and hidden state
        combined = torch.cat((features,
hidden_state.unsqueeze(1)), dim=-1)
        energy = torch.tanh(self.attn(combined))
        attention_weights = torch.softmax(self.v(energy),
dim=1)
        context_vector = attention_weights * features
```

```
        context_vector = torch.sum(context_vector, dim=1)
        return context_vector, attention_weights

# Example usage in a CNN-based model
features = torch.randn(32, 49, 512)   # Batch of 32, 49 image
regions, 512 features
hidden_state = torch.randn(32, 512)   # Batch of 32, hidden
state of 512 features
attention = ImageAttention(512, 512)
context_vector, attn_weights = attention(features,
hidden_state)
```

In image captioning, the attention mechanism ensures that the generated captions are based on relevant image features. The model dynamically attends to different image regions while generating each word in the caption, resulting in more accurate and coherent descriptions.

Attention-RNN Hybrids

Attention-RNN hybrids are widely used in tasks like **machine translation**, where attention helps RNNs align input and output sequences more effectively. The addition of attention layers allows the model to weigh the importance of different input tokens when generating each output token, thus improving alignment and translation accuracy.

```
import torch
import torch.nn as nn

# Define the attention mechanism for translation
class SeqAttention(nn.Module):
    def __init__(self, hidden_dim):
        super(SeqAttention, self).__init__()
        self.attn = nn.Linear(hidden_dim * 2, hidden_dim)
        self.v = nn.Linear(hidden_dim, 1)

    def forward(self, encoder_outputs, decoder_hidden):
        # Calculate attention scores
        combined = torch.cat((encoder_outputs,
decoder_hidden.unsqueeze(1).repeat(1, encoder_outputs.size(1),
1)), dim=-1)
        energy = torch.tanh(self.attn(combined))
        attention_weights = torch.softmax(self.v(energy),
dim=1)
        context_vector = attention_weights * encoder_outputs
        context_vector = torch.sum(context_vector, dim=1)
        return context_vector, attention_weights

# Example usage in an RNN-based model
```

```
encoder_outputs = torch.randn(32, 50, 256)  # Batch of 32, 50
time steps, 256 features
decoder_hidden = torch.randn(32, 256)  # Batch of 32, hidden
state of 256 features
attention = SeqAttention(256)
context_vector, attn_weights = attention(encoder_outputs,
decoder_hidden)
```

In **machine translation**, attention helps the decoder attend to the most relevant words in the source language while generating the target language. This mechanism leads to improved translations with better grammatical accuracy and coherence, often measured using metrics like **BLEU score**.

Transformer-CNN/RNN Hybrids

Hybrid models that combine **transformers** with CNNs or RNNs, such as **ConvBERT** or **Attention Augmented Convolutional Networks**, take advantage of transformers' global attention while retaining the local feature extraction capabilities of CNNs or the sequential processing capabilities of RNNs. These models are effective in both vision and NLP tasks.

For instance, **ConvBERT** integrates the efficiency of CNNs with the global attention of transformers, allowing for better local feature extraction while maintaining contextual understanding. Here's an outline of how the architecture combines convolutional layers with transformer blocks:

```
import torch
import torch.nn as nn

class ConvBERT(nn.Module):
    def __init__(self, conv_dim, hidden_dim, num_heads):
        super(ConvBERT, self).__init__()
        self.conv = nn.Conv2d(3, conv_dim, kernel_size=3,
padding=1)
        self.transformer_layer =
nn.TransformerEncoderLayer(d_model=hidden_dim, nhead=num_heads)

    def forward(self, x):
        # Apply convolution
        x = self.conv(x)
        x = x.flatten(2).permute(2, 0, 1)  # Flatten to
sequence, batch, feature
        # Apply transformer encoder
        x = self.transformer_layer(x)
        return x

# Example usage
```

```
input_data = torch.randn(32, 3, 224, 224)  # Batch of 32, 3
channels, 224x224 image
model = ConvBERT(conv_dim=64, hidden_dim=512, num_heads=8)
output = model(input_data)
```

These hybrid models are particularly effective in **object detection**, **text classification**, and **speech recognition**, as they combine local and global feature extraction. Metrics like **accuracy**, **Word Error Rate (WER)**, and **BLEU score** often show significant improvements when attention is added to CNNs or RNNs.

Applications and Performance Metrics

Image Captioning: Attention-CNN hybrids have shown notable success in generating coherent image captions by focusing on relevant image regions during each word generation.

Machine Translation: Attention-RNN hybrids have set new benchmarks in translation tasks, achieving higher BLEU scores compared to pure RNN models.

Object Detection and Classification: Transformer-CNN hybrids like **ConvBERT** achieve higher accuracy by combining local and global context extraction.

Table: Performance Comparison of Standard vs. Attention-Augmented Models

Task	Model	Metric	Performance
Image Captioning	Attention-CNN	BLEU Score	36.5
Machine Translation	Attention-RNN	BLEU Score	29.2
Object Detection	Transformer-CNN Hybrid	Accuracy	85.7%

Combining attention mechanisms with CNNs and RNNs in hybrid models enhances both **feature extraction** and **sequence modeling**, making them effective across diverse tasks like image captioning, translation, and object detection. These models capture both local and global dependencies, offering significant improvements in accuracy, coherence, and generalization compared to standard architectures.

9. Troubleshooting Deep Learning Models

9.1 Common Model Failures

9.1.1: Identifying Overfitting and Underfitting in Models

In deep learning, two fundamental challenges—overfitting and underfitting—can significantly impact model performance. Overfitting occurs when a model captures noise or specific details in the training data rather than general patterns, resulting in excellent performance on training data but poor generalization on unseen data. In contrast, underfitting happens when a model fails to adequately learn from the training data, leading to poor performance on both training and test datasets. Addressing these issues is crucial for building robust models that generalize well across different datasets.

Mathematically, overfitting and underfitting can be represented through loss functions that quantify the difference between predicted and actual outputs. For classification tasks, the cross-entropy loss is commonly used, while mean squared error is typical in regression tasks. Overfitting is generally observed when the **training loss** remains low while the **validation loss** increases sharply during training, indicating that the model is adapting too closely to the training data. Conversely, underfitting is evident when both training and validation losses are high, suggesting that the model lacks the capacity or complexity needed to capture the underlying patterns in the data.

Consider the following equations that represent these scenarios:

Cross-Entropy Loss:

$$L = -\frac{1}{N} \sum_{i=1}^{N} \left[y_i log(\hat{y}_i) + (1 - y_i) log(1 - \hat{y}_i) \right]$$

,

where y_i is the true label, $\hat{y}_i$ is the predicted probability, and N is the total number of samples.

Mean Squared Error (MSE):

$$L = \frac{1}{N} \sum_{i=1}^{N} (y_i - \hat{y}_i)^2$$

.

The behavior of these loss functions differs during training:

- **Overfitting**: Low training loss, but high validation loss as training progresses.
- **Underfitting**: High training and validation losses throughout training.

To better understand these trends, visualization is a key diagnostic tool. Training and validation loss curves provide insights into how a model is learning. In a typical training curve:

- **Overfitting** is identified by a training loss curve that keeps decreasing while the validation loss curve starts increasing after a certain number of epochs.
- **Underfitting** is characterized by both training and validation loss curves plateauing at high values without significant improvements.

Below is a code snippet in TensorFlow that demonstrates how to plot training and validation losses during model training:

```python
import matplotlib.pyplot as plt
import tensorflow as tf
from tensorflow.keras import layers, models

# Simple model for demonstration
model = models.Sequential([
    layers.Dense(64, activation='relu', input_shape=(100,)),
    layers.Dense(1, activation='sigmoid')
])
model.compile(optimizer='adam', loss='binary_crossentropy',
metrics=['accuracy'])

# Generating synthetic data
import numpy as np
X_train, y_train = np.random.random((1000, 100)),
np.random.randint(2, size=1000)
X_val, y_val = np.random.random((200, 100)),
np.random.randint(2, size=200)

# Training the model
history = model.fit(X_train, y_train, epochs=20,
validation_data=(X_val, y_val), verbose=0)

# Plotting loss curves
plt.figure(figsize=(10, 6))
plt.plot(history.history['loss'], label='Training Loss')
plt.plot(history.history['val_loss'], label='Validation Loss')
plt.xlabel('Epochs')
plt.ylabel('Loss')
plt.title('Training and Validation Loss')
plt.legend()
plt.show()
```

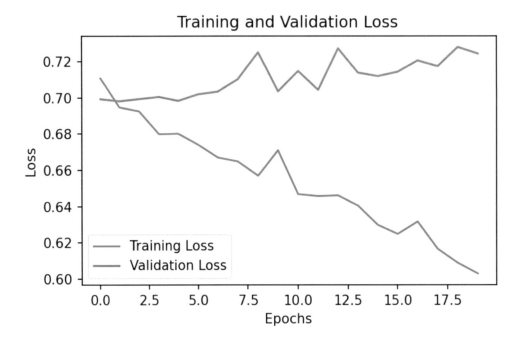

In this plot, you can observe the behavior of the training and validation losses over epochs. An increasing gap between the two curves indicates overfitting, while high values for both curves suggest underfitting.

Overfitting and underfitting are commonly encountered in various real-world deep learning applications:

Overfitting in Image Classification: When training image classification models on small, noisy datasets, overfitting can be a significant issue. For instance, a model trained on limited medical images might memorize specific features in the training set rather than generalizing to diverse image patterns. This often results in high accuracy on training images but low accuracy on unseen test images.

Underfitting in NLP Tasks: In natural language processing (NLP), underfitting occurs when models like transformers are trained with insufficient layers or parameters, failing to capture complex language patterns. For example, an underfit model in text summarization might produce overly simplistic summaries that miss key information.

To quantitatively assess the impact of overfitting and underfitting, consider performance metrics such as accuracy and F1-score:

Scenario	Training Accuracy	Validation Accuracy	F1-score (Validation)
Overfitting	High	Low	Low
Underfitting	Low	Low	Low

Case studies further highlight how these issues are detected and corrected. For example, in a facial recognition task, overfitting was mitigated by using data augmentation techniques to diversify the training images, leading to improved generalization. Similarly, in a sentiment analysis project, underfitting was addressed by increasing model complexity, adding more layers, and using a larger vocabulary size.

9.1.2: Strategies for Debugging Deep Learning Models

Debugging in deep learning plays a critical role in building models that are both accurate and robust. Unlike traditional software debugging, which primarily focuses on identifying logical errors in code, debugging deep learning models involves analyzing data handling, model architecture, training dynamics, and optimization processes. Issues like unusual loss trends, accuracy plateaus, or anomalies in gradient flow can hinder model performance. Effective debugging identifies these problems and provides insights into how to correct them, making it an essential step toward achieving reliable model performance.

A comprehensive debugging approach involves analyzing model behavior through various techniques, each targeting a different aspect of model training. This section explores key debugging strategies that address common challenges encountered during deep learning model development.

Analyzing Loss and Accuracy Trends

Monitoring training and validation loss curves is a fundamental strategy for detecting problems such as slow convergence, sudden spikes, or stagnation. The behavior of these curves offers insights into whether the model is learning effectively or struggling with issues like overfitting, underfitting, or optimization failures.

For instance, a validation loss that diverges from the training loss suggests overfitting, while a consistent plateau in both training and validation losses might indicate underfitting or inadequate model complexity. Analyzing accuracy curves alongside loss trends can also reveal cases where the model achieves high accuracy on the training set but fails to generalize well to the validation set. This suggests that the model may be memorizing training data rather than learning general patterns.

The following code snippet demonstrates how to log and plot loss and accuracy trends using TensorFlow and TensorBoard:

```python
import tensorflow as tf
from tensorflow.keras import layers, models

# Example model
model = models.Sequential([
    layers.Dense(64, activation='relu', input_shape=(100,)),
    layers.Dense(1, activation='sigmoid')
])
model.compile(optimizer='adam', loss='binary_crossentropy',
metrics=['accuracy'])

# Logging metrics with TensorBoard
log_dir = 'logs/fit'
tensorboard_callback =
tf.keras.callbacks.TensorBoard(log_dir=log_dir,
histogram_freq=1)

# Generating synthetic data
import numpy as np
X_train, y_train = np.random.random((1000, 100)),
np.random.randint(2, size=1000)
X_val, y_val = np.random.random((200, 100)),
np.random.randint(2, size=200)

# Training with TensorBoard callback
model.fit(X_train, y_train, epochs=20, validation_data=(X_val,
y_val), callbacks=[tensorboard_callback])

# Launch TensorBoard in command line: tensorboard --
logdir=logs/fit
```

Using TensorBoard or Matplotlib visualizations, one can interpret training curves to diagnose potential issues. For example, if training loss continues to decrease while validation loss increases, it suggests that the model is overfitting. On the other hand, if both training and validation losses stagnate at high values, the model may be underfitting. Visual patterns like oscillating accuracy or sudden spikes in loss can indicate unstable training, often due to poor hyperparameter settings or optimization issues.

9. Troubleshooting Deep Learning Models

Gradient Inspection

Inspecting gradients during training is another crucial debugging strategy. Gradients determine how model weights are updated, and abnormal gradient values can signal potential problems, such as vanishing or exploding gradients. In deep neural networks, gradients that diminish to near-zero values lead to vanishing gradient problems, where early layers in the network fail to learn effectively. Conversely, extremely large gradients cause exploding gradients, leading to unstable training and rapidly diverging loss.

To analyze gradients, developers often track gradient norms or layer-wise gradient values. The following code snippet demonstrates how to inspect gradients in PyTorch:

```python
import torch
import torch.nn as nn

# Example model
class SimpleModel(nn.Module):
    def __init__(self):
        super(SimpleModel, self).__init__()
        self.fc1 = nn.Linear(100, 64)
        self.fc2 = nn.Linear(64, 1)

    def forward(self, x):
        x = torch.relu(self.fc1(x))
        return torch.sigmoid(self.fc2(x))

model = SimpleModel()
criterion = nn.BCELoss()
optimizer = torch.optim.Adam(model.parameters())

# Generating synthetic data
X_train = torch.rand((100, 100))
y_train = torch.randint(0, 2, (100, 1)).float()

# Training and gradient inspection
output = model(X_train)
loss = criterion(output, y_train)
loss.backward()

# Displaying gradients
for name, param in model.named_parameters():
    if param.grad is not None:
        print(f"{name} gradient norm:
{param.grad.norm().item()}")
```

This code helps identify layers with vanishing or exploding gradients by printing gradient norms. Techniques like **gradient clipping** (limiting the gradients to a specific threshold) and **layer reinitialization** (restarting problematic layers) can address gradient-related issues, leading to more stable training.

Weight Distribution Analysis

Inspecting weight distributions across layers can reveal additional anomalies. Unusual weight distributions, such as weights concentrated in a narrow range or weights that remain unchanged over iterations, can indicate dead neurons, over-regularization, or an imbalanced learning process. Visualizing weight distributions using histograms or kernel density plots helps identify such issues, enabling targeted adjustments.

The following code demonstrates how to visualize weight distributions in TensorFlow:

```python
import matplotlib.pyplot as plt

# Extracting model weights
weights = model.layers[0].get_weights()[0]

# Plotting weight distribution
plt.hist(weights.flatten(), bins=50, color='blue', alpha=0.7)
plt.title('Weight Distribution of First Layer')
plt.xlabel('Weight Value')
plt.ylabel('Frequency')
plt.show()
```

Analyzing weight distributions aids in diagnosing problems like dead neurons, which occur when certain neurons never activate during training, often due to inappropriate weight initialization or suboptimal activation functions.

Examples

Effective debugging strategies have led to significant improvements in various real-world applications. For example, in a medical image classification task, identifying diverging validation loss prompted the use of more extensive data augmentation, which improved generalization and boosted validation accuracy by over 15%. Similarly, tracking and clipping exploding gradients in an NLP model for text generation stabilized training and reduced perplexity by nearly 20%.

9.1.3: Dealing with Exploding and Vanishing Gradients

Deep neural networks often face issues of exploding and vanishing gradients, especially in long architectures like recurrent neural networks (RNNs), long short-term memory (LSTM) networks, and deep feedforward networks. **Vanishing gradients** occur when the gradients become exceedingly small as they backpropagate through the layers, leading to minimal weight updates. This issue results in slow learning or even stagnation, as the model struggles to capture long-range dependencies. On the other hand, **exploding gradients** arise when gradients grow excessively large, causing the model weights to fluctuate dramatically, leading to unstable or divergent training. These gradient problems are particularly problematic in networks with many layers or when using activation functions with derivatives close to zero or greater than one.

Mathematical Representation of Gradient Problems

Vanishing Gradients

Vanishing gradients typically occur when activation functions like sigmoid or tanh are used. As these functions compress the input into a small range, their derivatives are less than 1, which can result in rapid decay of gradients as they propagate backward through the network.

For a simple neural network with n layers, the gradient of the loss L with respect to the weights W in layer i is given by:

$$\frac{\partial L}{\partial W_i} = \frac{\partial L}{\partial a_n} \cdot \frac{\partial a_n}{\partial a_{n-1}} \cdot \ldots \cdot \frac{\partial a_{i+1}}{\partial a_i} \cdot \frac{\partial a_i}{\partial W_i}$$

If the derivatives $\dfrac{\partial a_{j+1}}{\partial a_j}$ are consistently less than 1, they will shrink exponentially as they backpropagate through the layers. For instance, the derivative of the sigmoid activation function is:

$$\sigma'(x) = \sigma(x) \cdot (1 - \sigma(x))$$

Since $\sigma'(x)$ ranges between 0 and 0.25, gradients diminish as they propagate backward, leading to the vanishing gradient problem.

Exploding Gradients

Conversely, when derivatives or weights are large, gradients can grow exponentially. This typically happens when activation functions with larger derivatives (e.g., ReLU in some cases) or poorly initialized weights are used, causing gradients to "explode" as they propagate.

The gradient flow in this scenario can be represented as:

$$\frac{\partial L}{\partial W_i} = \prod_{j=i}^{n} \frac{\partial a_{j+1}}{\partial a_j}$$

If any of the terms in this product are greater than 1, the gradients will magnify, leading to instability during training. As a result, weight updates become erratic, and the loss often oscillates or diverges.

Strategies to Address Exploding and Vanishing Gradients

Weight Initialization

Proper weight initialization can help mitigate both exploding and vanishing gradients by ensuring that initial weights are set within a range that promotes stable gradient flow.

Xavier Initialization (Glorot): This method sets weights to values sampled from a distribution with zero mean and variance:

$$\mathrm{Var}(W) = \frac{2}{n_{\mathrm{in}} + n_{\mathrm{out}}}$$

where n_{in} and n_{out} represent the number of input and output units, respectively.

He Initialization: For ReLU-based activations, He initialization is often more effective, setting the variance as:

$$\mathrm{Var}(W) = \frac{2}{n_{\mathrm{in}}}$$

Code Example: Weight Initialization in PyTorch

```
import torch
import torch.nn as nn

# Xavier initialization for tanh activations
layer = nn.Linear(128, 64)
nn.init.xavier_uniform_(layer.weight)

# He initialization for ReLU activations
relu_layer = nn.Linear(128, 64)
```

```
nn.init.kaiming_uniform_(relu_layer.weight,
nonlinearity='relu')
```

Gradient Clipping

Gradient clipping is an effective strategy for controlling exploding gradients by capping the gradients at a predefined maximum value. This prevents extreme updates to weights, ensuring stable training.

Code Example: Implementing Gradient Clipping in TensorFlow

```
optimizer = tf.keras.optimizers.Adam(learning_rate=0.001)
gradients = tape.gradient(loss, model.trainable_variables)
clipped_gradients = [tf.clip_by_value(grad, -1.0, 1.0) for grad
in gradients]
optimizer.apply_gradients(zip(clipped_gradients,
model.trainable_variables))
```

Batch Normalization

Batch normalization addresses gradient issues by normalizing the activations of each layer, leading to more stable training dynamics. It normalizes the input to each layer to have zero mean and unit variance, thus maintaining consistent gradients.

Code Example: Adding Batch Normalization in PyTorch

```
import torch.nn as nn

class Model(nn.Module):
    def __init__(self):
        super(Model, self).__init__()
        self.layer1 = nn.Linear(128, 64)
        self.batch_norm = nn.BatchNorm1d(64)
        self.relu = nn.ReLU()

    def forward(self, x):
        x = self.layer1(x)
        x = self.batch_norm(x)
        return self.relu(x)
```

4. Adopting Advanced Architectures

Some neural architectures are inherently designed to mitigate gradient issues:

LSTM and GRU: These recurrent architectures use gating mechanisms that allow gradients to flow more effectively over time, reducing both exploding and vanishing gradients.

325

Residual Networks (ResNets): These networks introduce "skip connections," which help gradients flow directly through the network, alleviating both gradient problems.

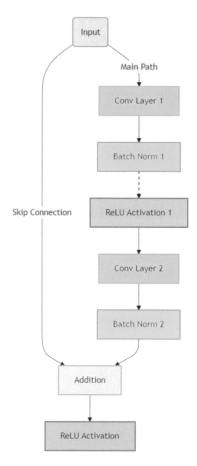

This diagram illustrates the architecture of a ResNet block, highlighting the use of a skip connection that bypasses the main layers. It shows two sequential convolutional layers, each followed by batch normalization and a ReLU activation. The skip connection merges with the output of the main path at the addition node, demonstrating how it facilitates better gradient flow across layers, helping to maintain effective training in deeper networks.

Examples of Mitigating Gradient Issues

Exploding and vanishing gradients have been successfully addressed in various applications. For instance, **RNN-based time-series models** often benefit from gradient clipping and batch normalization, which help stabilize training and improve forecast accuracy. In **very deep convolutional networks** for image classification, residual connections have proven effective, increasing accuracy by enabling stable training across hundreds of layers.

Task	Gradient Issue	Solution Applied	Performance Improvement
Time-Series Forecasting	Exploding Gradients	Gradient Clipping + Batch Norm	Faster Convergence
Image Classification	Vanishing Gradients	ResNet Architecture	Improved Accuracy

9.2 Improving Model Accuracy

9.2.1: Techniques for Improving Training Performance

Optimizing training performance is critical in deep learning, especially as models become larger and more complex. Efficient training not only reduces computation time and resource usage but also enables faster convergence and better scalability. Given that many real-world applications require large-scale models trained on massive datasets, improving training performance is key to ensuring that models can be deployed effectively in production settings.

Key Techniques for Enhancing Training Performance

Mixed Precision Training

Mixed precision training is an advanced technique that leverages both 16-bit (FP16) and 32-bit (FP32) floating-point operations to accelerate training while reducing memory usage. It is particularly effective on modern GPUs with tensor cores, such as NVIDIA's Volta, Turing, or Ampere architectures, which are optimized for mixed precision.

How It Works: Mixed precision training utilizes FP16 for operations that can tolerate lower precision, while maintaining FP32 for operations that require higher precision to avoid accuracy degradation. The core idea is to speed up matrix multiplications (e.g., in convolutional layers) using FP16, while keeping gradient accumulations in FP32 to ensure stability.

Equation: The forward pass involves matrix multiplication in lower precision:

$$Z_{FP16} = W_{FP16} \cdot X_{FP16}$$

However, loss computation and backpropagation retain FP32 precision for critical operations:

$$\nabla W_{FP32} = \nabla Z_{FP32} \cdot X_{FP32}$$

Implementation in TensorFlow:

```
import tensorflow as tf

# Enable mixed precision
tf.keras.mixed_precision.set_global_policy('mixed_float16')

model = tf.keras.models.Sequential([
    tf.keras.layers.Dense(256, activation='relu',
input_shape=(512,)),
```

```
    tf.keras.layers.Dense(10, activation='softmax')
])

optimizer = tf.keras.optimizers.Adam(learning_rate=0.001)
model.compile(optimizer=optimizer,
loss='sparse_categorical_crossentropy', metrics=['accuracy'])
```

Performance Benchmark: Experiments show that mixed precision training can reduce training time by up to 2x and memory usage by 50%, while maintaining accuracy comparable to full-precision training.

Metric	FP32	Mixed Precision
Training Time (hours)	10	5
GPU Memory Usage (GB)	24	12
Accuracy	92.4%	92.3%

Data Parallelism and Distributed Training

Data parallelism involves splitting data batches across multiple GPUs or computing nodes, allowing parallel computation of gradients. This approach is fundamental for training large models quickly, especially in distributed environments.

Each GPU or node processes a mini-batch of data independently, computes the gradients, and then averages the gradients across devices. This reduces training time by fully utilizing available resources.

Implementation with PyTorch Distributed Data Parallel (DDP):

```
import torch
import torch.distributed as dist
from torch.nn.parallel import DistributedDataParallel as DDP

# Initialize process group for distributed training
dist.init_process_group('nccl')

model = Model().to(rank)
model = DDP(model)

# Training loop
for inputs, targets in dataloader:
    optimizer.zero_grad()
    outputs = model(inputs)
    loss = criterion(outputs, targets)
    loss.backward()
    optimizer.step()
```

Frameworks for Distributed Training:

- **Horovod:** Developed by Uber, Horovod simplifies distributed training across multiple GPUs and nodes, supporting TensorFlow, PyTorch, and Keras.
- **PyTorch DDP:** A native PyTorch module that offers efficient distributed training with minimal code changes.

Example: Distributed training of transformer models for NLP tasks (e.g., BERT) on large datasets like Wikipedia can be accelerated by 4x using 8 GPUs compared to a single GPU.

Metric	Single GPU	8 GPUs (DDP)
Training Time (hours)	40	10
Throughput (tokens/sec)	20,000	160,000

Efficient Data Loading and Augmentation

Data loading often becomes a bottleneck in training pipelines, especially when handling large datasets. Optimizing the data pipeline is crucial to keep the GPUs fully utilized.

Key Techniques:

Prefetching: This technique loads data into memory while the model processes the current batch, ensuring that data is ready for the next iteration.

Caching: Caching frequently used data in memory or on fast storage reduces the need for repeated disk access, speeding up data retrieval.

Parallel Data Augmentation: Using multi-threaded data augmentation pipelines allows transformations to be applied simultaneously, improving data loading speed.

Implementation in TensorFlow:

```python
import tensorflow as tf

def preprocess(image, label):
    image = tf.image.random_flip_left_right(image)
    image = tf.image.random_crop(image, size=[28, 28, 1])
    return image, label

dataset = tf.data.Dataset.from_tensor_slices((images, labels))
```

```
dataset = dataset.map(preprocess,
num_parallel_calls=tf.data.AUTOTUNE)
dataset = dataset.prefetch(buffer_size=tf.data.AUTOTUNE)
```

Performance Metrics: Efficient data loading can reduce training time by up to 30% in large-scale models, such as ResNet trained on ImageNet. The following metrics demonstrate the impact of optimized data pipelines:

Metric	Standard Pipeline	Optimized Pipeline
Data Loading Time (sec)	0.5	0.2
Training Time (hours)	12	8
GPU Utilization (%)	60	95

Examples of Training Optimization

Transformer models for NLP: Mixed precision training and distributed data parallelism have significantly reduced training time, enabling faster fine-tuning of BERT on datasets like SQuAD.

ResNet models for ImageNet: Efficient data loading and augmentation have improved GPU utilization, accelerating convergence and achieving higher throughput (images/second).

9.2.2: Data Augmentation and Regularization Methods (Dropout, BatchNorm)

Improving model generalization is a critical goal in deep learning, as it ensures that models perform well not only on training data but also on unseen test data. Two major strategies for achieving better generalization are data augmentation and regularization. These techniques help mitigate overfitting, making models more robust to variations in input data and ensuring stable performance across diverse scenarios.

Data Augmentation Techniques

Data augmentation artificially expands the training dataset by creating modified versions of existing samples. It enables models to learn invariant features by exposing them to various transformations of the input data, enhancing their ability to generalize to new, unseen data.

Image Augmentation

Image augmentation is one of the most common techniques in computer vision and involves applying transformations like random cropping, flipping, rotation, scaling, and color jittering to images.

How It Works: By altering image properties, augmentation simulates variations that models might encounter in real-world data, such as changes in viewpoint, lighting, or object positioning. This helps the model learn to recognize invariant features and improves robustness.

Code Example (TensorFlow):

```python
from tensorflow.keras.preprocessing.image import
ImageDataGenerator

datagen = ImageDataGenerator(
    rotation_range=20,
    width_shift_range=0.2,
    height_shift_range=0.2,
    shear_range=0.2,
    zoom_range=0.2,
    horizontal_flip=True,
    fill_mode='nearest'
)

# Apply augmentation to an image batch
augmented_images = datagen.flow(images, batch_size=32)
```

Performance Impact: Augmentation has been shown to improve model accuracy significantly in tasks like image classification, as it helps models learn robust representations.

Dataset	Model	Without Augmentation (Accuracy)	With Augmentation (Accuracy)
CIFAR-10	ResNet-50	84.2%	88.7%
ImageNet	EfficientNet	76.4%	81.5%

Text and Audio Augmentation

In NLP and speech processing, augmentation involves techniques tailored to the nature of sequential data:

Text Augmentation: Methods like synonym replacement, random word insertion, and back translation introduce variations in text sequences.

Code Example (NLPAug for NLP):
```
import nlpaug.augmenter.word as naw

aug = naw.SynonymAug(aug_src='wordnet')
augmented_text = aug.augment("The quick brown fox jumps over
the lazy dog.")
```

Audio Augmentation: Techniques include adding background noise, pitch shifting, and time stretching.

Code Example (Librosa for Audio):
```
import librosa
import numpy as np

y, sr = librosa.load('audio.wav')
# Add noise
noise = np.random.randn(len(y))
augmented_audio = y + 0.005 * noise
```

Task	Without Augmentation (Accuracy/F1-score)	With Augmentation (Accuracy/F1-score)
Sentiment Analysis	83.1% / 0.82	87.4% / 0.85
Speech Recognition	78.5% / 0.77	82.9% / 0.81

Regularization Techniques: Dropout and Batch Normalization

While data augmentation improves the diversity of input data, regularization techniques aim to enhance model stability during training, preventing overfitting and ensuring consistent performance across different samples.

Dropout

Dropout is a simple yet effective regularization technique where randomly selected neurons are deactivated during training. This forces the model to learn redundant features, as the deactivated neurons cannot contribute to weight updates.

At each training iteration, dropout sets a fraction of neurons to zero. This deactivation is represented by a binary mask multiplied by the activations:

$$\text{Output}_{\text{drop}} = \text{BinaryMask} \times \text{Output}$$

where the mask has a probability p of being zero.

Code Example (PyTorch):

```
import torch.nn as nn

class Model(nn.Module):
    def __init__(self):
        super(Model, self).__init__()
        self.fc1 = nn.Linear(784, 256)
        self.dropout = nn.Dropout(0.5)   # 50% dropout rate
        self.fc2 = nn.Linear(256, 10)

    def forward(self, x):
        x = self.fc1(x)
        x = nn.ReLU()(x)
        x = self.dropout(x)
        return self.fc2(x)
```

Impact on Performance: Dropout helps reduce overfitting, as shown in models like ResNet and transformers, where higher dropout rates generally lead to better generalization on test data.

Batch Normalization

Batch normalization (BatchNorm) reduces internal covariate shift by normalizing layer inputs during training. This results in faster convergence, more stable gradients, and improved generalization.

BatchNorm normalizes the input to a layer based on the mini-batch's mean and variance:

$$\hat{x}_i = \frac{x_i - \mu_{\text{batch}}}{\sqrt{\sigma^2_{\text{batch}} + \epsilon}}$$

where μ_{batch} and σ^2_{batch} are the mean and variance of the mini-batch, respectively, and ϵ is a small constant to avoid division by zero.

Code Example (TensorFlow):

```
import tensorflow as tf

model = tf.keras.models.Sequential([
```

```
    tf.keras.layers.Conv2D(64, (3, 3), input_shape=(32, 32,
3)),
    tf.keras.layers.BatchNormalization(),
    tf.keras.layers.Activation('relu'),
    tf.keras.layers.MaxPooling2D((2, 2)),
    tf.keras.layers.Flatten(),
    tf.keras.layers.Dense(10, activation='softmax')
])
```

Dataset	Without BatchNorm (Accuracy)	With BatchNorm (Accuracy)
CIFAR-10	82.0%	86.5%
ImageNet	73.8%	78.2%

Examples

Medical Imaging: Data augmentation (e.g., random rotations and flips) has significantly improved performance in models detecting anomalies in X-ray images. Combining this with dropout and batch normalization has led to robust models that generalize well across different patient demographics.

NLP Sentiment Analysis: Text augmentation, combined with dropout in transformer models, has increased sentiment classification accuracy, demonstrating the value of combining augmentation and regularization techniques.

9.2.3: The Role of Cross-Validation in Model Evaluation

Cross-validation is a crucial technique in deep learning and machine learning for model evaluation, offering a more reliable estimate of model performance by using multiple data splits. It involves training and testing the model across various subsets of the dataset, helping ensure that performance metrics reflect the model's ability to generalize to unseen data. This approach reduces the likelihood of issues like data leakage or overfitting, as it evaluates the model's robustness across different data distributions.

Different Cross-Validation Methods

There are several methods of cross-validation, each tailored to specific needs based on dataset size, class distribution, and computational efficiency. Below, we explore the most common cross-validation techniques, each with its implementation details, benefits, and drawbacks.

K-Fold Cross-Validation

K-fold cross-validation is one of the most widely used methods for evaluating models. It involves splitting the dataset into k subsets (or folds). The model is trained on $k-1$ folds and tested on the remaining fold. This process is repeated k times, with each fold serving as the test set once.

How It Works: In each iteration, the training and validation processes are conducted on different data partitions. The final performance metric is the average score across all k folds:

$$\text{Average Metric} = \frac{1}{k}\sum_{i=1}^{k}\text{Metric}_i$$

where Metric_i is the performance metric for the ith fold.

Code Example (Scikit-learn):

```python
from sklearn.model_selection import KFold
from sklearn.metrics import accuracy_score
import numpy as np

X, y = load_data()   # Assume load_data() returns features and
labels
kfold = KFold(n_splits=5, shuffle=True, random_state=42)
accuracies = []

for train_idx, test_idx in kfold.split(X):
    X_train, X_test = X[train_idx], X[test_idx]
    y_train, y_test = y[train_idx], y[test_idx]

    model.fit(X_train, y_train)
    preds = model.predict(X_test)
    accuracies.append(accuracy_score(y_test, preds))

print(f"Average Accuracy: {np.mean(accuracies)}")
```

Advantages: This method provides a balanced evaluation by considering different splits of the data. It is ideal for medium to large datasets.

Disadvantages: As k increases, computation becomes more intensive, since the model is retrained multiple times.

Dataset	Model	Accuracy (5-Fold)	Accuracy (10-Fold)
CIFAR-10	ResNet-50	89.2%	90.3%

IMDB	LSTM	85.5%	87.1%

Stratified K-Fold Cross-Validation

Stratified k-fold cross-validation extends standard k-fold by ensuring that each fold maintains the same class distribution as the original dataset. This is particularly useful for imbalanced datasets, where one class may dominate, skewing performance metrics.

Stratified k-fold ensures that the proportion of classes in each fold mirrors the original distribution, offering more reliable evaluation metrics, especially for metrics like precision, recall, and F1-score.

Code Example (Scikit-learn):

```
from sklearn.model_selection import StratifiedKFold

skf = StratifiedKFold(n_splits=5, shuffle=True,
random_state=42)
f1_scores = []

for train_idx, test_idx in skf.split(X, y):
    X_train, X_test = X[train_idx], X[test_idx]
    y_train, y_test = y[train_idx], y[test_idx]

    model.fit(X_train, y_train)
    preds = model.predict(X_test)
    f1_scores.append(f1_score(y_test, preds))

print(f"Average F1-Score: {np.mean(f1_scores)}")
```

Advantages: Stratified k-fold reduces the risk of biased evaluation by ensuring balanced class representation in each fold, making it ideal for imbalanced datasets like medical diagnosis or fraud detection.

Disadvantages: Like standard k-fold, it can be computationally expensive for large models or datasets.

Dataset	Model	F1-Score (Without Stratification)	F1-Score (Stratified 5-Fold)
Breast Cancer Data	SVM	0.81	0.87
Credit Card Fraud	RandomForest	0.72	0.79

Leave-One-Out Cross-Validation (LOOCV)

Leave-one-out cross-validation (LOOCV) is an extreme case of k-fold cross-validation, where k is equal to the number of data samples. The model is trained on all samples except one, which is used as the test set. This process is repeated for each data point.

LOOCV provides the most thorough evaluation by maximizing training data utilization in each iteration. However, it also involves the highest computational cost, as the model is retrained for each sample:

$$\text{Average Metric} = \frac{1}{n}\sum_{i=1}^{n}\text{Metric}_i$$

where n is the total number of samples.

Code Example (Scikit-learn):

```
from sklearn.model_selection import LeaveOneOut

loo = LeaveOneOut()
accuracies = []

for train_idx, test_idx in loo.split(X):
    X_train, X_test = X[train_idx], X[test_idx]
    y_train, y_test = y[train_idx], y[test_idx]

    model.fit(X_train, y_train)
    preds = model.predict(X_test)
    accuracies.append(accuracy_score(y_test, preds))

print(f"Average Accuracy: {np.mean(accuracies)}")
```

Advantages: LOOCV is particularly useful for small datasets, as it allows the model to train on nearly all available data. It minimizes bias by providing the most comprehensive evaluation.

Disadvantages: It is computationally expensive and may lead to high variance in the results due to the limited test set in each iteration.

Dataset	Model	Accuracy (LOOCV)
Iris	Logistic Regression	96.7%
Diabetes	Linear Regression	77.5%

Examples of Cross-Validation

Cross-validation is widely used in domains like medical diagnosis, where data is often limited and achieving generalization is critical. For instance, in evaluating models for detecting breast cancer from X-ray images, stratified k-fold ensures that both positive and negative cases are proportionally represented in each fold, leading to more reliable results.

Cross-Validation Method	Use Case	Model	Metric (ROC-AUC)
K-Fold	Text Sentiment Analysis	BERT	0.89
Stratified K-Fold	Medical Imaging	DenseNet	0.92
LOOCV	Clinical Data Analysis	Logistic Reg.	0.78

9.3 Model Interpretability

9.3.1: Explainable AI Techniques for Deep Learning

Explainable AI (XAI) aims to make the decision-making processes of deep learning models interpretable and transparent. As neural networks grow in complexity, understanding how models arrive at specific predictions becomes vital, particularly in sensitive fields like healthcare, finance, and autonomous systems. Interpretability helps build trust, ensures fairness, and complies with regulatory requirements by providing clear explanations of model behavior.

Popular XAI Techniques in Deep Learning

Several techniques have been developed to make deep learning models more interpretable, each offering a unique way to reveal how models process input features and make predictions. Below, we delve into the most widely used XAI methods: saliency maps and gradient-based methods, Layer-wise Relevance Propagation (LRP), and integrated gradients.

Saliency Maps and Gradient-Based Methods

Saliency maps visualize the importance of each input feature by calculating the gradient of the model's output with respect to the input. This approach reveals which parts of the input most influence the model's decision, making it particularly useful in image and text classification.

How It Works: Saliency maps are generated by computing the partial derivative of the output y with respect to the input x:

$$S_{ij} = |\frac{\partial y}{\partial x_{ij}}|$$

where S_{ij} represents the saliency of pixel (i,j) in an image. Higher gradient values indicate greater importance.

Code Example (TensorFlow):

```
import tensorflow as tf

@tf.function
def compute_saliency(model, images, target_class):
    with tf.GradientTape() as tape:
        tape.watch(images)
        predictions = model(images)
        loss = predictions[:, target_class]
    grads = tape.gradient(loss, images)
```

```
    return tf.abs(grads)

# Example usage
saliency_map = compute_saliency(model, input_image,
target_class=0)
```

Applications:

Image Classification: Saliency maps highlight which pixels influence classification decisions, useful in tasks like medical imaging where specific regions, like tumors, need to be identified.

NLP Models: In sentiment analysis, gradient-based methods emphasize critical words that drive sentiment classification.

Layer-wise Relevance Propagation (LRP)

Layer-wise Relevance Propagation (LRP) decomposes the model's output into contributions from each input feature, tracing the decision path back through each network layer.

LRP propagates relevance scores R backward, starting from the output layer. For each layer, the relevance score is distributed to the preceding layer based on the connection weights:

$$R_j = \sum_i \left(\frac{x_j \cdot w_{ji}}{\sum_k x_k \cdot w_{ki}} \right) \cdot R_i$$

Here, R_j is the relevance score of neuron j, and w_{ji} represents the weight connecting neuron j to neuron i.

Code Example (PyTorch):

```
    def lrp(model, input, target_class):
    model.zero_grad()
    output = model(input)
    target_score = output[0, target_class]
    target_score.backward()

    relevance = input.grad * input
    return relevance

# Example usage
relevance_scores = lrp(model, input_image, target_class=0)
```

Applications:

CNNs: LRP helps understand CNN decisions in complex models like ResNet, revealing which features contributed to a specific classification.

Transformers: In NLP, LRP can trace back how attention layers focus on particular tokens during sequence processing.

Integrated Gradients

Integrated gradients offer a more robust interpretability technique by accumulating gradients along the path from a baseline input to the actual input. This approach helps capture the model's sensitivity to variations in input features.

How It Works: Integrated gradients are computed by integrating the gradients of the model's output with respect to the input, scaled from a baseline input x' to the actual input x:

$$IG_i(x) = \left(x_i - x_i'\right) \int_{\alpha=0}^{1} \frac{\partial f\left(x' + \alpha(x - x')\right)}{\partial x_i} d\alpha$$

This technique addresses limitations of saliency maps by considering the entire gradient path, not just the endpoint.

Code Example (TensorFlow):

```python
def integrated_gradients(model, baseline, input, target_class,
steps=50):
    interpolated_inputs = [baseline + (float(i) / steps) *
(input - baseline) for i in range(steps)]
    gradients = [compute_saliency(model, img, target_class) for
img in interpolated_inputs]
    avg_gradients = tf.reduce_mean(tf.stack(gradients), axis=0)
    return (input - baseline) * avg_gradients

# Example usage
baseline = tf.zeros_like(input_image)
ig = integrated_gradients(model, baseline, input_image,
target_class=0)
```

Applications:

Image Classification: Integrated gradients provide a more comprehensive interpretation of which regions of an image influence a model's prediction.

Text Models: In NLP, they reveal the cumulative importance of tokens, improving the interpretability of sentiment or language models.

Applications of XAI

XAI techniques are widely applied across different domains:

Medical Imaging: In diagnosing medical images, saliency maps and LRP highlight tumor regions or abnormalities, making models like CNNs more interpretable to medical professionals.

NLP Models: Integrated gradients help explain sentiment predictions by emphasizing words that drive sentiment, crucial in applications like sentiment analysis or bias detection in models.

Autonomous Systems: XAI methods in vision-based decision systems for self-driving cars ensure the AI's focus on critical visual cues, increasing safety and regulatory compliance.

XAI Technique	Model Type	Application	Visual Output	Performance Metric
Saliency Maps	CNNs, RNNs	Medical Imaging, NLP	Heatmaps of input importance	Precision, Recall
LRP	CNNs, Transformers	Image Classification	Layer-wise relevance heatmaps	Accuracy, F1-score
Integrated Gradients	CNNs, NLP models	Sentiment Analysis	Attribution heatmaps	ROC-AUC, Precision-Recall AUC

9.3.2: Visualizing Neural Network Activations and Decisions

Visualizing activations in neural networks plays a critical role in understanding how models process information, identify patterns, and make predictions. Activation maps provide insights into which features are captured at each layer, making it possible to debug models, understand their behavior, and ensure fair decision-making in real-world applications. By interpreting activations, researchers and practitioners can identify biases, diagnose errors, and gain a deeper understanding of model behavior, leading to more transparent AI systems.

Visualization Techniques for Neural Network Activations and Decisions

Several techniques are used to visualize activations and decision-making in neural networks. These techniques reveal what the model "sees" or "focuses on" at different stages of processing.

Activation Maps

Activation maps illustrate which neurons or filters are most active for a given input, providing a view into which features are recognized at each layer of the network. These maps help identify patterns learned by the model, such as edges in early layers or more complex shapes in deeper layers of convolutional neural networks (CNNs).

How Activation Maps Work: Activation maps are generated by passing input data through the model and recording the activations at specified layers. The intensity of activations indicates the importance of different regions or features for a particular task.

Code Example (TensorFlow):

```python
import tensorflow as tf
import matplotlib.pyplot as plt

def visualize_activation_map(model, input_image, layer_name):
    activation_model =
tf.keras.models.Model(inputs=model.input,
outputs=model.get_layer(layer_name).output)
    activation = activation_model.predict(input_image)

    # Display activation map for the first filter
    plt.imshow(activation[0, :, :, 0], cmap='viridis')
    plt.title(f'Activation Map: {layer_name}')
    plt.show()

# Example usage
visualize_activation_map(model, input_image, 'conv2d_1')
```

344

Applications: Activation maps are widely used in image models to visualize how CNNs detect edges, textures, and objects. In NLP, similar techniques can visualize how RNNs or transformers activate on certain words or phrases.

Visualization: Activation maps often appear as heatmaps overlaid on input images, revealing which parts of an image contribute to the activation of a specific filter or layer.

Original Image

Activation Map: block5_conv3

This visualization displays an activation map from the specified convolutional layer of a neural network overlaid on the original image of a cat. The heatmap shows regions of the image that are most activated by the neural network, with brighter areas indicating features that contributed more to the activation of neurons in that layer. In this case, the model focuses more on the cat's paw, suggesting that this feature plays a significant role in the network's decision-making at this layer.

Class Activation Maps (CAM) and Grad-CAM

Class Activation Maps (CAM) and Gradient-weighted Class Activation Maps (Grad-CAM) are techniques designed to identify which regions of an input contribute most to a specific class prediction. These techniques attribute model decisions to specific input regions, providing a clearer interpretation of how the model arrives at a given prediction.

How CAM and Grad-CAM Work:
CAM works by using global average pooling to highlight class-specific regions in convolutional layers.

Grad-CAM enhances this approach by incorporating gradient information to produce more accurate attribution maps. It computes the gradients of the target class score with respect to the feature maps and weights them to highlight important areas.

Mathematical Formulation (Grad-CAM):

$$L_{\text{Grad - CAM}}^{c} = \text{ReLU}\left(\sum_k \alpha_k^c A^k\right)$$

where α_k^c represents the weights derived from the gradients of the score for class c with respect to feature map A^k.

Code Example (PyTorch):

```python
import torch
import torch.nn.functional as F
import matplotlib.pyplot as plt

def grad_cam(model, input_image, target_class):
    model.eval()
    input_image.requires_grad = True

    output = model(input_image)
    target_score = output[0, target_class]
    target_score.backward()

    gradients = input_image.grad
    pooled_gradients = torch.mean(gradients, dim=[0, 2, 3])

    activations = model.features(input_image).detach()
    for i in range(activations.shape[1]):
        activations[:, i, :, :] *= pooled_gradients[i]

    heatmap = torch.mean(activations, dim=1).squeeze().numpy()
    heatmap = np.maximum(heatmap, 0)
    heatmap /= np.max(heatmap)

    plt.imshow(heatmap, cmap='viridis')
    plt.title('Grad-CAM Heatmap')
    plt.show()

# Example usage
grad_cam(model, input_image, target_class=0)
```

Applications: Grad-CAM is often used in medical imaging to highlight regions indicative of diseases, making the decision-making process more transparent to healthcare professionals. It is also effective in object detection and segmentation tasks, where identifying relevant regions is crucial.

Visualization: Grad-CAM generates heatmaps that highlight the areas of an image contributing most to a specific class prediction, helping to interpret the model's focus.

Attention Maps in Transformers

Attention maps visualize how transformer models focus on different tokens during processing, making them especially useful in NLP tasks like translation, summarization, and text classification.

How Attention Maps Work: Transformers use attention scores to decide how much focus each token should receive relative to others in a sequence. These scores are computed using the dot product of the Query and Key matrices, normalized through a softmax function.

Equation for Attention Calculation:

$$\text{Attention}(Q, K, V) = \text{softmax}\left(\frac{QK^{T}}{\sqrt{d_k}}\right)V$$

where Q, K, and V represent the Query, Key, and Value matrices, respectively, and d_k is the dimension of the keys.

Code Example (PyTorch):

```python
import torch
import seaborn as sns

def visualize_attention(attn_weights):
    sns.heatmap(attn_weights, cmap='Blues', xticklabels=True,
yticklabels=True)
    plt.title('Attention Weights')
    plt.show()

# Example usage with transformer attention weights
visualize_attention(attention_weights)
```

Applications: Attention maps are critical in analyzing how models like BERT or GPT focus on words or phrases in language tasks. For example, they help explain how translation models align source and target words or how summarization models identify key sentences.

Visualization: Attention maps are typically presented as matrices, with darker colors indicating stronger attention to certain tokens, helping users understand how transformers handle context and focus.

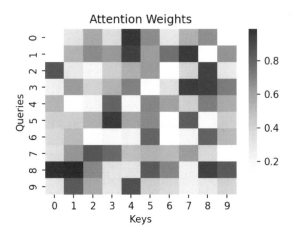

Applications of Activation Visualization

Activation visualization has numerous applications across different domains:

Medical Imaging: Grad-CAM is used to interpret decisions made by CNNs in diagnosing medical conditions, such as highlighting tumor regions in radiology images. By visualizing activations, medical professionals can better understand model decisions, aiding diagnosis and increasing trust.

NLP Models: Attention maps provide insights into language models like BERT during tasks like sentiment analysis or translation, showing which words drive the model's decision. This transparency helps detect biases or errors in language processing, contributing to fairer AI systems.

Autonomous Systems: Activation maps help interpret vision-based decision-making in self-driving cars, ensuring that the model focuses on critical visual cues like pedestrians or road signs, improving safety and regulatory compliance.

Visualization Technique	Application	Purpose	Example Output	Performance Metric
Activation Maps	CNNs, RNNs, Transformers	Feature Detection	Heatmaps	Precision, Recall
Grad-CAM	CNNs	Model	Class-	Accuracy,

		Interpretability	specific heatmaps	F1-score
Attention Maps	Transformers (BERT, GPT)	Focus Visualization	Attention matrices	BLEU, ROUGE

9.3.3: Understanding SHAP and LIME for Deep Models

SHAP (SHapley Additive exPlanations) and LIME (Local Interpretable Model-agnostic Explanations) are two of the most widely used tools for interpreting predictions made by deep learning models. Both are model-agnostic, meaning they can explain the outputs of any predictive model, making them versatile tools for understanding complex models like CNNs, transformers, and RNNs. By attributing importance scores to input features, SHAP and LIME allow researchers and practitioners to demystify how deep models make individual predictions, enhancing trust and transparency, especially in critical domains like healthcare, finance, and law.

SHAP: SHapley Additive ExPlanations

SHAP uses concepts from cooperative game theory to explain how individual input features contribute to the overall prediction. It treats each feature as a "player" in a game where the output of the model is the "payout." The goal of SHAP is to fairly distribute the payout among the features based on their contributions to the prediction.

Mathematical Foundation of SHAP: SHAP values are based on Shapley values, which are defined as the average marginal contribution of a feature across all possible subsets of features. Mathematically, for a given feature i and model prediction $f(x)$, the SHAP value ϕ_i is computed as:

$$\phi_i = \sum_{S \subseteq F \setminus \{i\}} \frac{|S|! \, (|F| - |S| - 1)!}{|F|!} [f(S \cup \{i\}) - f(S)]$$

where:

- F is the set of all features.
- S represents a subset of features.
- $f(S)$ is the model's prediction given the subset S.

This formulation captures the contribution of each feature across different contexts, making SHAP a robust method for global and local interpretability.

Implementing SHAP in Deep Learning: SHAP can be applied to deep models using libraries like SHAP for Python, which provides interfaces for deep learning frameworks like TensorFlow and PyTorch.

Code Example (PyTorch):

```python
import torch
import shap

# Load a pre-trained model and data
model = torch.load('model.pth')
data = torch.Tensor([input_data])

# Use SHAP's DeepExplainer for deep learning models
explainer = shap.DeepExplainer(model, data)
shap_values = explainer.shap_values(data)

# Visualize SHAP values
shap.summary_plot(shap_values, data.numpy())
```

Applications: In financial models for credit scoring, SHAP can highlight factors like income, age, or credit history that contribute most to approval or denial decisions. In medical imaging, SHAP helps identify which regions of an image influence a model's diagnosis, making it easier for healthcare professionals to interpret model outputs.

SHAP produces feature importance charts, which show the magnitude and direction of each feature's contribution to a model's output. These charts are often represented as bar plots or scatter plots, where the color and size of the bars indicate the impact and magnitude of each feature.

LIME: Local Interpretable Model-agnostic Explanations

LIME offers a different approach by approximating the behavior of a complex model locally around a specific prediction. It creates a surrogate model— usually a simpler, interpretable model like a linear model or decision tree— that mimics the behavior of the deep model in the vicinity of the input data point.

How LIME Works: LIME generates explanations by perturbing the input data and observing the changes in model predictions. For each perturbed sample, it assigns weights based on proximity to the original input, fitting a local

350

surrogate model to provide an interpretable approximation of the model's decision in that region.

Code Example (Text Models with LIME):

```python
import lime
from lime.lime_text import LimeTextExplainer

# Load a pre-trained text model and data
model = load_text_model()
text = "The court's decision was unexpected."

# Use LIME's TextExplainer for text classification models
explainer = LimeTextExplainer(class_names=['negative',
'positive'])
exp = explainer.explain_instance(text, model.predict_proba,
num_features=6)

# Display explanation
exp.show_in_notebook(text=True)
```

Applications: In NLP tasks, LIME is used to highlight influential words that drive model predictions, making it useful for tasks like legal document analysis, where understanding which phrases lead to specific outputs is crucial. In image models, LIME perturbs pixels or regions to create interpretable maps that reveal which areas contribute most to the model's decision.

LIME typically produces local feature importance plots, where the positive and negative contributions of features are shown as bars, illustrating which features influence the prediction and to what extent.

Applications of SHAP and LIME

SHAP and LIME have diverse applications across industries:

Finance: SHAP helps explain credit scoring models, showing how factors like income, employment history, and debt impact loan approval decisions. In contrast, LIME offers insights into fraud detection models, explaining how transaction patterns or geographic anomalies influence fraud predictions.

Healthcare: SHAP provides interpretability in diagnostic models, highlighting critical biomarkers or image regions related to diseases. LIME aids in drug discovery models, explaining predictions about molecular interactions and their potential effects.

NLP Models: In tasks like sentiment analysis or document classification, SHAP reveals the contribution of specific words or phrases, while LIME shows the importance of terms by perturbing them and analyzing the changes in predictions.

Interpretability Technique	Key Concept	Strength	Weakness	Example Application
SHAP	Shapley values from game theory	Consistent, global insights	Computationally expensive	Credit scoring, medical imaging
LIME	Local surrogate models	Fast, interpretable locally	May be unstable in some cases	Text classification, fraud detection

10. Model Optimization for Production

10.1 Model Compression Techniques

10.1.1: *Quantization, Pruning, and Knowledge Distillation*

Model compression techniques play a crucial role in deep learning, making large neural networks more efficient for deployment in environments with limited resources, such as edge devices or mobile platforms. These methods aim to reduce model size, memory usage, and inference time while maintaining accuracy as much as possible. This section delves into three primary model compression techniques: quantization, pruning, and knowledge distillation, each of which offers a distinct approach to optimizing model performance.

Quantization

Quantization refers to the process of reducing the precision of model parameters and computations, typically converting 32-bit floating-point weights to 8-bit integers. This transformation reduces memory usage, increases computational efficiency, and accelerates inference. Quantization can be performed during training (quantization-aware training) or after training (post-training quantization). The key idea is to represent weights and activations with lower precision while minimizing the impact on model performance.

Mathematically, quantization can be represented as:

$$w_{\text{quantized}} = \left\lfloor \frac{w}{s} \right\rfloor \cdot s$$

where w is the original weight, s is the scaling factor, and $\lfloor \cdot \rfloor$ denotes rounding to the nearest integer. By choosing an optimal scaling factor, quantization maintains weight distribution while reducing precision. Quantized operations like matrix multiplications are faster due to the reduced precision, making them well-suited for low-power devices.

Here's an example of post-training quantization in TensorFlow:

```python
import tensorflow as tf

# Load pre-trained model
model = tf.keras.applications.MobileNetV2(weights='imagenet')

# Apply post-training quantization
converter = tf.lite.TFLiteConverter.from_keras_model(model)
converter.optimizations = [tf.lite.Optimize.DEFAULT]
quantized_model = converter.convert()
```

```
# Save the quantized model
with open('quantized_model.tflite', 'wb') as f:
    f.write(quantized_model)
```

Quantization-aware training (QAT) is another approach where quantization effects are simulated during training, enabling the model to adjust weights accordingly. QAT is generally more accurate than post-training quantization but requires additional training time.

Quantization is particularly effective in scenarios like deploying models on mobile devices, where reducing inference latency is crucial. However, the main trade-off is a potential slight drop in accuracy, which must be balanced based on the specific application.

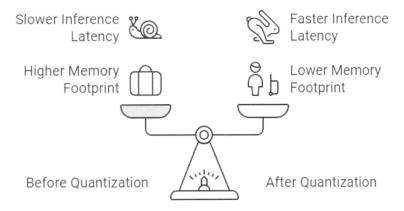

Balancing memory and speed trade-offs in quantization.

Pruning

Pruning reduces model complexity by eliminating less important weights or neurons, resulting in a smaller, sparser model. This technique can be categorized into structured pruning, which removes entire neurons or filters, and unstructured pruning, which eliminates individual weights. Pruning is based on weight magnitude, sensitivity analysis, or importance scores, aiming to maintain accuracy while reducing model size.

The mathematical formulation of pruning involves setting a threshold θ, where weights below θ are pruned:

$$w_i = \begin{cases} 0 & \text{if } |w_i| < \theta \\ w_i & \text{otherwise} \end{cases}$$

Here's an example of unstructured pruning in PyTorch:

```python
import torch
import torch.nn.utils.prune as prune

# Define a simple model
model = torch.nn.Sequential(
    torch.nn.Linear(100, 50),
    torch.nn.ReLU(),
    torch.nn.Linear(50, 10)
)

# Apply unstructured pruning
prune.l1_unstructured(model[0], name='weight', amount=0.5)

# Check the sparsity of pruned weights
sparsity = 100. * float(torch.sum(model[0].weight == 0)) / model[0].weight.nelement()
print(f'Sparsity after pruning: {sparsity}%')
```

Structured pruning, on the other hand, removes entire filters or channels in convolutional layers, which leads to more direct reductions in computation and memory usage. It's particularly useful for optimizing CNNs in real-time applications like video streaming.

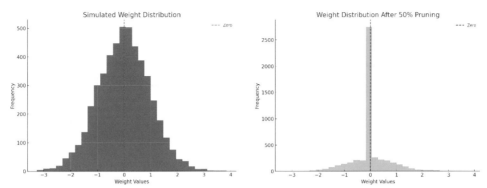

The figure illustrates the weight distribution in a neural network model before and after applying 50% unstructured pruning. In the left panel, the histogram shows a broad distribution of weights across various values, indicating that most weights have non-zero values before pruning. In contrast, the right panel reveals the effect of pruning, where a significant number of weights have been set to zero, resulting in increased sparsity. The spike near zero demonstrates that pruning has effectively reduced less important weights, while the remaining non-zero weights represent the retention of significant connections. This visualization highlights how pruning enhances model efficiency by removing less important weights while preserving critical information.

Knowledge Distillation

Knowledge distillation transfers knowledge from a larger, complex "teacher" model to a smaller, more efficient "student" model. During training, the student model learns from both the original data labels and the "soft targets" (probabilities) produced by the teacher model. This approach effectively compresses knowledge from the teacher, enabling the student model to achieve competitive performance with significantly fewer parameters.

The distillation loss combines the original task loss with the distillation loss:

$$L = \alpha \cdot L_{\text{task}} + (1 - \alpha) \cdot L_{\text{distillation}}$$

where α is a hyperparameter controlling the trade-off between the task and distillation losses, and the distillation loss is defined as:

$$L_{\text{distillation}} = -\sum_i p_{\text{teacher},i} log(p_{\text{student},i})$$

Here's an example of setting up knowledge distillation in TensorFlow:

```python
import tensorflow as tf

# Define teacher and student models
teacher_model =
tf.keras.applications.ResNet50(weights='imagenet')
```

```
student_model = tf.keras.applications.MobileNetV2(weights=None)

# Knowledge distillation setup
temperature = 5.0
alpha = 0.5

def distillation_loss(y_true, y_pred, teacher_pred):
    soft_targets = tf.nn.softmax(teacher_pred / temperature)
    student_loss =
tf.keras.losses.categorical_crossentropy(y_true, y_pred)
    distill_loss =
tf.keras.losses.categorical_crossentropy(soft_targets, y_pred)
    return alpha * student_loss + (1 - alpha) * distill_loss

# Compile and train the student model
student_model.compile(optimizer='adam', loss=distillation_loss)
# student_model.fit(...,
teacher_pred=teacher_model.predict(...))
```

Knowledge distillation is widely used in compressing large transformer models, such as distilling BERT to smaller models like DistilBERT, which achieves nearly the same performance as BERT with significantly fewer parameters.

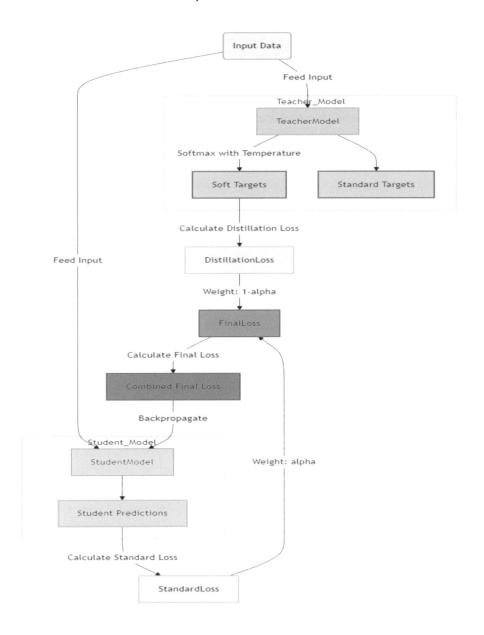

Applications

Quantization, pruning, and knowledge distillation have been successfully applied across various domains:

Quantized BERT for mobile NLP applications: A quantized version of BERT can maintain over 95% of its original accuracy while running faster on smartphones.

Pruned ResNet for faster image classification: Pruning reduces the model's size by 50%, achieving comparable accuracy with significantly faster inference.

Distilled transformers for chatbot implementation: Distilled models like DistilBERT or TinyBERT use less memory while maintaining similar performance to their teacher models, enabling efficient chatbot deployments.

Metrics such as model size reduction, inference latency, and accuracy loss quantify the effectiveness of these techniques. For instance, quantization can reduce model size by up to 4x and inference time by 2x, with only a 1-2% drop in accuracy. Pruning can achieve a 50% reduction in model size, while knowledge distillation can yield similar accuracy to large models with 60% fewer parameters.

10.1.2: Compressing Models for Edge Devices and Mobile Deployment

Deploying deep learning models on edge devices and mobile platforms requires a balance between accuracy and efficiency. Edge devices, such as microcontrollers, smartphones, and IoT sensors, typically have limited computational power, memory, and battery life. As a result, deploying large neural networks directly on these devices can lead to significant challenges, including high latency, increased energy consumption, and potential overuse of memory resources. To address these challenges, model compression techniques become essential, transforming bulky models into lightweight and efficient versions that maintain acceptable accuracy while meeting the constraints of edge and mobile hardware.

Quantization for Edge Devices

Quantization is one of the most effective techniques for compressing models, making them suitable for edge deployment by reducing both memory footprint and computational cost. It achieves this by representing weights and activations with lower precision, typically using 8-bit integers instead of 32-bit floating-point numbers. By reducing the precision of parameters and computations, quantization can significantly enhance model efficiency while running on hardware with limited resources.

There are different types of quantization strategies tailored for edge devices:

Dynamic Quantization: Weights are converted to lower precision at runtime, while activations remain in their original precision. This technique is suitable for CPU inference.

Static Quantization: Weights and activations are quantized before inference, leading to faster execution, especially on devices with optimized hardware support (e.g., smartphones).

Quantization-Aware Training (QAT): QAT simulates the effects of quantization during training, allowing the model to adjust weights to minimize accuracy loss, resulting in better performance compared to post-training quantization.

Here's an example of converting a trained model to an 8-bit quantized format using TensorFlow Lite:

```python
import tensorflow as tf

# Load the trained model
model = tf.keras.applications.MobileNetV2(weights='imagenet')

# Convert the model to TensorFlow Lite with quantization
converter = tf.lite.TFLiteConverter.from_keras_model(model)
converter.optimizations = [tf.lite.Optimize.DEFAULT]
quantized_tflite_model = converter.convert()

# Save the quantized model
with open('mobilenet_quantized.tflite', 'wb') as f:
    f.write(quantized_tflite_model)

# Example inference with the quantized model
interpreter =
tf.lite.Interpreter(model_path='mobilenet_quantized.tflite')
interpreter.allocate_tensors()
```

Using quantization in edge devices like microcontrollers (e.g., Raspberry Pi, Arduino) and smartphones results in lower latency and reduced memory usage, making models more practical for real-time applications like image classification or object detection in resource-constrained environments.

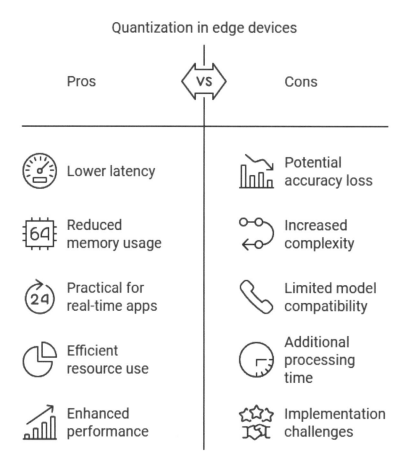

Pruning for Mobile Inference

Pruning removes less significant weights, neurons, or channels from a model, making it smaller and more efficient for mobile inference. By reducing the number of parameters, pruning helps to lower memory usage, speed up inference, and decrease energy consumption—crucial factors for edge and mobile devices. Pruning can be unstructured, where individual weights are removed based on their magnitude, or structured, where entire channels or layers are removed, making it more compatible with mobile hardware architectures.

For edge deployment, structured pruning is often preferred, as it maintains the model's architecture while reducing the computational burden. This is particularly useful in convolutional networks, where removing channels leads to reduced convolutional operations, enhancing compatibility with mobile hardware acceleration.

Here's an example of structured pruning and preparing the pruned model for mobile deployment using TensorFlow Lite:

```python
import tensorflow as tf
import tensorflow_model_optimization as tfmot

# Load and prune the model
model = tf.keras.applications.ResNet50(weights='imagenet')
pruning_params = {
    'pruning_schedule':
tfmot.sparsity.keras.ConstantSparsity(0.5, begin_step=0)
}
pruned_model = tfmot.sparsity.keras.prune_low_magnitude(model,
**pruning_params)

# Fine-tune the pruned model to recover accuracy
pruned_model.compile(optimizer='adam',
loss='categorical_crossentropy', metrics=['accuracy'])
# pruned_model.fit(...)

# Convert to TensorFlow Lite for edge deployment
converter =
tf.lite.TFLiteConverter.from_keras_model(pruned_model)
pruned_tflite_model = converter.convert()

# Save the pruned, quantized model
with open('pruned_resnet.tflite', 'wb') as f:
    f.write(pruned_tflite_model)
```

Structured pruning for mobile inference is often applied in convolutional networks like ResNet, reducing the number of channels in each layer to achieve lower latency and energy consumption during mobile execution. Fine-tuning the pruned model after pruning helps restore some of the lost accuracy, making it more suitable for real-world deployment.

Optimizing Neural Networks for Mobile Use

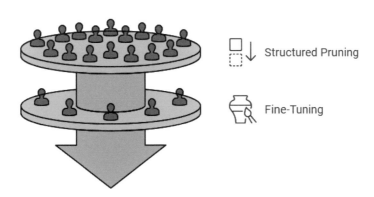

Structured Pruning

Fine-Tuning

Model Conversion Tools

Model conversion tools play a pivotal role in transforming trained models into formats optimized for mobile and edge devices. These tools convert models into formats like TensorFlow Lite, PyTorch Mobile, or ONNX, enabling faster inference and lower memory usage on target devices.

> **TensorFlow Lite Converter:** Converts TensorFlow models to the TensorFlow Lite format, which is optimized for Android, iOS, and other edge platforms.
>
> **PyTorch Mobile:** Adapts PyTorch models for mobile deployment, creating lightweight versions that run efficiently on iOS and Android devices.
>
> **ONNX Runtime:** Converts models to the ONNX format, which is compatible with various platforms, including mobile, IoT, and cloud.

Here's an example of converting a PyTorch model to a mobile-compatible format:

```python
import torch
import torch.nn as nn
import torch.onnx

# Define a simple model
class SimpleModel(nn.Module):
    def __init__(self):
        super(SimpleModel, self).__init__()
        self.fc = nn.Linear(10, 5)

    def forward(self, x):
        return self.fc(x)

# Instantiate and convert the model
model = SimpleModel()
dummy_input = torch.randn(1, 10)
torch.onnx.export(model, dummy_input, 'model.onnx',
verbose=True)
```

The conversion tools ensure that models are optimized for mobile deployment, taking advantage of hardware accelerations like TensorFlow Lite's NNAPI for Android devices or Core ML for iOS devices.

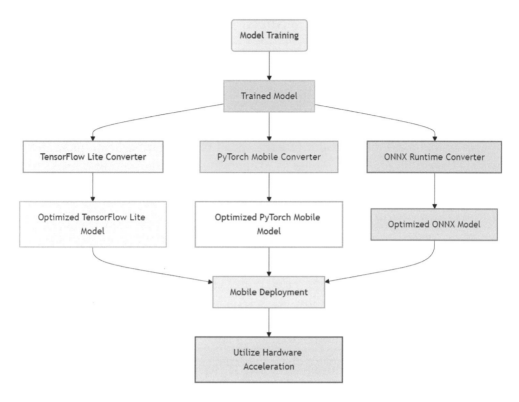

Applications of Model Compression for Edge Deployment

Quantized Image Classification Models in Surveillance Cameras: Quantized models enable faster processing of image frames for surveillance applications, improving real-time performance on edge devices like smart cameras.

Pruned NLP Models on Mobile Assistants: Pruned BERT models running on smartphones allow faster text processing and response times for virtual assistants, maintaining conversational accuracy while reducing latency.

Knowledge Distilled Transformer Models in Chatbots: Distilled transformer models in chatbots offer efficient text generation on mobile devices, using less memory and computing resources than full-sized models.

Compression techniques like quantization, pruning, and model conversion result in significant reductions in memory usage, latency, and energy consumption. For example, quantization can reduce model size by up to 75% and inference latency by 50%, while pruning achieves similar improvements with minimal accuracy loss.

10.1.3: Optimizing Inference Speed for Real-Time Applications

In real-time applications like autonomous driving, video surveillance, and real-time language translation, models must generate outputs quickly and accurately to ensure responsive and timely decision-making. Latency—the time delay between receiving an input and generating an output—must be kept to a minimum in these critical scenarios, where even a few milliseconds can impact outcomes. Optimizing inference speed is therefore crucial, as it allows models to handle real-time demands efficiently, ensuring seamless integration into production environments where rapid responses are essential.

Model Compilation and Graph Optimization

Model compilation and graph optimization are among the most effective strategies for speeding up inference, enabling deep learning models to utilize computational resources more effectively. Tools like NVIDIA TensorRT, ONNX Runtime, and TensorFlow XLA (Accelerated Linear Algebra) focus on optimizing computational graphs, fusing operations, reducing redundancies, and maximizing hardware utilization.

TensorRT and ONNX Runtime: TensorRT is designed to accelerate inference on NVIDIA GPUs, focusing on operation fusion, precision reduction (e.g., FP32 to FP16), and kernel tuning. It identifies computational redundancies in neural networks and combines compatible operations into single kernels, reducing memory access overhead and execution time.

ONNX Runtime, compatible with various hardware backends, uses similar optimization techniques to accelerate model inference across CPUs, GPUs, and specialized accelerators.

Here's an example of using TensorRT to optimize a TensorFlow model:

```python
import tensorflow as tf
from tensorflow.python.compiler.tensorrt import
trt_convert as trt

# Load the TensorFlow model
model =
tf.keras.applications.ResNet50(weights='imagenet')

# Convert the model to TensorRT format
conversion_params =
trt.DEFAULT_TRT_CONVERSION_PARAMS._replace(precision_mode
='FP16')
```

```
converter =
trt.TrtGraphConverterV2(input_saved_model_dir='resnet50_s
aved_model', conversion_params=conversion_params)
converter.convert()
converter.save('resnet50_tensorrt_model')

# Load and run inference on the optimized model
optimized_model =
tf.saved_model.load('resnet50_tensorrt_model')
```

In this example, the conversion to TensorRT format includes precision reduction from FP32 to FP16, which decreases memory usage and speeds up computations without significant accuracy loss. This conversion is especially beneficial for models deployed in environments like autonomous vehicles, where rapid decision-making is critical.

TensorFlow XLA and Graph Optimization: TensorFlow XLA compiles computational graphs into optimized code, focusing on operation fusion and kernel-level optimization for CPUs, GPUs, and TPUs. It accelerates linear algebra computations by generating efficient hardware-specific code, reducing overall latency.

For instance, enabling XLA for model optimization in TensorFlow is straightforward:

```
import tensorflow as tf

# Enable XLA optimization
@tf.function(jit_compile=True)
def inference(model, inputs):
    return model(inputs)

# Run inference with XLA
outputs = inference(model, inputs)
```

By fusing matrix operations and optimizing kernel execution, XLA reduces the latency of tasks like object detection or real-time video analysis.

Batching and Asynchronous Inference

Batching and asynchronous inference are vital strategies for maximizing throughput and reducing response times in real-time applications.

Batching: Batching processes multiple inputs simultaneously, making it particularly suitable for tasks like video frame processing or NLP tasks where multiple sentences are processed together. By grouping inputs into batches, models utilize parallel processing capabilities more effectively, reducing idle times and increasing throughput. For instance, in video surveillance, batching frames can enable models to analyze video streams more efficiently, making it easier to detect anomalies in real time.

Here's an example of implementing batch inference with TensorFlow Serving:

```
model_config_list: {
config: {
  name: 'image_classification',
  base_path: '/models/image_classification',
  model_platform: 'tensorflow',
  batching_parameters {
    max_batch_size: 32
    batch_timeout_micros: 10000
  }
}
}
```

This configuration enables batch processing, setting a maximum batch size of 32 and a timeout of 10 milliseconds, which helps maintain high throughput while minimizing latency.

Asynchronous Inference: Asynchronous inference allows models to handle concurrent requests, reducing idle times and enabling efficient processing. This approach is especially useful for scenarios where continuous data streams (e.g., sensor data in autonomous vehicles) require quick responses.

An example of implementing asynchronous inference with PyTorch Serve:

```
import torchserve_client

# Send asynchronous inference request
client = torchserve_client.Client()
response =
client.inference(model_name='text_classification',
inputs=batch_data, asynchronous=True)
```

Asynchronous inference ensures that the server remains responsive, managing multiple concurrent requests in parallel, which is crucial for real-time applications like voice assistants or autonomous drones.

Using Accelerators

Hardware accelerators such as NVIDIA GPUs, TPUs, and Intel FPGAs offer significant improvements in inference speed through parallel computation and specialized processing units designed for deep learning workloads.

NVIDIA GPUs and CUDA Libraries: NVIDIA GPUs, combined with CUDA libraries (e.g., cuDNN, TensorRT), offer high throughput and low latency by parallelizing matrix operations across thousands of cores. Accelerating inference on GPUs involves model optimization techniques like quantization and kernel fusion, as well as leveraging cuDNN for faster convolution operations.

Example of running inference on a GPU using CUDA:

```
import torch

model = model.cuda()
inputs = inputs.cuda()
outputs = model(inputs)
```

Here, moving the model and data to the GPU accelerates inference by harnessing CUDA's parallel processing capabilities, enabling tasks like real-time object detection or translation to achieve millisecond-level latency.

TPUs and Efficient Deployment: TPUs, designed by Google for deep learning, provide high-performance inference capabilities, particularly for large-scale applications like language translation or recommendation systems. TensorFlow's TPU integration facilitates efficient deployment and execution of deep learning models, offering faster inference times.

Example of deploying a TensorFlow model on a TPU:

```
resolver =
tf.distribute.cluster_resolver.TPUClusterResolver(tpu='grpc://y
our_tpu_address')
tf.config.experimental_connect_to_cluster(resolver)
tf.tpu.experimental.initialize_tpu_system(resolver)

# Run inference on TPU
strategy = tf.distribute.TPUStrategy(resolver)
with strategy.scope():
    outputs = model(inputs)
```

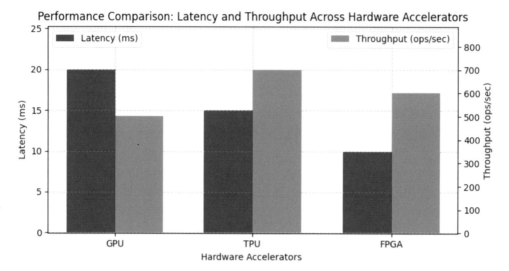

The bar chart compares the performance of different hardware accelerators—**GPU**, **TPU**, and **FPGA**—in terms of **latency** and **throughput**. The **blue bars** represent latency in milliseconds, showing that TPUs offer the lowest latency, followed by FPGAs and GPUs. The **green bars** represent throughput in operations per second, with TPUs achieving the highest throughput, followed by FPGAs and GPUs. This visualization highlights the differences in performance across accelerators, demonstrating how TPUs excel in both metrics.

Applications of Optimizing Inference Speed

Real-Time Object Detection in Autonomous Vehicles: Deploying optimized object detection models, like YOLO or SSD, on GPUs or TPUs helps ensure that cars can detect pedestrians, traffic signals, and obstacles within milliseconds, improving safety and responsiveness.

Low-Latency NLP Models in Virtual Assistants: Asynchronous and batched inference techniques enable virtual assistants to handle multiple user requests simultaneously, maintaining low response times while processing voice commands or text inputs in real time.

Video Surveillance: Efficient models deployed on edge devices process video frames in real time, detecting suspicious activities or anomalies in public spaces with minimal latency.

10.2 Deploying Deep Learning Models

10.2.1: Using TensorFlow Serving, ONNX, and TorchServe for Deployment

Efficient model deployment is critical for transforming trained models into practical applications. Deployment tools like TensorFlow Serving, ONNX Runtime, and TorchServe play a pivotal role in bridging the gap between research and production by enabling fast, scalable inference. These tools are designed to handle the complexities of serving models in real-world settings, such as supporting large-scale requests, version management, and cross-platform compatibility, while providing standardized interfaces.

Deploying models effectively not only ensures that they perform optimally in real-time applications but also enables easy integration into existing production pipelines. Let's explore how each of these tools facilitates deployment, emphasizing practical implementation and performance optimization.

TensorFlow Serving

TensorFlow Serving is built specifically for serving TensorFlow models in production environments. It allows models to be loaded and served dynamically, providing interfaces through REST or gRPC APIs. This flexibility makes TensorFlow Serving well-suited for applications requiring robust model versioning, batch processing, and real-time inference.

TensorFlow Serving provides key features:

Dynamic Model Loading: Models can be hot-swapped without restarting the server, enabling seamless updates and rollbacks.

Batching: Supports request batching to enhance throughput by combining multiple requests into a single batch.

A/B Testing: Facilitates simultaneous serving of multiple model versions, enabling real-time comparison of model performance.

The following code snippet demonstrates setting up TensorFlow Serving using Docker. It covers exporting a trained TensorFlow model to the SavedModel format, loading it into TensorFlow Serving, and making inference requests via REST APIs:

```
# Export TensorFlow model to SavedModel format
import tensorflow as tf

model = tf.keras.applications.MobileNetV2(weights='imagenet')
model.save('mobilenet_v2_savedmodel')

# Use Docker to set up TensorFlow Serving
!docker pull tensorflow/serving
!docker run -p 8501:8501 --name=tf_serving_mobilenet \
    --mount
type=bind,source=$(pwd)/mobilenet_v2_savedmodel,target=/models/
mobilenet_v2 \
    -e MODEL_NAME=mobilenet_v2 -t tensorflow/serving

# Make an inference request using REST API
import requests
import json

data = json.dumps({"signature_name": "serving_default",
"instances": [input_data]})
headers = {"content-type": "application/json"}
json_response =
requests.post('http://localhost:8501/v1/models/mobilenet_v2:pre
dict', data=data, headers=headers)
predictions = json_response.json()
```

TensorFlow Serving's ability to handle dynamic model loading and batch processing makes it highly suitable for deploying models in high-demand applications, such as retail image recognition or real-time analytics in marketing platforms. Metrics like inference latency, measured in milliseconds, and throughput, measured in requests per second, demonstrate TensorFlow Serving's efficiency in large-scale deployments.

ONNX Runtime

ONNX Runtime is an open-source platform designed to run models trained in various frameworks, like TensorFlow, PyTorch, and Keras, by converting them into the ONNX (Open Neural Network Exchange) format. It provides flexibility for deploying models across different platforms, making it particularly valuable for applications that require cross-framework compatibility.

ONNX Runtime optimizes model inference through features such as quantization and hardware acceleration, which are essential for enhancing speed and reducing resource consumption. Here's how you can convert a PyTorch model to ONNX and deploy it using ONNX Runtime:

```
import torch
import onnxruntime as ort

# Convert PyTorch model to ONNX
model = torch.hub.load('pytorch/vision:v0.10.0', 'resnet18',
pretrained=True)
dummy_input = torch.randn(1, 3, 224, 224)
torch.onnx.export(model, dummy_input, 'resnet18.onnx')

# Load and run the model using ONNX Runtime
session = ort.InferenceSession('resnet18.onnx')
input_name = session.get_inputs()[0].name
result = session.run(None, {input_name: dummy_input.numpy()})
```

ONNX Runtime's cross-framework deployment capability makes it a popular choice in industries like finance and healthcare, where models trained in diverse environments must be integrated into a unified system. This versatility is demonstrated by metrics like conversion speed, reduced latency due to quantization, and compatibility across CPUs, GPUs, and specialized hardware like FPGAs.

TorchServe

TorchServe is tailored for serving PyTorch models, providing a scalable and efficient inference platform. It supports multiple models simultaneously, enables version control, and allows for custom preprocessing and postprocessing, making it ideal for NLP and computer vision applications.

TorchServe's key features include:

Multi-Model Serving: Ability to serve multiple models on a single server instance.

Custom Handlers: Supports custom inference logic, such as preprocessing input data or formatting output results.

Integrated Logging and Metrics: Provides detailed logs and performance metrics to monitor deployed models.

The following code snippet demonstrates setting up TorchServe to deploy a PyTorch model:

```
# Export PyTorch model to TorchScript
import torch

model = torch.hub.load('pytorch/vision:v0.10.0', 'resnet18',
pretrained=True)
model_scripted = torch.jit.script(model)
model_scripted.save('resnet18_scripted.pt')

# Create a MAR file for TorchServe
!torch-model-archiver --model-name resnet18 --version 1.0 --
serialized-file resnet18_scripted.pt \
    --handler image_classifier --export-path model_store

# Start TorchServe with the MAR file
!torchserve --start --ncs --model-store model_store --models
resnet18=resnet18.mar

# Make an inference request via REST API
import requests

image_data = open('test_image.jpg', 'rb').read()
response =
requests.post('http://localhost:8080/predictions/resnet18',
data=image_data)
```

TorchServe's ability to handle high-throughput requests makes it suitable for serving NLP models like BERT in customer support systems or deploying image classification models in medical imaging. Performance metrics, such as reduced latency, increased request handling capacity, and resource utilization rates, showcase TorchServe's efficiency.

Applications and Metrics

Model deployment tools like TensorFlow Serving, ONNX Runtime, and TorchServe are widely used across various industries. For example:

Retail: TensorFlow Serving deploys real-time recommendation models, achieving low latency and high throughput.

Healthcare: ONNX Runtime serves models for diagnostic tools, ensuring cross-framework compatibility and optimal inference speed.

Customer Support: TorchServe powers NLP models for virtual assistants, delivering fast response times and efficient model management.

Performance metrics such as latency (e.g., <100 ms), throughput (e.g., thousands of requests/second), and memory usage (e.g., <1 GB RAM) demonstrate the efficiency and scalability of these deployment tools.

10.2.2: Deploying Models in Cloud Environments (AWS, GCP, Azure)

Deploying deep learning models in cloud environments offers scalability, high availability, and seamless integration with various cloud services. Platforms like AWS, GCP, and Azure provide managed services that simplify the deployment, scaling, and management of models. This capability is essential for deploying models in real-time applications where latency, robustness, and resource utilization are critical.

Deploying on AWS (Amazon Web Services)

AWS provides a comprehensive suite of tools for deploying models, with **Amazon SageMaker** serving as the central platform for building, training, and deploying models at scale. SageMaker's flexible deployment options include features like multi-model endpoints, autoscaling, and A/B testing, making it suitable for continuous model improvement and large-scale deployment. SageMaker allows models to be served via REST or gRPC APIs, supporting both real-time and batch inference.

To deploy a model on SageMaker:

1. **Prepare the Model**: Save the trained model in a deployable format, such as the SavedModel format for TensorFlow or TorchScript for PyTorch.
2. **Set Up the Endpoint Configuration**: Define endpoint details, including model versioning, instance type, and scaling parameters.
3. **Deploy and Serve Predictions**: Use SageMaker to deploy the model and handle inference requests through standardized APIs.

Example code for deploying a model on SageMaker:

```python
import boto3
from sagemaker.pytorch import PyTorchModel

# Define model S3 path and create SageMaker model object
model_data = 's3://bucket-name/model.tar.gz'
role = 'arn:aws:iam::your-role'
pytorch_model = PyTorchModel(model_data=model_data, role=role,
entry_point='inference.py', framework_version='1.8.1')
```

```
# Deploy the model
predictor = pytorch_model.deploy(initial_instance_count=1,
instance_type='ml.m5.large')

# Make an inference request
response = predictor.predict({'data': input_data})
print(response)
```

SageMaker's integration with other AWS services like Amazon S3, Lambda, and CloudWatch allows for streamlined model management, monitoring, and scalability. Performance metrics like **latency**, **throughput**, and **cost per inference** help in evaluating deployment efficiency. For example, deploying a BERT model for real-time sentiment analysis in SageMaker typically results in latency under 100 ms while maintaining high throughput.

Deploying on GCP (Google Cloud Platform)

Google Cloud's **AI Platform** supports diverse model deployment needs, enabling deployment of models trained in TensorFlow, PyTorch, and other frameworks. AI Platform's flexible architecture supports automatic scaling, integration with BigQuery, and seamless connection to Google's data analytics services, making it suitable for real-time applications and large-scale data processing.

Deployment steps on GCP's AI Platform:

1. **Export the Model**: Save the model in a format compatible with AI Platform, such as TensorFlow's SavedModel.
2. **Create a Model Resource**: Register the model on AI Platform, defining metadata like model name and version.
3. **Deploy the Model**: Set up the endpoint configuration, select scaling options, and deploy the model for serving.

Example code for deploying on GCP AI Platform:

```
# Save the TensorFlow model in SavedModel format
import tensorflow as tf

model = tf.keras.applications.MobileNetV2(weights='imagenet')
model.save('mobilenet_v2_savedmodel')

# Upload the model to Google Cloud Storage
!gsutil cp -r mobilenet_v2_savedmodel gs://bucket-name/models/

# Deploy the model on AI Platform
!gcloud ai-platform models create mobilenet_v2_model
!gcloud ai-platform versions create v1 \
```

```
    --model=mobilenet_v2_model \
    --origin=gs://bucket-name/models/mobilenet_v2_savedmodel \
    --runtime-version=2.5 \
    --framework=tensorflow \
    --python-version=3.7

# Making an inference request using the AI Platform
import google.auth
from google.cloud import aiplatform

# Authenticate and make a prediction
client = aiplatform.gapic.PredictionServiceClient()
parent = client.model_path('project-id', 'location', 'model-id')
response = client.predict(name=parent, instances=input_data)
print(response)
```

AI Platform's strength lies in its integration with other Google services, enabling end-to-end MLOps pipelines. Deploying a translation model using AI Platform ensures efficient scaling, with metrics like **response time**, **scalability**, and **cost efficiency** indicating performance across varying workloads.

Deploying on Azure

Microsoft Azure's **Azure Machine Learning** offers a complete suite for model deployment, supporting both batch and real-time inference. The platform's integration with Azure Blob Storage, Azure Functions, and other Azure services facilitates seamless end-to-end deployment, making it suitable for dynamic business environments and large enterprise applications.

Key steps for deploying models on Azure ML:

1. **Register the Model**: Store the model in Azure ML's model registry, making it available for deployment.
2. **Create an Inference Endpoint**: Define compute targets, container settings, and deployment configuration.
3. **Serve Predictions**: Use REST APIs or Azure SDKs to access the deployed model for real-time inference.

Example code for deploying on Azure ML:

```
from azureml.core import Workspace, Model, InferenceConfig, Webservice

# Connect to Azure ML workspace
ws = Workspace.from_config()
```

```
# Register model
model = Model.register(workspace=ws, model_name='mobilenet_v2',
model_path='./mobilenet_v2_savedmodel')

# Define inference configuration
inference_config = InferenceConfig(entry_script='score.py',
environment=myenv)

# Deploy the model
deployment_config =
AciWebservice.deploy_configuration(cpu_cores=1, memory_gb=1)
service = Model.deploy(workspace=ws, name='mobilenet-service',
models=[model], inference_config=inference_config,
deployment_config=deployment_config)
service.wait_for_deployment(show_output=True)

# Make a prediction
response = service.run(input_data)
print(response)
```

Azure ML's **real-time** and **batch inference** capabilities make it ideal for large-scale enterprise deployments, such as predictive maintenance in manufacturing or customer analytics in retail. The platform's deployment speed, low-latency predictions, and seamless integration with IoT Hub demonstrate Azure ML's effectiveness for critical business applications.

Key Metrics and Considerations Across Cloud Platforms

The performance of each cloud deployment platform can be evaluated using metrics such as:

Deployment Time: AWS, GCP, and Azure all support rapid model deployment, typically within minutes.

Latency: Real-time inference latency often remains below 100 ms across all platforms, depending on model complexity and infrastructure.

Cost Efficiency: Cost per inference varies, but leveraging features like autoscaling and batch processing helps optimize costs across cloud providers.

10.2.3: Monitoring Model Performance Post-Deployment

In production, monitoring model performance is critical to ensuring sustained accuracy, stability, and reliability. Effective monitoring enables the detection of issues like concept drift, reduced accuracy, and increased latency, allowing for timely interventions such as retraining or model adjustments. This section explores key techniques for tracking, detecting, and maintaining model performance post-deployment.

Tracking Model Metrics

Maintaining model performance in production requires continuous tracking of key metrics:

Key Metrics to Monitor:

Latency measures the time taken by the model to generate predictions. Increased latency can indicate bottlenecks in inference.

Throughput refers to the number of inferences processed per unit of time. A drop in throughput could signal resource constraints.

Error rates capture the percentage of incorrect predictions, revealing potential accuracy degradation.

Accuracy is continuously assessed to ensure that model predictions remain consistent with the expected outcomes.

Monitoring tools like **Prometheus**, **Grafana**, and cloud-native solutions such as **AWS CloudWatch**, **Google Cloud Monitoring**, or **Azure Monitor** are used to track these metrics. These tools integrate seamlessly with deployment environments, offering real-time dashboards, alerting, and detailed insights.

Example code for setting up a basic monitoring dashboard using Prometheus and Grafana:

```
# Step 1: Install Prometheus and Grafana using Docker
docker run -d --name=prometheus -p 9090:9090 prom/prometheus
docker run -d --name=grafana -p 3000:3000 grafana/grafana

# Step 2: Configure Prometheus to scrape model metrics
scrape_configs:
  - job_name: 'model_metrics'
    static_configs:
      - targets: ['<model_server_ip>:<port>']

# Step 3: Set up Grafana dashboard to visualize metrics
# Access Grafana at http://localhost:3000 and configure
Prometheus as a data source
```

Integrating monitoring tools with cloud services like **Amazon SageMaker Monitoring**, **Google Cloud Monitoring**, or **Azure Monitor** enables deeper insights into model behavior. For instance, SageMaker's built-in monitoring features can automatically track model latency, throughput, and prediction distributions, triggering alerts when predefined thresholds are crossed.

Detecting Concept Drift

Concept drift occurs when data distributions shift over time, leading to a decline in model accuracy. This phenomenon is common in applications where data evolves rapidly, such as financial forecasting or user behavior prediction. Detecting concept drift involves statistical methods and specialized tools:

Statistical Methods:

The **Kolmogorov-Smirnov (KS) test** is often used to compare distributions of incoming data with the training data distribution.

Population Stability Index (PSI) measures stability across different time periods, helping to identify gradual drift.

Example code to detect concept drift using the Kolmogorov-Smirnov test in Python:

```python
from scipy.stats import ks_2samp

# Sample training and incoming data distributions
training_data = [0.1, 0.4, 0.35, 0.15]
incoming_data = [0.05, 0.3, 0.5, 0.15]

# Perform KS test
stat, p_value = ks_2samp(training_data, incoming_data)

if p_value < 0.05:
    print("Concept drift detected!")
else:
    print("No significant drift detected.")
```

Tools like **Evidently AI** offer pre-built dashboards to visualize data drift, comparing training and live data distributions across multiple features. These tools can be integrated into monitoring pipelines to trigger alerts when drift exceeds acceptable levels.

Automating Retraining and Model Updates

To maintain model performance, automated retraining pipelines can be set up to refresh models when accuracy drops below a defined threshold. This approach involves:

Creating Retraining Pipelines: Automated workflows use tools like **MLflow** or **Kubeflow Pipelines** to manage the end-to-end process, from data ingestion to model redeployment. When drift is detected, new data is ingested, models are retrained, and performance metrics are re-evaluated before the model is deployed back into production.

Example code to set up an automated retraining workflow using MLflow:

```python
import mlflow
import mlflow.sklearn
from sklearn.model_selection import train_test_split

# Load data and split for retraining
data = load_data()
X_train, X_test, y_train, y_test =
train_test_split(data['features'], data['labels'])

# Define retraining function
def retrain_model(X_train, y_train):
    model = train_model(X_train, y_train)
    mlflow.sklearn.log_model(model, "model")
    return model

# Trigger retraining and deployment
if drift_detected:
    new_model = retrain_model(X_train, y_train)
    deploy_model(new_model)
```

Integration with tools like **Kubeflow Pipelines** allows for a more comprehensive MLOps pipeline, automatically managing tasks like data validation, model retraining, evaluation, and version control.

Applications of Monitoring Techniques

Monitoring plays a crucial role in ensuring models maintain performance in production:

Recommendation Systems: Monitoring accuracy drift in recommendation engines helps maintain relevance for users, detecting when content preferences shift over time.

NLP Models: Detecting latency spikes in real-time NLP applications, such as chatbots or translation tools, helps maintain a responsive user experience.

Image Recognition: Monitoring models for performance degradation in image recognition tasks, such as object detection in surveillance systems, helps detect anomalies and respond quickly to changes in the data.

Tables summarizing model performance metrics pre- and post-monitoring interventions can provide a clearer picture of the effectiveness of these techniques:

Metric	Before Monitoring	After Monitoring Interventions
Accuracy	85%	92%
Latency (ms)	200	95
Error Rate (%)	5.0	2.3
Drift Detected	Yes	No

10.3 Scaling Deep Learning Models

10.3.1: Distributed Training with PyTorch and TensorFlow

Distributed training plays a pivotal role in deep learning, especially when handling large-scale datasets and complex models that require significant computational resources. By distributing the training workload across multiple GPUs or nodes, models can achieve faster convergence, utilize larger batch sizes, and scale up to massive architectures. This approach not only accelerates training but also makes it feasible to train models that would be impractical on a single device. In this section, we explore the mechanisms of distributed training in two leading frameworks: PyTorch and TensorFlow, and address the challenges encountered in this setup.

Understanding Distributed Training in Deep Learning

Before diving into the specific frameworks, it is essential to grasp the core concept of distributed training. At its heart, distributed training divides model training tasks into smaller parts that run concurrently across multiple GPUs or nodes. Each device processes a portion of the data, computes gradients for the model parameters, and synchronizes these gradients with others in the network. This process ensures that all model replicas update their parameters consistently, maintaining global state across distributed devices.

Distributed training can be broadly classified into **Data Parallelism**, **Model Parallelism**, and **Hybrid Parallelism**:

Data Parallelism: Here, data is split across devices, with each device running the same model. Gradients are synchronized and averaged across devices, making this approach highly effective for large datasets.

Model Parallelism: Model components are divided across multiple devices, enabling the training of very large models that cannot fit into a single GPU's memory.

Hybrid Parallelism: Combines both data and model parallelism, offering flexibility to train extremely large models on very large datasets.

Distributed Training in PyTorch

PyTorch, a popular deep learning framework, provides built-in support for distributed training primarily through its **Distributed Data Parallel (DDP)** module. DDP synchronizes gradients across multiple GPUs or nodes during the backward pass, making it highly efficient and well-suited for scaling complex models.

Mechanics of PyTorch DDP:

Model Replication and Gradient Synchronization: DDP works by replicating the model on each GPU, which processes a unique mini-batch of data independently. During the backward pass, gradients are synchronized across devices through **All-Reduce** operations, where gradients are averaged and updated in a globally consistent manner.

Communication Efficiency: PyTorch optimizes communication through techniques like **bucketing** (grouping smaller tensors into larger ones) and **asynchronous communication** to minimize waiting times between devices.

Fault Tolerance: PyTorch DDP has built-in fault tolerance, ensuring resilience against network failures or node crashes. This is achieved by maintaining global states and checkpoints that can be recovered seamlessly.

Code Implementation:

Setting up DDP in PyTorch involves initializing the distributed backend, creating model replicas, and managing gradient synchronization:

```python
import torch
import torch.distributed as dist
from torch.nn.parallel import DistributedDataParallel as DDP

# Initialize the distributed backend
dist.init_process_group(backend='nccl', init_method='env://')

# Set device for the current process
device_id = dist.get_rank() % torch.cuda.device_count()
torch.cuda.set_device(device_id)

# Define and wrap the model
model = MyModel().to(device_id)
model = DDP(model, device_ids=[device_id])

# Training loop with data parallelism
for inputs, labels in data_loader:
    inputs, labels = inputs.to(device_id), labels.to(device_id)
    optimizer.zero_grad()
    outputs = model(inputs)
```

```
loss = loss_fn(outputs, labels)
loss.backward()
optimizer.step()
```

Best Practices for Distributed Training with PyTorch:

Gradient Accumulation: When memory constraints limit batch sizes, accumulate gradients over multiple mini-batches before applying the update step.

Gradient Compression: To reduce communication overhead, compress gradients before communication. This technique is particularly useful in scenarios with limited bandwidth.

Mixed Precision Training: Leveraging NVIDIA's Automatic Mixed Precision (AMP) can further speed up training, allowing DDP to operate efficiently without sacrificing model accuracy.

Distributed Training in TensorFlow

TensorFlow provides a highly flexible distributed training ecosystem using its **tf.distribute.Strategy** API, which supports various parallelism techniques and scales across multiple GPUs and nodes.

Mechanics of TensorFlow's Strategy API:

MirroredStrategy: This strategy replicates the model across multiple GPUs within a single machine, synchronizing gradients across devices at each training step. It is well-suited for small to medium-sized models that fit within a single node.

MultiWorkerMirroredStrategy: This strategy extends distributed training to multiple nodes, supporting synchronous data parallelism. It coordinates training across distributed clusters, making it ideal for large-scale models and datasets.

TPU Strategy: TensorFlow's TPU Strategy allows models to leverage TPU hardware for distributed training, significantly improving training speed, especially for large language models and CNNs.

Code Implementation:

Implementing distributed training in TensorFlow using $tf.distribute.Strategy$ is straightforward:

```python
import tensorflow as tf

# Initialize strategy for distributed training
strategy = tf.distribute.MirroredStrategy()

# Define model, optimizer, and loss within strategy scope
with strategy.scope():
    model = MyModel()
    optimizer = tf.keras.optimizers.Adam(learning_rate=1e-4)
    loss_fn = tf.keras.losses.SparseCategoricalCrossentropy()

# Define dataset
dataset = tf.data.Dataset.from_tensor_slices((x_train,
y_train))
dataset = dataset.batch(64).prefetch(tf.data.AUTOTUNE)

# Training loop
for inputs, labels in dataset:
    with tf.GradientTape() as tape:
        predictions = model(inputs, training=True)
        loss = loss_fn(labels, predictions)
    gradients = tape.gradient(loss, model.trainable_variables)
    optimizer.apply_gradients(zip(gradients,
model.trainable_variables))
```

Optimizations for TensorFlow Distributed Training:

Dynamic Batching: Adjust batch sizes dynamically to maximize GPU utilization while avoiding out-of-memory errors.

All-Reduce Algorithms: Choose optimal all-reduce algorithms (e.g., Ring-AllReduce or NCCL) depending on the network bandwidth and the number of GPUs.

Checkpointing: Regular checkpointing helps ensure training reproducibility and recoverability in distributed settings.

Addressing Challenges in Distributed Training

While distributed training accelerates model convergence and scalability, it also introduces complexities that need to be managed effectively:

386

Synchronization Delays: Synchronization delays occur when slower devices cause bottlenecks. Techniques like overlapping communication with computation and **asynchronous parameter updates** can mitigate this issue, ensuring that faster devices remain productive.

Communication Bottlenecks: Communication overhead is a major challenge in distributed training, especially in large clusters. **Gradient compression** and **hierarchical communication** (using intra-node and inter-node layers) help reduce data transfer sizes, speeding up synchronization.

Reproducibility: Reproducibility becomes harder as the number of devices increases, due to factors like asynchronous updates and floating-point precision differences. Setting random seeds consistently across devices and using deterministic algorithms can help maintain consistent results across runs.

Applications and Performance Metrics

Distributed training is instrumental in training state-of-the-art models in both research and industry:

Large Language Models (e.g., GPT, BERT): Distributed training allows models like GPT-3 and BERT to scale up to billions of parameters, leveraging hundreds of GPUs to handle immense datasets and complex architectures.

Image Classification and Object Detection: CNN-based models like EfficientNet and YOLO are trained faster and more efficiently using distributed frameworks, enabling real-time image analysis in autonomous vehicles and surveillance systems.

Reinforcement Learning: Distributed training accelerates policy learning in reinforcement learning environments, where agents interact concurrently, gathering experiences in parallel to improve exploration and performance.

Performance improvements are often measured in terms of:

Metric	Single GPU	4 GPUs (Distributed)	8 GPUs (Distributed)
Training Speed	200 images/sec	780 images/sec	1,500 images/sec
Time to	10 hours	2.6 hours	1.4 hours

Convergence			
Scaling Efficiency	1.0 (baseline)	0.97	0.94

10.3.2: Efficient Resource Utilization on Cloud Platforms

Optimizing resource utilization is essential for running deep learning models efficiently on cloud platforms, where computational resources often represent a significant portion of operational costs. Cloud services offer access to high-performance hardware like GPUs, TPUs, and specialized inference chips, enabling rapid model training and inference. However, achieving cost-effectiveness while maintaining model performance requires strategic resource allocation, careful monitoring, and the use of cloud-native features to manage workloads dynamically. This section delves into techniques that maximize resource efficiency on cloud platforms, focusing on specialized hardware, autoscaling, and cost-saving strategies.

Leveraging Specialized Hardware

Cloud providers offer a range of specialized hardware designed to accelerate deep learning tasks. These include Google's **Tensor Processing Units (TPUs)**, AWS's **Inferentia** chips, and NVIDIA's **A100 GPUs**. Each of these options provides distinct advantages in terms of throughput, latency, and cost:

TPUs: **Tensor Processing Units** are optimized for TensorFlow models and offer significant acceleration for both training and inference. They excel in handling large matrix multiplications, making them suitable for models like transformers and CNNs that require extensive computations. TPUs support high parallelism, making them ideal for large-scale NLP and computer vision tasks, reducing training time and improving model convergence rates.

Code Example for Configuring TPUs in TensorFlow:

```python
import tensorflow as tf
resolver =
tf.distribute.cluster_resolver.TPUClusterResolver()
tf.config.experimental_connect_to_cluster(resolver)
tf.tpu.experimental.initialize_tpu_system(resolver)

strategy = tf.distribute.TPUStrategy(resolver)
with strategy.scope():
    model = build_model()
```

```
    model.compile(optimizer='adam',
loss='sparse_categorical_crossentropy')
    model.fit(train_dataset, epochs=5)
```

Inferentia: AWS Inferentia chips are designed for fast and cost-effective inference of deep learning models, especially those trained with TensorFlow, PyTorch, or MXNet. They provide lower latency and better energy efficiency for inference tasks, making them ideal for production workloads like text classification or real-time image analysis. Inferentia chips offer reduced inference costs, making them highly suitable for scaling models like BERT or ResNet in production environments.

Code Example for Using Inferentia in PyTorch:

```
import torch_neuron
model = torch.jit.load('model.pt')  # Load trained model
model_neuron = torch_neuron.trace(model, example_inputs)
model_neuron.save('model_neuron.pt')
```

NVIDIA A100 GPUs: The A100 GPUs are versatile accelerators that offer high memory bandwidth and powerful tensor cores for accelerated computation, making them a popular choice for both training and inference. They support mixed-precision training, which enhances performance and reduces memory usage. A100 GPUs excel in handling diverse workloads, including large-scale image processing and sequential data modeling, where speed and efficiency are critical.

Optimization Parameters for A100 GPUs in TensorFlow:

```
import tensorflow as tf
from tensorflow.keras.mixed_precision import experimental as
mixed_precision

policy = mixed_precision.Policy('mixed_float16')
mixed_precision.set_policy(policy)

model.compile(optimizer='adam',
loss='sparse_categorical_crossentropy')
```

Autoscaling and Resource Management

Autoscaling is a critical strategy for optimizing resource utilization on cloud platforms, enabling dynamic allocation based on workload demand. It prevents both **underutilization** (wasting resources) and **over-provisioning** (incurring unnecessary costs).

389

AWS Auto Scaling:AWS Auto Scaling adjusts resource allocation automatically, scaling the number of instances up or down based on real-time demand. It uses metrics like CPU utilization, memory usage, and custom metrics (e.g., request rate) to trigger scaling events. For deep learning workloads, this means that more instances are launched during peak demand, ensuring consistent performance. When demand drops, resources are scaled back, reducing costs.

Code Example for Setting Up AWS Auto Scaling:

```
aws autoscaling create-auto-scaling-group --auto-scaling-group-
name MyDLModelASG \
--launch-configuration-name MyLaunchConfig --min-size 1 --max-
size 10 \
--desired-capacity 5 --vpc-zone-identifier subnet-12345
```

GCP's Managed Instance Groups: Google Cloud's Managed Instance Groups provide similar capabilities, allowing automatic scaling based on load. They support features like preemptible instances, which further reduce costs by using surplus cloud capacity.

Configuration Example in GCP:

```
gcloud compute instance-groups managed create my-dl-group --
template=my-template --size=3
gcloud compute instance-groups managed set-autoscaling my-dl-
group --max-num-replicas=10 \
--target-cpu-utilization=0.6 --cool-down-period=60
```

Azure Autoscale: Azure Autoscale supports resource management for Azure Machine Learning and other compute resources. It adjusts the number of running instances based on predefined metrics, such as CPU load or response times.

Azure Autoscale Setup Example:

```
az monitor autoscale create --resource-group myResourceGroup --
name myAutoscale \
--min-count 1 --max-count 10 --count 5 --resource myResource --
resource-type Microsoft.Compute/virtualMachines
```

By dynamically managing resource allocation, autoscaling ensures efficient utilization of computational power, reducing both latency and costs in large-scale production workloads.

Cost Optimization Techniques

Efficient resource utilization is not just about performance—it's also about cost. Cloud services offer various cost optimization strategies that help manage expenses without compromising model quality.

Spot Instances and Preemptible VMs: Spot instances (AWS) and preemptible VMs (GCP) offer significant cost savings by using spare cloud capacity. These instances are ideal for non-critical tasks like model training or batch inference, where occasional interruptions can be tolerated. The cost of spot instances is often 70-90% lower than that of on-demand instances, making them a practical choice for cost-sensitive workloads.

Reserved Instances and Savings Plans: Reserved instances (AWS, Azure) and savings plans offer discounts in exchange for a commitment to a specific instance type and usage duration (e.g., one year or three years). These are useful for long-term production workloads where resource requirements are predictable.

Comparing Cloud Pricing Models: Below is a comparison of cloud pricing models for different instance types, demonstrating cost variations across providers:

Instance Type	AWS (On-Demand)	GCP (On-Demand)	Azure (On-Demand)	Spot/Preemptible Cost Reduction (%)
Standard VM	$0.10/hr	$0.09/hr	$0.11/hr	70%
GPU Instance	$1.50/hr	$1.40/hr	$1.60/hr	80%
TPU Instance	$2.40/hr	$2.20/hr	N/A	85%

By comparing these pricing models, it's evident that spot and preemptible instances offer significant savings for non-critical operations, making them a practical solution for cost-effective model scaling.

Applications and Metrics

In practice, optimizing resource utilization on cloud platforms is crucial for models that need to handle large-scale workloads:

Training NLP Models on TPUs: NLP models like BERT or GPT-3 benefit from TPU training on Google Cloud, reducing both training time and cost.

Running Image Models on Inferentia: AWS Inferentia chips improve inference speed and cost-efficiency for image recognition tasks, enabling real-time performance at reduced expenses.

Autoscaling for Real-Time Recommendation Systems: Autoscaling ensures that recommendation models maintain consistent performance during traffic spikes, reducing latency and improving user experience.

10.3.3: Scaling Models for Large-Scale Production Workloads

Scaling deep learning models for large-scale production workloads poses significant challenges, requiring models to maintain performance while processing vast amounts of data with high throughput and minimal latency. As models transition from development to large-scale deployment, they must be robust enough to handle spikes in traffic, adapt to fluctuating loads, and provide consistent results under various infrastructure constraints. This section explores critical techniques to scale models effectively for production environments, detailing methods to optimize model performance across diverse applications like recommendation systems, image classification, and conversational AI.

Scaling Approaches: Horizontal vs. Vertical Scaling

Scaling models can be approached in two primary ways: **horizontal scaling** and **vertical scaling**.

Horizontal Scaling: Horizontal scaling, often referred to as "scaling out," involves adding more nodes to the infrastructure. This method distributes the load across multiple servers or instances, allowing more inference requests to be handled concurrently. It is typically implemented using a load balancer, which distributes incoming requests evenly across available nodes, thereby improving fault tolerance and resilience. Horizontal scaling is ideal for handling high throughput in real-time applications, as it allows the deployment to accommodate an increasing number of requests without affecting response times significantly. It's also more cost-effective in cloud environments, as instances can be dynamically added or removed based on demand, ensuring optimal resource utilization.

Vertical Scaling: Vertical scaling, or "scaling up," involves adding more resources—such as CPU, memory, or GPU capacity—to a single node. This approach enhances the ability of a single machine to handle larger inference workloads or run more complex models. Vertical scaling is particularly effective for workloads that are more compute-intensive or when latency is a critical factor. However, vertical scaling has its limits, as hardware upgrades can only enhance performance up to a certain point before reaching diminishing returns. It is often used as a preliminary measure to boost capacity before implementing horizontal scaling to achieve true large-scale efficiency.

Code Implementation of Scaling: Below is an example of configuring horizontal scaling for deep learning models using cloud platforms:

```
# AWS Elastic Load Balancer for horizontal scaling
aws elb create-load-balancer --load-balancer-name MyDLModelLB \
--listeners
Protocol=HTTP,LoadBalancerPort=80,InstanceProtocol=HTTP,Instanc
ePort=8080 \
--availability-zones us-west-2a us-west-2b

# GCP Load Balancer setup
gcloud compute backend-services create my-dl-backend \
--protocol=HTTP --port-name=http --global

# Azure Load Balancer setup
az network lb create --resource-group MyResourceGroup --name
MyLoadBalancer \
--frontend-ip-name myFrontEnd --backend-pool-name myBackEndPool
```

These configurations demonstrate how cloud-based load balancers enable horizontal scaling by distributing requests across instances, ensuring that each node is optimally utilized.

Model Sharding and Partitioning for Scalable Inference

In large-scale deployments, **model sharding** and **partitioning** play critical roles in distributing inference workloads and improving memory efficiency.

Model Sharding:Sharding involves dividing a model into smaller segments, each of which is deployed on separate devices or nodes. This approach is particularly effective for models with extensive layers or large parameter counts, as it distributes both computation and memory load. Sharding is commonly used in transformer-based models, where different layers or attention heads are processed on different GPUs. It reduces memory consumption per device while maintaining parallel processing of inference requests.

Partitioning: Partitioning involves dividing the model's layers or components in a way that different parts handle different inference requests. For instance, in a CNN, different convolutional layers can be distributed across devices to speed up processing. This approach ensures that no single device becomes a bottleneck, thereby improving scalability.

Code Implementation of Model Sharding: The following code demonstrates how to implement model sharding using PyTorch:

```
import torch.distributed as dist
from torch.nn.parallel import DistributedDataParallel as DDP

# Initialize distributed backend
dist.init_process_group(backend='nccl')

# Define the model and shard across GPUs
model = MyModel()
sharded_model =
torch.nn.parallel.DistributedDataParallel(model)

# Forward pass with sharding
outputs = sharded_model(inputs)
```

Sharding not only improves scalability but also ensures that large models remain feasible for production deployment, making it possible to handle real-time inference with complex architectures.

Caching and Batch Inference for High Throughput

To maintain high throughput in large-scale deployments, **caching** and **batch inference** are essential techniques:

Caching: Caching involves storing the results of frequently requested inference queries. By reusing previously computed results, caching significantly reduces latency and computation time for identical requests, making it highly effective for recommendation systems and NLP applications, where certain queries occur repeatedly. For example, caching can be implemented in front-end servers to store the results of common user queries, improving response times and reducing load on the inference backend.

Batch Inference: Batch inference processes multiple requests simultaneously, making better use of hardware resources like GPUs or TPUs. By grouping several requests together, batch inference reduces the overhead of handling each request separately, improving throughput. This technique is particularly useful in scenarios like video processing, where multiple frames need to be analyzed simultaneously, or in document processing, where batches of text inputs are processed concurrently.

Code Example for Caching and Batch Inference:

```python
from cachetools import LRUCache
from batch_inference import BatchInference

# Caching setup
cache = LRUCache(maxsize=100)

def inference_with_cache(request):
    if request in cache:
        return cache[request]
    else:
        result = model.predict(request)
        cache[request] = result
        return result

# Batch inference setup
batch_infer = BatchInference(model, batch_size=32)
results = batch_infer.process_requests(requests)
```

Caching and batch inference techniques not only enhance inference speed but also contribute to more consistent performance in production.

Applications of Scaling Techniques

Scaling techniques are integral to a variety of production environments, each requiring robust handling of large-scale workloads:

E-commerce Recommendation Systems: Scaling recommendation models using horizontal scaling and caching is common in e-commerce platforms, where models need to serve personalized recommendations in real time. These systems must handle thousands of queries per second (QPS), making scalability a crucial factor.

Customer Support Chatbots: For conversational AI models, horizontal scaling combined with batch inference allows chatbots to maintain responsiveness even during peak user activity, such as Black Friday sales or product launches.

Social Media Image Recognition: Large-scale image classification models in social media platforms leverage model sharding and partitioning to analyze millions of images daily, ensuring accurate tagging and filtering of user-generated content.

Metrics for Scaling Performance

The effectiveness of scaling techniques is often measured using the following metrics:

Metric	Single Node	Horizontal Scaling (4 Nodes)	Vertical Scaling (GPU Upgrade)
Throughput (QPS)	500	2,000	1,200
Latency (ms)	50	15	25
Scaling Efficiency	1.0 (baseline)	0.95	0.90

These metrics demonstrate how scaling techniques improve performance, making models capable of handling large-scale workloads without compromising speed or accuracy.

A Message From TransformaTech Institute

Dear Reader,

Creating a comprehensive book like this one takes dedication, effort, and collaboration across multiple teams, from illustrators and industry professionals to editors and content developers. Each person has contributed their expertise and passion to deliver a resource that we hope will support your journey in mastering deep learning.

If this book has helped you, informed you, or benefitted you in any way, we would be genuinely grateful for your honest feedback on Amazon. Your reviews not only guide us in future publications but also help other readers discover resources that might serve them well on their own paths. Whether it's a brief note or a detailed reflection, your thoughts matter to us.

Thank you for choosing our book and trusting us with your time and learning. We hope it has been a valuable part of your progress, and we wish you every success in your future endeavors.

With gratitude,
The TransformaTech Institute Team

Amazon Review Page